alps
Story Maker

Using fiction as a resource for accelerated learning

STEPHEN BOWKETT

Published by Network Educational Press Ltd
PO Box 635
Stafford
ST16 1BF

ISBN 1 855 39 076 0

Managing Editor: Anne Oppenheimer
Design: Neil Hawkins – Network Educational Press Ltd
Illustrations: Annabel Spenceley
Illustrations from *Double Dare Gang* stories by Jamie Egerton
Illustration on page 193 by Stella Hender

Printed in Great Britain by
MPG Books Ltd., Bodmin, Cornwall

Contents

Foreword

The Accelerated Learning Series attempts to pull together new and innovative thinking about learning. The titles in the series offer contemporary solutions to old problems. The series is held together by the accelerated learning model which, in turn, is underwritten by an informed theoretical understanding.

The term 'Accelerated Learning' can be misleading. The method is not for a specific group of learners, nor for a given age range, nor for a category of perceived ability. The method is not about doing the same things faster. It is not about fast tracking or about hot housing. It is a considered, generic approach to learning based on research drawn from disparate disciplines and tested with different age-groups and different ability levels in very different circumstances. As such, it can be adapted and applied to very different challenges.

The books in the Accelerated Learning series build from the accelerated learning cycle. The cycle starts by attending to the physical, environmental and social factors in learning. It proposes the worth of a positive and supportive learning environment. It then deliberately attempts to connect to, and build upon, prior knowledge and understanding whilst presenting an overview of the learning challenge to come. Participants set positive outcomes and define targets towards reaching those outcomes. Information is then presented in visual, auditory and kinaesthetic modes and is reinforced through different forms of intelligent response. Frequent, structured opportunities to demonstrate understanding and to rehearse for recall are the concluding feature of the cycle.

Humans are habitual story-makers. We import meanings to every experience. The meanings are unique to each individual. We cannot stop ourselves making stories of our lives. If we stopped making stories we would enter a world of dislocation and dysfunction. So we create stories about ourselves and then run them in our heads. We live the stories. We internalise them and then, without necessarily wishing to, we become our own stories. Steve Bowkett has written a marvellous book about making stories. He has called it *ALPS StoryMaker*. It draws on the learning model described in *The ALPS Approach* and takes it into new territory.

We story-make in ways which are idiosyncratic, are particular yet also transferable. When we share the stories that we make, we transfer ourselves into a more public space. Steve Bowkett talks about insight and separates the term 'in' and 'sight': 'it's a form of 'looking' in', he says. Stories encourage 'looking in' – making sense of ourselves. I would add at the same time, stories encourage 'outsight' – looking out. Sharing the sense we are making. Comparing our stories with those of others.

In the 21st century the opportunities to do so have proliferated and the space in which we can exchange our stories has become larger. We share stories through conversation. This is the time worn method. Conversation – or shared story-making – ranges across a wide territory and includes all sorts of tools: analysis, attention to detail, considered reflection, gossip, exaggeration, gross generalisations, scandalmongering. Shared story-making in the 21st century also operates across different media. The story-making media can be broadcast – the mass appeal of television, newspapers, radio, advertising – or narrowcast – the instruction book, the specialist channel, the fanzine. Story-making can be through shared public activities such as the arts. It can be through community activity. It could be through the celebrations that we shape our lives with. We story-make through the sporting events which provide their own strange and enduring compulsion. We are a species of habitual story-makers. What's more, there is something strangely attractive about anyone who can convey a good story!

Steve Bowkett tells a good story. He is a very skilled story-teller. I watched Steve Bowkett tell stories to a group of 7-year-olds. (He tells similar stories to adults in prisons – the principles are the same, the content differs!) The 7-year-olds were transfixed. They were inhabiting the world of the Double Dare Gang. As they heard about Old Man Jones and the forbidden fruit in his allotment, their mouths and eyes widened. Steve very skilfully allowed them to complete their own pictures and to splash them with as much colour and detail as they wished. He used language which was inviting and had a hypnotic quality. He allowed them space to process their pictures. He held them in thrall to their own imaginations. They became spellbound.

Within the pages of *ALPS StoryMaker* you will find a brilliant array of tools to help children construct more vivid stories. Through the sophisticated techniques here you can help children paint even more colourful images of their own lives and those of the others who inhabit their imagination. They can make themselves spellbound!

A lot of the skills of reading and thus engaging fully in story-making, lie in our brain's capacity to identify, rehearse and manipulate sounds. Story-making starts with exploration of sound. According to Professor John Stein of the University of Oxford nearly 2/3rds of the differences in 11-year-olds' reading ability in the United Kingdom can be explained by auditory and visual transient sensitivity. This means that the brain is not yet good enough at tracking subtle changes in sounds nor in tracking the changing shapes of words represented on a page as the eyes move across that page. Developmental dyslexics are known to be less sensitive to changes in sound frequency and intensity. Illiterate subjects have different patterns of brain activation to literates when asked to do language activities that do not require reading.

We are all born with an equal potential to learn any language. At six months we begin to build the phonemes specific to our native language. Then we get an opportunity to practice manipulating the sounds. With luck we will have a coach who will help is with our manipulations, repeat them, rehearse them and reward our successes with them. We call this coach a parent. A lot of the evidence shows that poor reading skills can be traced in many cases to poor language learning skills and that as many as 30 per cent of children start school with poor language learning skills. Much of classroom teaching is language based. Listening to stories helps prepare the brain to make its own.

The basic unit of language is the phoneme. Learning phonemes starts in the pram or earlier. Children in the bottom 20 per cent in phonological awareness in Year One are likely to be reading about two and a half years or more below reading age by Year Five. In a project run by Betty Hart and Todd Risley simultaneously in Kansas and in Alaska, four-year-olds from welfare families were found to have up to 14 million fewer words of cumulative language experience than four-year-olds from more advantaged blue- and white- and blue-collar families. When all socio-economic, class, and ethnicity variables were stripped out, what seemed to have made the difference to learning performance was the extent to which the child had encountered language in the first four years of life.

The best three bits of guidance that a parent can be given to help his or her child become a confident reader are:
1. provide a normal caring home environment with lots, but not too much, of sensory stimulation
2. check your child's eyesight and hearing
3. speak positively, and often, to, with, and around your child.

Later in life, developing a love of story can build on that positive supportive learning environment. In some cases, catching the love of story before it gets lost forever, can go along way to compensating for some of the physical difficulties with reading and talking which may have characterised the early years.

Michelangelo is reputed to have said, 'a man paints with his brain and not with his hands'. When we tell ourselves and others stories, when we learn through the medium of story, we paint pictures in our heads. If the pictures are uniquely ours, if they are compelling and distinctive, if they connect sufficiently to our lives, then the pictures remain.

Neuroscientists – scientists who study the brain – tell us that different parts of the brain are involved in seeing words, hearing words, speaking words and thinking about using words. When we read or listen to a story, when we tell ourselves our own stories, we activate the brain. We know that the corpus callosum – an area of the brain connecting the right and left hemispheres – is thinner in illiterates. Does this mean their stories are less vivid, less pictorial, less fanciful? Or more so?

Reading also activates specific visual centres in the brain. This is so for different types of reader. Work done at Oxford University by Dr Simon Baron-Cohen showed that the visual cortex is activated when individuals blinded after the age of 14 read Braille. A cognitive neuroscientist, Dr Martha Farah, asserts that 'when the child is listening to a story, the hippocampal and visual cortex areas of a child's brain are activated'. The hippocampus is an area of the brain which contributes to visual and spatial recall in memory; the visual cortex helps us rehearse the look of something. Story-making elicits long-term visual memories.

What other physiological phenomena does story-making tap into? This is what Dr Marilyn Albert, Professor of Psychology at Harvard Medical School says about emotion in learning,

'We know there's a part of the brain ... that gets activated when we're very emotional, and it increases our ability to remember things. When there's emotion attached to something we're more likely to remember it.'

Has there ever been a better mechanism, tried in different cultures across centuries, to engage the emotions than story? What a thrill to hide under the blankets in your childhood bedroom reading by torchlight late into the night. So, our rationale for the development of the ALPS StoryMaker techniques is transparent.

Stories can engage and enhance the language centres of the brain, and, almost coincidentally activate visual processing centres and those contributing to visual and spatial memory. This activity can, and often will, lead to a higher level of emotional arousal and the release of the chemical 'messengers' associated with that physical state. Emotions lock in the experience and related memories.

What do schools do to catch the love of story? Provide environments for learning where there is structured exploration of language, where risks can be taken and where the exploration of the external and internal worlds of story can occur. Encourage parents to do the same. Develop the skills of professional staff in telling stories and helping children tell theirs. Arguing the case for structured oral work around story in class. Bringing in others who can share their stories and listen to those of the children. Finally, remember that there is a sound neurological basis for structured language exchange at all phases of learning and because of this, stories leave sounds, pictures and feelings which never fade...

Alistair Smith
July 2001

Using this book

As with my previous books, *Imagine That* and *Self-Intelligence*, the activities in StoryMaker are designed for use across the age and ability range. A glance at the contents page will show that activities have been grouped into what are intended to be handy categories such as characters, plot, genre, etc, and arranged with simpler activities at the beginning of a section and more elaborate ones towards the end. However, this organisation is only a guide. Feel free to mix and match ideas to suit yourself and your children's requirements. Some children will easily be able to cope with several activities at once, which combine to form a complex exploration. Other children might be most beneficially challenged with a simple exercise which, when they've done it well, will boost their confidence and allow them to progress to greater adventures.

However StoryMaker resources are employed, their effect will be cumulative. Children will become familiar and comfortable with their use, applying them and the thinking skills they utilise to fiction more generally, and in the end across the range of school subjects and beyond them into the wider arena of life. You will find that 'StoryMaking' equips children with an empowering attitude towards language, creative thinking and learning. These are practised through the activities and in turn sustain and nourish the attitude which supports them.

Throughout the book activities are cross-referenced as appropriate; though you may discover many other links as you use them. An index at the end makes specific reference to principles of brain-based learning, and an extensive bibliography is offered if you want to explore certain aspects of accelerated learning in more depth.

In a nutshell; take an eclectic approach. Use what works for you as you work with your children. Discard what doesn't sit comfortably in your domain, and feel free to adopt, adapt and extend the rest.

Acknowledgements

With thanks to Alistair Smith and Nicola Call for bringing excitement to accelerated learning; to Jamie Egerton and Stella Hender for startling visualisations; to Anne Oppenheimer for her wonderfully efficient editing (as ever); to Jim Houghton and the staff of NEP for making it all possible; and to the children I've worked with across the country who have proved to me that story-making is a natural human process.

Stephen Bowkett
June 2001

Section One:

The creative mind

When someone looks at the moon
The fool looks at the finger
But the wise man looks at the moon.

Traditional Chinese proverb

Overview of Section One: The creative mind

Page	Topic/activity	Story element covered	Accelerated learning link
11	A model of the mind		Left/right-brain thinking
13	Principles of brain-based learning		The optimal learning environment
14	Reactive and creative thinking	*Generating ideas*	Association as a learning device
16	The mind–brain question and some helpful metaphors	*The use of metaphor*	Metacognition – encouraging thinking about thinking
17	Thinking tools and tasks		The 'thinking tools' analogy
18	Intelligent behaviours		Fields of potential, multiple intelligences and 'the new 3Rs'
19	Scoring goals	*Planning and plotting*	Goals, targets and strategies
20	Intention – output – effect	*Early planning*	Decision-making and consideration of consequences (3Rs)
21	Story summary templates	*Preview and overview of the story*	The preview-do-review process and the Big Picture
23	Story organiser	*Early organisation of ideas/incorporating the advice of others*	'Chunking', time management and prioritisation of tasks
25	Anticipating outcomes	*Planning*	Strategic flexibility, fixed goals, arranging win-win situations
25	Sleep on it	*Generating ideas*	Preprocessing and the use of nonconscious resources
26	Picture work	*Visual stimulus for story-making*	VAK and multisensory thinking
27	VAK-splats	*Attention to descriptive details*	VAK and multisensory thinking / nonconscious visual reminders
32	Picture this	*Visual stimulus/key words, themes and motifs*	Peripheral learning devices
33	Pole-bridging	*Free flow of ideas*	Pole-bridging, self-guiding, the use of nonconscious resources
33	The without-trying game	*Free flow of ideas / separating the generation of ideas from their evaluation*	Self-guiding and the use of nonconscious resources
34	Link-it	*Free flow of ideas/using a 6x6 grid template*	Flexibility of thinking through association/brainstorming
35	Link-it using side bars	*Generation of ideas using a variety of stimuli*	Flexibility of thinking through the use of templates/organisation of initial ideas
36	The ethos of intuition – diffusions, downtime and attention skills		The use of nonconscious resources/ ultradian rhythms / concentration spans / daydreaming
38	Questioneering	*Exploration of any story element*	Questioning techniques / manipulation and personalisation of information
39	Meaning-making	*Early development of one's own writing style and 'voice'*	Brainscape – mindscape – wordscape and the power of language
40	Challenging the language	*Awareness of language patterns/limiting beliefs in writing*	Metacognition/metal model questioning/challenging limiting beliefs

41	Connective prompts	*Awareness of language patterns/limiting beliefs in writing/breaking writer's block*	Metacognition/metal model questioning/challenging limiting beliefs
42	Many endings	*Awareness of multiple options' thinking*	Development of a menu of strategies/exploration of limiting beliefs
42	Menu of options	*Exploration of any story element*	Development of a menu of strategies/exploration of limiting beliefs
43	Wordplay	*Exploration of any story element*	Development of a menu of strategies/exploration of limiting beliefs
44	Representing the knowledge	*Awareness of multiple options thinking*	True understanding of knowledge / flexibility of strategies for achievement and success

Stories contain the
wisdom of the species.

Joe Griffin / Ivan Tyrrell

The creative mind

◆ A model of the mind

Naming and investigating the parts of the brain responsible for the mind's various functions and metacognition – thinking about thinking – are useful things to do when it comes to raising awareness of the mind's vast repertoire of capabilities. Albert Einstein believed that 'Things should be made as simple as possible – but no simpler', and so in respect of that advice a brief guide is offered here which can act as a platform for subsequent StoryMaker activities.

There are two guiding principles in understanding how the mind works:

- The mind and body are fundamentally linked, so that thoughts, feelings and physical states and behaviours are profoundly interconnected.
- Each of us has a conscious aspect and a subconscious (or nonconscious) aspect to our lives.

We can therefore make a distinction – albeit a rather artificial one – between our conscious thoughts, feelings and behaviours, and our subconscious ones. Conscious 'stuff' is stuff that we're aware of at the time, for reasons we understand. We also have a greater degree of control over our conscious lives. So, a conscious thought is one we know we're thinking, and we know why we're thinking it…

Think of a pleasant place right now. Take a little time to notice visual details. Imagine some sounds associated with this place. Explore the textures: imagine you can reach out and feel the surfaces of things. Make the place vivid and powerful in your mind. This is a conscious visualisation – you know you are thinking about it and you know why (because I asked you to). You also have a high degree of control over this process. Perhaps you based your imagined scene on a memory. Make a gentle effort of will now to change some aspects of the place. Alter the colour of something perhaps. Add something incongruous. Change a sound or two. Pick something up from and make it hotter, larger, heavier… This is the capacity of imagination, to manipulate information in new ways.

Now – effortlessly notice a few new and interesting details that have some significance for you…

Perhaps you know how those details are significant, or maybe insights (in-sights, lookings-in) will come later. Given that the details you noticed were spontaneous rather than anticipated, we can say that you allowed the subconscious part of your mind to supply them. You might also have noticed feelings associated with your visualisation. If so, were you aware that those feelings caused more extensive physiological responses? Perhaps your facial expression or breathing changed, your pulse quickened or slowed; possibly your blood pressure altered; maybe you tensed or displayed a range of micro movements in the muscles – especially if you were 'in the picture' – as you recalled a posture you assumed when you were last in that place in reality.

All of these aspects of thinking to create this simple visualisation can be utilised through a menu of activities to accelerate children's learning. In summary:

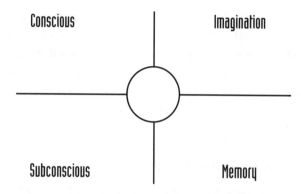

- Thinking–feeling–acting is an elegant dance of energy between these aspects of mind and body.
- We see with the mind's eye, hear with the mind's ear, touch with the mind's hands, feel with the mind's heart.
- What we conceive and admit, we believe. What we believe, we act upon.
- Experiences are 'anchored' in our lives, both past and future; strung like beads on a necklace consciously – drawn like locations on a map subconsciously.

Accelerated learning makes use of both the conscious and subconscious aspects of an individual's personality, and recognises that learning is as much an emotional/physiological experience as it is a mental/intellectual process.

◆ Principles of brain-based learning

Alistair Smith and Nicola Call in *The ALPS Approach* identify nine principles which guide us in the endeavour to create the optimal environment for children to learn. These are:

1 The brain develops best with high levels of sensory stimulation and sustained cognitive challenge – though I would add that cognition (conscious, left-hemisphere, intellectually-oriented thinking) is itself helped and supported by the use of subconscious thinking tools.

2 The best conditions for learning combine high mental challenge with low threat. 'Threat' in this case usually means the threat of getting the wrong answer or otherwise doing badly in comparison with others. Competitive and judgemental activities and testing perhaps have their place in an educational environment, but they do tend to invite reactive rather than creative thinking skills – see below.

3 Be sensitive to the emotional and physical readiness of the learner to learn. We are talking here of the 'inner environment' of the child. The fact that the law requires children to gather in designated areas at specified times in order to learn does not mean that they will inevitably do so, or do so most effectively. Recognising and understanding children's emotional and physical states – and being able to intervene positively to modify those states – is a powerful ability for any teacher (and learner!) to possess, relating as it does to the whole broad and growing field of emotional resourcefulness.

4 The brain thrives on immediate feedback and choice. Human beings have been called 'meaning-making' beings: our natural tendency is to want to make sense of the world and ourselves. This tendency is best satisfied when our conclusions are swiftly verified through feedback, and when we have a wide range of options in order to form those conclusions and then act upon them.

5 Use the whole range of the brain's capabilities (i.e. both left- and right-hemisphere specialisms) through a wide variety of learning experiences. Notice and utilise different attentional states. For example, facing front and paying attention engages conscious, externalised concentration and evokes (or at least implies the usefulness of) rational intellectual thought. Visualisation work (or systematic daydreaming as creative people call it) internalises the attention and creates conscious passivity. This allows for insightfulness and greater intuition as the subconscious offers up the results of its assimilation of information – i.e. its meaning-makings.

6 Each brain is unique and 'plastic'. As individuals we carry with us unique 'maps of reality' based on our own life experiences. Those experiences act upon the range of 'intelligences' or potentials we all possess, perhaps inhibiting some, possibly stimulating others to flourish most effectively. We are also highly adaptable in the way in which we assimilate and utilise, at whatever level, the experiences life brings our way; although it must be said that some experiences inhibit and limit personal growth. Any civilised educational environment will recognise these principles and endeavour to develop any learner's full repertoire of talents.

7 Learning takes place at a number of levels. It has been wisely said that we know more than we realise we know: we amount to much more than we appreciate. The comparison has also been made between people and onions – both make you cry sometimes, and both have many layers. Robert Dilts (see Bibliography) has postulated the following 'neurological levels' of thinking, feeling and behaving, which reflects this notion:

- environment – where and when we do things

- behaviour – what we do as we do things

- capabilities – how we employ strategies to do things

- beliefs and values – why we do the things we do

- identity – who we think we are as a basis for doing things

Interventions are possible on any of these levels to explore and remove learning blocks, and to maximise the learning potential of the individual.

8 Memory is a series of processes rather than locations. Effective retention and recall of information depends upon strategies which are active and participative rather than passive, and which are involving, accessible and rich in context.

9 We are 'hard wired' for language. As Jean Aitchison (in *Words in the Mind*) and other researchers assert, human beings come into the world with the ability to learn, recognise and utilise language, that supposedly abstract and unquestionably highly elaborate system of sounds and shapes which allows us to communicate. It is, however, a use-it-or-lose-it scenario in a child's early life; and a 'language-poor' environment at any time during childhood severely limits the development of one's overall learning capability.

◆ Reactive and creative thinking

Following the above principles allows for the construction of a rich, vibrant, stimulating and supportive learning environment where children's individual needs and requirements are taken into account, and where every child's contribution is recognised, celebrated and used. Such an environment allows creative thinking to flourish. The mathematician Henri Poincaré suggested four stages in the ongoing process of creative thought:

1 **preparation** – which can be as general as simply accumulating experience as you live in the world, or as precise and systematic as researching a specific problem or topic area.

2 **assimilation** – where the meaning-making occurs. This is largely a subconscious process, although, clearly, conscious logical connections will be made as one attempts to make sense of diverse pieces of information and draw them together into a rational conclusion. Subconscious assimilation can be exploited by, for instance, assuming a state of 'relaxed alertness' when deeper insights become conscious; or by 'pole-bridging' –

muttering one's understanding in a quiet and spontaneous way. This process is embodied in the epithet of, 'How do I know what I think until I hear what I say?'

3 **illumination** – that Eureka Moment when the answer comes, as it were, out of the blue. Often enough you just *know* it's right, but even so we feel compelled to verify our understandings above and beyond simple reliance upon our intuitions (inner tuitions). Illuminations are usually accompanied by powerful positive emotions which help make creative thinking highly enjoyable. And there is no need to 'wait for the Muse to bless you'. Creativity is not a mysterious or vicarious process, but one that can be trained and exploited at will through the use of various strategies.

4 **verification** – testing the understanding. People who are habitually creative (who are, as the writer David Gerrold says, 'perpetual notion machines') tend to be flexible and adaptable in their strategies to stimulate creative thinking, and rather independent and self-reliant in their judgements. Even so, we probably all feel the need to verify our insights and the products of those insights. A writer will return to a story weeks or months later and read it with 'fresh eyes', and will tend to want others' opinions. Verification can therefore occur individually and internally, and by using external resources. The creative thinker will think creatively about any number of ways of testing the veracity, quality or usefulness of her ideas!

Creative thinkers reveal themselves in a number of other ways too. They will tend to have confidence in their ability to learn, since they are flexible in their approach to learning and have previously verified useful resources and strategies for doing so. They will tend to rely on their own judgements and not be fearful of discriminating between what they see as relevant and what is not. They are not frightened of being 'wrong', recognising that you need to have lots of ideas to have good ideas, and that all ideas are more or less useful in the end. Creative thinkers will tend to learn through enquiry: they will ask questions, including questioning their own assumptions; observe, deduce and speculate. They will make extensive use of definitions and metaphors (frequently self-generated) in their thinking. They understand the usefulness of goals, and maintain confidence in a variety of strategies as moveable feasts in the attainment of those goals; and yet creative thinkers are not usually driven by the need to have a final resolution to every problem. In short, creative thinkers make effective learners through a range of behaviours, many of which involve the elegant use of language.

Reactive thinkers tend to lack what creative thinkers possess and hold dear. Reactive thinking has been called 'guess-the-right-answer' thinking. A typical scenario might involve the teacher who on Monday tells his class; 'Don't forget that Paris is the capital of France. I'll be asking you for that answer later in the week.' When that moment comes, children will be required to recall the answer and feed it back unaltered to the teacher. Notice that the information (the single simple link between 'capital' and 'France') has not been manipulated inside the learners' heads in any way. It has only been retained and recalled – usually without the teacher supplying specific strategies for the retention and recollection of information!

'So, what is the capital of France?' At this point some children will struggle to remember. They might be fearful of getting the wrong answer, and so might try to guess the right answer, perhaps by noticing subtle behavioural cues from the teacher or other students. They might 'try hard' to recall the answer they were given on Monday, and may feel a sense of failure if they don't. That sense of failure might be exacerbated when one child gives the right answer and is praised for it. Such experiences, if repeated as part of a 'reactive thinking environment' can inhibit learning and lead to the development of limiting self-beliefs.

In a learning environment where creative thinking is valued and where the principles of brain-based learning are utilised, the information (the idea in-formation) that Paris was the capital of France would form the starting point of a greater, richer and more interactive context of enquiry. So, the teacher might wonder:

- Why do you think Paris is the capital of France?
- How can we find out why it is?
- What conditions might need to be satisfied for any place to become the capital of a country?
- What common features of other capitals can we find to check our ideas on the above question?
- Can the place which is the capital of a country ever change? What factors might lead to a change of capital, do you think?
- What would things be like if *your* home town was the capital of the country?

… etcetera. The list could be much longer than this, of course. And notice how thinking about the questions utilises a broader range of processes, and is much more satisfying and much more fun, than remembering (or struggling to remember) that Paris is the capital of France. In this creative thinking environment, driven by open enquiry, the process is teacher-led initially. But soon enough, children will personalise the approach (Why do *I* think Paris is the capital of France?) and in so doing participate more profoundly in the acceleration of their own learning abilities.

◆ The mind—brain question and some helpful metaphors

It is a moot point whether the operations of mind are merely the by-products of brain chemistry, or whether the brain is simply the vehicle which allows the mind to express itself in the world. The question need not impinge upon our use of models of the mind, or knowledge of how the brain develops to optimise children's learning. One interesting way of raising children's (and one's own) awareness of how the mind works is by the use of metaphor. So:

- the mind is a lake. Thoughts flow from the shallows to the depths and back.
- the mind is a tree. The roots of our thinking go deep, sap rises to all the branches and we pick the fruit of our ideas.
- the mind is an orchestra. The conscious conductor directs our thinking, and the subconscious musicians work together to create complex harmony.
- the brain is a spider-web. It has many connections and is very sensitive to influences coming from outside.

- the brain is a prism. It breaks down white light into many colours and allows us to see those colours.
- the brain is a map. It has many locations where special things occur, yet all those places are connected one to another.
- the mind is a mirror...
- the mind is a story...
- the mind is a detective...
- the brain is an encyclopedia...
- the brain is a computer...
- the brain is a playground...

... and so on. A great website called Neuroscience Resources for Kids extends this exercise and offers a menu of ideas, information and activities to allow children to learn more about thinking, the brain and the nervous system. Go to:

http://faculty.washington.edu/chudler/metaphor.html

◆ Thinking tools and tasks

One very useful metaphor is to consider the mind as a toolbox – or a cross between a toolbox and a treasure chest. Inside you'll find some tools that were used once upon a time, when we were children and rehearsed the world through play; when we possessed 'beginner's minds' filled with possibilities, but which now lie rusting in a corner. And there are other tools that perhaps have never been taken out of their wrappings; and others which we have relied upon over the years to get us through school. These we take for granted, and might never think to use them in different combinations, or to rest them and let other implements do the job in other, innovative ways. As the saying goes, if the only tool you think you've got is a hammer, you'll see every problem as a nail. Solving problems, therefore, becomes a matter of finding other tools, or pretending the problems aren't nails.

Look at this list and reflect upon how often and under what circumstances you use these thinking tools and tasks for yourself and the children you teach:

absorb, analyse, anticipate, apply, associate, attend, brainstorm, categorise, choose, conclude, critique, daydream, debate, decide, deconstruct, deduce, describe, dissociate, discriminate, discuss, draft, enquire, evaluate, experiment, explain, explore, feed back, imagine, integrate, intuit, judge, listen, make up, memorise, model, notice, observe, perform, plan, pretend, preview, question, rationalise, read, recite, recollect (re-collect), reflect, reiterate, relate, remember, reminisce, replan, research, review, speculate, synthesise, tell, verify

It would be worth taking some time a) to decide what you understand is involved in these varied processes and b) to review your current classroom practices and note which thinking tools are used to carry them out. StoryMaker aims to involve children in all or most of the above and in a variety of contexts.

◆ Intelligent behaviours

Alistair Smith and Nicola Call in *The ALPS Approach* quote Professor Arthur Costa of the Institute of Intelligence at Berkeley, who postulated that intelligence – explained elegantly in Howard Gardner's sense of multiple intelligences or 'fields of potential' – is defined by and manifested as a range of behaviours which may be inherited and /or acquired. In any event, these intelligent behaviours can and should be cultivated within any civilised educational environment. Costa's list includes:

persistence, managing impulsivity, empathy, flexibility of mental and emotional response, metacognition, verifying accuracy and precision, questioning, problem-posing, applying previous knowledge, using language and thought with precision, gathering data in a multisensory way, ingenuity (using the 'inner genius'), insightfulness, curiosity, transference of knowledge, insight and creative process from one field to another

Creative thinking, utilising a broad range of thinking tools and tasks, results in intelligent behaviours which accelerate the learning process. This, in turn, boosts further creative thinking in a synergistic cycle. The greatest power and benefit of such a cycle implies a sense of responsibility on the part of both the teacher and learner. Responsibility is here defined as 'response-ability'; the ability to respond to the needs and requirements of the learner within the educational environment, meanwhile dealing with the pressures imposed on that environment from outside. Although external agencies seek to verify the effectiveness of their policies through a limited range of testing procedures, one should keep in mind that the ultimate aim of any truly educational system is to build within each and every child the attributes of responsibility, resilience and resourcefulness – the 'New 3Rs' which will allow our children to flourish lifelong:

Resilience	**Resourcefulness**	**Responsibility**
Positive feedback form peers, adults, one's own experiences	Acquiring a diversity of resources, and making up one's own resources.	The ability to respond, emotional resourcefulness, independent assessment, enquiry.

◆ Scoring goals

Creating a story is an effective way of developing target- and goal-setting skills. The 'finished product' amounts to a highly organised structure that can be broken down into smaller and smaller elements; chapters, scenes, paragraphs, sentences, words – each with its own component purposes and meanings. By considering the polished draft of a story as the goal to which you have aspired, an awareness of its constituent features – targets, strategies, techniques, tasks – can be raised and developed at the appropriate time.

Activities relating to goal- and target-setting are to be found throughout the StoryMaker materials. For now, here are the basics:

➡ GOAL – 'a dream within a timescale.' A goal is a fixed, simply-expressed, longer-term aspiration.

➡ TARGETS – these are measurable and verifiable points en route to the realisation of a goal: milestones along the path towards your final destination.

➡ STRATEGIES – are moveable means of reaching the fixed goal. Strategies are processes, plans of action, that can be composed and recomposed of different elements for greatest effectiveness. Entire strategies can be changed if necessary. Flexibility in using strategies is a key element in achieving one's goals.

➡ TECHNIQUES – these are the mechanisms, activities and devices that build into strategic skills which allow for the completion of tasks so that we can reach our targets and achieve our goals.

➡ TASKS – are what we do to practise and develop our technical skills. They are the building blocks of the strategies we choose.

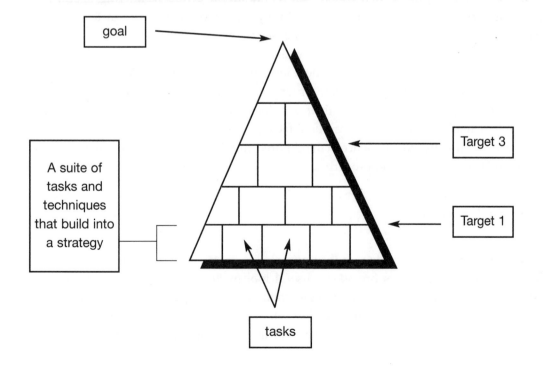

◆ Intention – output – effect (IOE)

There are three parts to making a story:

> the thinking time – the writing time – the reflecting time

Effective writing means that the author has considered her intentions with regard to the effects she wishes the writing to have on her readers. This process can be made explicit in the following way...

Use this template to introduce the idea of the IOE process. Have children focus on their intentions behind their writing. When the writing is done, have them test the work and get feedback on its effect from others.

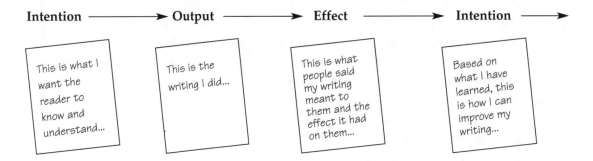

Intention	Output	Effect	Intention
This is what I want the reader to know and understand...	This is the writing I did...	This is what people said my writing meant to them and the effect it had on them...	Based on what I have learned, this is how I can improve my writing...

Intentionality is a focusing mechanism which operates throughout the story-making journey and at all levels. It is a process of frequent self-reminding, a gentle wondering about, for instance: What purposes does this character serve? Why did I choose this word instead of that word? How can I make the reader feel uneasy as I describe this particular setting?

Ongoing intention implies the use of independent judgement and decision-making. All writers build towards this, although initially young writers will continually be asking for help and advice, and perhaps for someone to make their decisions for them. Be sensitive to how much support a child actually needs: laziness can be a factor, or perhaps an echo of the old fear of 'getting it wrong'. Cultivate independence in the children and they will soon draw strength from relying upon themselves. As the old proverb says, 'The work will show you how to do it.'

◆ Story summary templates

Whether children are making up their own stories or studying someone else's, the use of summary templates provides a useful tool in the preview–do–review process. They offer the Big Picture and allow children to anticipate the story experience. 'Preprocessing' also occurs as children gather up (often largely subconsciously) ideas, information and experiences associated with the story they are going to read or make.

◆ Story Summary Template

Title: The Allotment Ghost (from *The Double Dare Gang*)

Plot:

The Double Dare Gang plan to raid Old Man Jones's allotment and steal some fruit. Shortly before they do so, they read his obituary in the local paper but decide to go ahead anyway. During the raid the 'ghost' of Old Man Jones appears and scares the kids away. This was a ploy by Jones, who faked his own obituary, to teach them the lesson of their lives – don't steal another man's apples!

Characters:

- Steve – tall, gangly, fair curly hair, introverted, unconfident, sensitive. Narrator voice.

- Nigel Lloyd – small, scruffy, rebellious, mischievous. Leader of the gang.

- Anthony Morris – thin, cheap glasses, fast runner, poor family. Typical street kid.

- Kevin Howells – thick-lensed glasses, dark curly hair, quiet, sensible, academic. Common sense balance.

- Neil Butler – plain, plump, slow, low self-esteem. The protected one.

- Brian Roberts – large, powerful, slow-witted, very loyal. The bodyguard.

- Anna Williams – tall, reasonably pretty, strong-willed, sensible, mature. Female counterbalance.

Background: Kenniston, 'mid-Atlantic' town, modern day.

Motifs

- Allotment (your 'lot', domain, the framework of your life, forbidden zone to others).

- Apples (autumn, plenty, temptation).

- Chain link fencing (barrier, territory, privacy).

- Old Man Jones (adult, hostility, aggression, unknown and not understood, old age, the monster, nemesis).

- Friday (start of free time, opportunity for adventure, freedom to play and imagine).

- Scar (marked by life, learning through pain, badge of courage).

Themes:

Daring to defy/Forbidden fruit/What lies 'over the line'?/Innocence and experience.

◆ Story Summary Template

Title:

Plot:

Characters:

Background:

Motifs

Themes:

During writing, the template helps children to keep to the point. Inconsistencies can easily occur within stories as writers forget previous details or lose track of plot threads – a mild-mannered character with blue eyes, for example, can unintentionally turn into a green-eyed fury simply because it seemed like a good idea at the time. Frequent reference to a summary template can help writers avoid this kind of error.

As review devices, story templates gather up relevant information and present it in an accessible way. The worked example given shows how a detailed overview can be fitted onto a single sheet. The template blank offers one format, but many others are possible, depending upon your requirements. Summary templates need not look quite so stark: space can be made for drawings and sketches, while borders can be colourfully decorated, perhaps with motifs and other features that appear in the story.

Bookmarks

◆ **B**ookmarks made by the children can feature key ideas and key words relevant to a story. They can be visually attractive and act as subliminal learning devices, as readers see them often but take little conscious notice of what they contain (see the section on subliminals, peripherals and nonconscious learning).

Story organiser

◆ **M**ost children are familiar with organisers, homework diaries and the like. Build on current good practice by introducing story-making organisers as part of your goal-setting programme. There are many ways of doing this – for example, see 'Countdown to a Story'(p.75) and 'Story Flowchart' in *Imagine That* (pp.184-5). Templates are also useful insofar as they can be configured for various tasks, levels of detail and scale.

Example 1. Using *The Allotment Ghost* as though a child had just written the first draft:

To do in order:	Whole story	Scenes	Technical
1	Check I've got the time-of-year right all the way through – mid to late September.		
2		Check map of Kenniston. Can you get to the allotments by going down Auriga Street? (or is it Auriga Road?)	
3			Am I using too many commas?
4		Not much description of Steve's mum. Do I need to add some?	
5	Steve worries about stealing the fruit. Do the other characters worry too? Should they? Decide about this.		

Example 2. Preparing to write the next story in the series – *The Long School Photograph* – in light of feedback from peers and the teacher:

Tasks:	My ideas	Teacher's advice	Readers' comments
Must do! – by end of week	Check old panoramic photos and how they were taken. Can you run from one side to the other in time?	Mr Houghton said that the best ghost stories were spooky rather than gory. He suggested I think about atmosphere and recommended some stories to read.	Deepak liked the bit in The Allotment Ghost when Old Man Jones chased the kids away. He said I should put a 'shocky' bit in my next story...But what? Think about this.
Consider doing these soon	I want to base the character of Specky on my friend John Reynolds. Must ask John's permission.	Check map of Kenniston to make sure the story locations are right.	Jenna thought 1) that there should be at least one female character in the DDG and 2) that the ghost of Specky should be inside Jethro's head. • Will there be time to introduce a female character? • Can I write the story so that Specky might have been real or imagined?

Before I write	Problem	Options	Action
1	The story plan talks about children cheating in tests. Could upset Mr Houghton, etc.	• Don't write about cheating. • Ask advice first. • Do it anyway.	I asked Mr Houghton and he didn't mind me writing about ways of cheating – He said it would be useful information for him when *we* do tests!
2	Will people understand about 'childish' and 'childlike'? We had an assembly on this once and I think the idea is really important.	• Leave that bit out. • Put it in and explain it a bit more. • Just mention it anyway hoping some readers will understand.	I've decided to mention it in passing. I don't want to sound 'preachy', but the whole point is that Jethro comes to learn more about Specky and what it's like to be a kid. Also, doing it this way won't make the story too long.
3	Jethro Evens is a really mean, cruel character, the kind of teacher everyone hates. It might annoy or upset some people if they are a bit like Jethro (or a lot like him!).	• Make Jethro nicer so people will sympathise with him. • Leave him as he is. • Have a different ending so Jethro turns out to be a nice guy in the end...	I asked a few people about this and decided in the end to keep Jethro cruel and mean. There are people like him, I'm not making it up. Anyway, I kind of feel sorry for Jethro in the end: he's such a lonely man, life has been a real disappointment to him.

Notice how organiser-templates like these make use of feedback, but support independence of judgement and accommodate individual decision-making. At times the entries resemble those you might find in a personal journal, which emphasises the essential nature of creative fiction. Compare the use of story organisers with 'Annotated Notebooks' (pp.133).

◆ Anticipating outcomes

Every child knows more or less explicitly that a story has a beginning, a middle and an end. When children have ideas for stories, they often have a (more or less vague) overview of the entire tale. In this sense, the outcome of the story has already been decided at the outset – although practising StoryMaker activities allows writers to understand that the 'fixed goal' of the story's conclusion can be reached by any number of routes. The notion of 'the inevitability of the ending being so' can be a wonderful benefit in priming the child for success. On the other hand, if it is conditioned into the child in a negative way – if the child thinks success is unwinnable – 'I can't write this story' – it may lead to an unfortunate self-fulfilling prophecy of failure.

Stories and the process of story-making can be used flexibly and powerfully as vehicles for goal-setting, envisioning achievable targets, anticipating successful outcomes and understanding the process of reaching those outcomes. Activities to enable this include:

- **Annotated Notebooks** – for previewing success, kickstarting preprocessing in the brain, logging the process of achieving goals.
- **Story Map** – for connecting the learning and seeing the Big Picture.
- **Story Tree** – for anticipating multiple outcomes, for planning the route(s) to desired outcomes, for smashing the myth of the inevitability of the outcome at the outset.
- **Story Path** – for 'chunking down' goals into strategies and strategies into specific tasks and techniques.

These activities will be found elsewhere in the book – see index.

◆ Sleep on it

The writer Douglas Hill relishes the prospect of starting a new story. Often his first ideas include a notion of some characters, a few details of setting, and the vital question, 'What's the problem?' which creates the essential conflict of the tale. He then follows the tried and tested method of:

- specifying the problem clearly and consciously
- reviewing all of the information he has available at the outset which is pertinent to the story
- reminding himself to be patient. Illumination (inspiration, ideas-out-of-the-blue) can be gathered systematically, but conscious impatience or pressure to achieve inhibits the subconscious creative flow)
- writing down ideas *as they arrive*. It is good practice to carry a notebook and pen around at all times, and to have them at the bedside if you wake (or are woken!) with a good idea in mind

● maintaining an easy assurance that useful material will come along. Once the creative subconscious has been stimulated to act by conscious clarity of direction, ideas will appear without effort – though hard work will be needed to evaluate and link them together into the 'finished product'.

Doug Hill loves nothing more than to write his characters into a cliffhanger situation and then to wonder, as he settles down to sleep, 'How will they get out of this fix?' Almost invariably he will wake with the solution in mind, and this acts as a platform for his writing that day.

The subconscious has been described as 'the ultimate multi-tasker'. It will routinely assimilate recent material into one's map of reality, but also has the capacity to work on specific problems once they have been consciously defined and the imperative to solve them has been articulated.

Although some aspects of sleep remain mysterious scientifically, it is widely accepted by artists and creative thinkers of all kinds that sleeping on a problem (while emphatically not worrying about it) stimulates a spray of ideas which can then be evaluated and acted upon consciously.

If you choose to use this technique with your children, take time to explain the basic model of the mind offered earlier. Run through the steps listed above, and check that the children have formulated their questions/problems/instructions clearly and simply. Tell them to read through these just before they go to sleep, and to notice their thoughts as they wake next morning – ideas can be subtle and fleeting. It is so easy to have a wonderful idea, only to have forgotten it moments later. Emphasise the importance of jotting down all ideas immediately, even if the notes are very sketchy: these will be the 'hooks' on which further material will hang later on.

Explain that if nothing comes along, children should be patient with themselves. Assimilation of material and the release of ideas is a process, and processes take time. It may well be that 'instructions' given on Monday night won't produce results until Wednesday morning – although the positive anticipation of success will stimulate subconscious preprocessing even more powerfully, and is likely to lead to a wealth of impressions ultimately.

◆ Picture work

It is wisely said that you can measure a circle by starting anywhere. Similarly, you can learn to think creatively/make a story by using any stimulus at any time. Pictures offer a powerful and accessible way of practising a range of thinking skills in this context. They also exert a strong influence subconsciously, because although we may use a dominant sensory modality (visual, auditory, kinaesthetic) to represent our understanding of the world, most of the information we absorb is visual. It is also the case that the subconscious thinks in a largely visual (and highly symbolic) way, which is why most people tend to recall dream images rather than sounds, textures, smells, etc.

Basic picture activity

Use a black-and-white picture as an initial stimulus.

Go through the following steps:

- What do you actually notice in the picture? (Say only what you can see.)
- If the picture was in colour, what colours would there be, do you think? (You can also ask children to explain why they opt for particular colours. You may get, 'Well, I just think his shirt would be blue' – which is fine, or the question might stimulate deductive reasoning and some interesting rationales).
- Now let's turn up the volume in the picture. What sounds do you hear?
- We're jumping into the picture – now! What else do you notice? (Further activities on associating/dissociating are suggested later.)

By this time, you have stimulated skills of observation, deduction and speculation (See *Self Intelligence* pp.28-32 for a more elaborate version of the activity) and have allowed children to notice the differences between these. You have also catered to the preferential learning styles within the group, inviting input from visual, auditory and kinaesthetic thinkers (if one can put it as simply as this). Further questions and prompts allow children to practise and draw pleasure from their non-dominant mode: ask auditory thinkers to notice where the light in the picture might be coming from: What's making it? What mood does it create in the picture? And so on.

The next step invites children to 'get into the mind' of the characters to explore emotions and motivations, and to anticipate outcomes.

- What do you think is going on in this picture? (It's from 'The Rope Swing' in *The Double Dare Gang*. This, and any other illustration featured, can be used independently of the story. Children won't need to have read the stories to do these activities.)

- What might have brought Nigel and Anna to this point? (Use 'Upside Down Tree' (see *Self Intelligence* p.190) as a way of exploring ideas.)

- Be Nigel and describe how you feel.

- Be Anna and describe how you feel.

- Be another member of the Double Dare Gang and describe how you feel about the situation.

- What might happen now?

- Have you ever been in any similar situation? If so, explain what happened and how you felt. If not, imagine such a situation and describe how you feel.

This step begins to separate out observations and 'facts' from opinions and value judgements. It also invites 'mind reading' – guessing what other people, fictional or otherwise, might be thinking. It's worth pointing out to children that although we can sometimes work out how someone feels from the way they look (posture, facial expression and nonverbal cues), it is usually unhelpful to mind read, especially if this leads to or reconfirms a negative self opinion – 'I know you're disappointed in me/I can tell you're angry/She always scowls when I've done something stupid… I'm just useless!'

Stepping-in and stepping-out of a picture or story scenario gives children greater control over their ability to associate with and dissociate from situations. This in turn develops flexibility in one's emotional response, both in the range of the emotions and in their intensity. So, instead of, say, getting upset or angry, one can stand back and decide if these emotions are justified, how assertively they should be expressed if they need to be, or whether some other response would be more helpful and/or beneficial. Such awareness, understanding and control of emotional response is the basis of so-called 'emotional literacy'.

A further benefit in the context of story-making and reading is that by practising stepping-in and stepping-out children can become more deeply involved in characters and situations, enjoying the experience of 'being there' while having the ability to dissociate so as to offer a wider perspective. Other benefits include:

- 'paying attention' becomes a learned skill whereby children are more richly and deeply involved in an educational experience. Disengaging from such attentiveness is accomplished elegantly and effectively through the use of 'brain breaks' (see *The ALPS Approach*, p.142), other break states, relaxation techniques, etc. Thus the process evolves into something much more deliberate, systematic and meaningful than paying attention or not! It also incorporates these sub-skills into a rich cluster forming part of the greater accelerated learning environment.

- ease-of-use in the skill of associating allows for the development of inter- and intrapersonal skills, including higher-order abilities such as empathy. Learning to understand how others feel might usefully proceed by exploring the characters in stories using a range of other StoryMaker activities.

- Stepping-In enhances VAK-ability – and vice versa! (See 'VAK-Splats' below).

- switching between states of association and dissociation encourages a more balanced use of the right and left cerebral hemispheres. A state of association, where information is absorbed and assimilated without great conscious effort, is the state of 'relaxed alertness' wherein creative thinking occurs without conscious interference – yet where the conscious mind is aware enough to receive and utilise intuitions (inner tuitions) which are the outcomes of such creative thought. Dissociating from that state 'switches down the volume' of the subconscious and focuses the conscious attention externally, so that the conscious tools of reflection, rationality and assessment can be used to hone and verify the intuitions gained earlier. (Incidentally, all authors must be familiar with such switching of states. They create first, through an easy flow of subconscious material, then edit and redraft within a more conciously active, 'intellectual' mode.)

◆ VAK-Splats

Although our predominant representational system may be visual, auditory or kinaesthetic, the subconscious 'map of reality' assimilates information in a multisensory way, reflecting the multisensory nature of our experiences. Enhancing children's skill in absorbing and expressing ideas across the range of their senses remains part of the accelerated learning 'mission' to give children as rich and meaningful an educational experience as possible. Developing 'VAK-ability' through the resource of fiction provides them with the necessary mental tools in an involving and enjoyable way.

The basic VAK-Splat technique brings children's attention repeatedly to the multisensory nature of what is being communicated in the story. Without this reminder, visual children might select out only the visual details, etc. A VAK-Splat icon acts as a visual anchor for the behaviour we seek…

> You could smell the apples, sweet and tempting, in the still September air. We were crouched down behind clumps of willow herb overlooking the allotments. The purply-pink flowers had withered and died, and by Christmas the patch would be nothing more than dried sticks, giving no cover at all. But for now we were camouflaged, hidden from everyone except a small terrier who came and sniffed at us before Brian scooted him on his way.

Stage one of VAK-Splatting encourages children to 'tease out' the multisensory nature of the text, perhaps by placing impressions in separate boxes. Stage two seeks to enhance those impressions by having children elaborate on the details; initially, again, in discrete boxes, but ultimately by writing pieces of polished text.

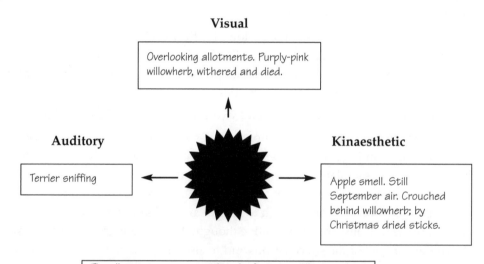

Visual

Overlooking allotments. Purply-pink willowherb, withered and died.

Auditory

Terrier sniffing

Kinaesthetic

Apple smell. Still September air. Crouched behind willowherb; by Christmas dried sticks.

So VAK-Splat it!

The allotments were a patchwork of greens, yellows and browns with some bright specks – oranges and reds – of late flowers.
The purply-pink willowherb also had some white feathery seedheads. The stalks were whitish-brown with darker brown patches.
The apples were mainly green with blotches of red and some brown spots.

The dry willowherb stalks crackled softly as the children crouched down. Kevin's watch ticked quickly and softly nearby.
The terrier's sniffing was fast and inquisitive.
Anthony's breathing was a bit wheezy.
Another dog barked far away in the distance.
An aeroplane droned a long way off in the sky.

The apples smelled sweet like flowers. The air was still and cool. There was also the smell of woodsmoke.
The willowherb stalks snapped easily if you bent them. The flowers were dry and a bit crackly. They had a dampish mouldy smell.
The terrier also smelled damp, a strong doggish smell. He had mud on his paws and they stank a bit.
I had pins-and-needles as I crouched with the Double Dare Gang.

Notice how easily a child associates with the story as she speculates on further multisensory details (see Stepping-In, Stepping-Out). And while VAK-Splatting is a somewhat explicit and extended process initially, with children being asked to write in boxes, eventually they reach a stage of nonconscious competence when it will become second nature to them to notice and express the richness of detail.

VAK-Splats can be used across the age and ability range and throughout the curriculum. Even the sometimes dry and rather abstract language of science would benefit from the technique – though it is important to state that in instances like this VAK-Splatting would not seek to detract from the descriptive precision of the language, but rather to enhance the child's experience of the process of science. An annotated science notebook (See 'Annotated Notebooks', p.31), for example, might contain an experiment written up conventionally on the right-hand page, while on the left the child's subjective VAK-Splatted impressions of what she did would allow the experience to be personalised and perhaps enriched with useful asides and insights.

Ultimately the simple inclusion of the VAK-Splat icon would be enough to trigger multisensory attention and assimilation of detail.

Because the sun is the biggest and heaviest thing in nearby space, it has the greatest gravitational pull. This means that the Earth, all the other planets, plus bits and pieces such as comets, asteroids and so on, are attracted towards it.

However, because of the speed with which these objects orbit the sun, they do not fall into it; instead, like a spaceship orbiting the Earth, they spin around in endless freefall, achieving balance and stability.

Imagine beads of various sizes rolling along as though they were on a sheet of glass, circling the central sun, and you've got a pretty good idea of what the Solar System looks like from way out in space.

During children's story writing, many variations on the theme of multisensory thinking become possible:

- characters could deliberately use sense-specific language to help raise readers' awareness of their own linguistic style. So, for example, Nigel could use visual language ('I see what you mean'/'Put me in the picture', etc.), while another member of the Double Dare Gang could be auditory, another kinaesthetic.
- visual thinkers could be encouraged to include auditory and kinaesthetic details; auditory thinkers to focus on kinaesthetic and visual; and kinaesthetic to notice visual and auditory.
- 'Annotated Notebooks' could come ready-written with VAK-Splat templates.

  (See *Self Intelligence*, Section 1: 'Developing sensory acuity'; *The ALPS Approach* p.180: 'VAK plus – See it, hear it, do it, be curious about it!' (Alistair Smith.))

Forbidden Fruit

Picture this:

Most younger children love to draw pictures to accompany stories, create coloured borders, sketch out maps of story locations and so on. All of this is to be encouraged, since it is a more kinaesthetically varied activity than actually writing, and creates a brain-break from the steady concentration required to compose text.

If children are to write on separate pieces of paper, at the very least offer sheets with plenty of border space for decoration, which could be a mixture of images, keywords, etc that you have chosen, and drawings made by the children themselves. The same technique can be used if children are keeping a journal of books they've read or writing a story review.

Border annotations are easily created in most modern word-processing packages. Encouraging children to use them at the PC gives them good practice in IT skills and allows for a very professional-looking finished product.

Temptation

◆ Pole-bridging

Pole-bridging has also been called 'muttering your understanding' (*The ALPS Approach* p.198), when neural pathways which link language sites with other 'poles' or points within the brain are created and strengthened. It is that self-absorbed state when you are engrossed in some task and talk yourself through it, quietly, effortlessly, often hardly realising you're doing so. Such a simple thing embodies elements of 'self-guiding' and the idea of 'How do I know what I think until I hear what I say?' Sometimes the very act of articulating an idea, problem, process, clarifies your understanding of it more than consciously thinking it through and 'trying hard' to succeed. The muttered information you get when Pole-bridging is largely subconscious: you might find that new connections are made and moments of illumination come frequently. The unselfconscious ease of Pole-bridging provides the insight that conscious effort is not and need not be involved.

Pole-bridging is a state of mind (and body) characterised by relaxed alertness, a lowering of the barriers between the subconscious mind and the object of attention, with murmured language as the link. When children read aloud to themselves in this state, you might notice them 'trying out' the characters' voices and even assuming their facial expressions and postures. Children also pole-bridge during writing, often as they spell a word or try out a sentence before they write it down. Some writers jump back a few sentences and re-read them as a stepping stone to the next bit of the story.

In a way you cannot try to Pole-bridge. Telling children, 'Right, class, we're going to do some Pole-bridging now!' is as profitless as demanding a daydream. But it is a state and a process that can be encouraged and woven into the texture of your lessons. Pole-bridge yourself as you work at your desk, so that children will notice what you're doing. Offer opportunities for children to model your behaviour, and praise them when you catch them doing it right. In the context of StoryMaking, mapping techniques ('Story Map', 'Story Tree', etc., pp.113–19, 139, 160) provide ideal situations for Pole-bridging to occur, while Annotated Notebooks (p.133) offers a vehicle for children to record their insights.

◆ The Without-Trying Game

Actually this can be any activity characterised by the ease and effortlessness of having ideas and making connections between them. You will recognise that Pole-bridging is a kind of 'without-trying' process, in which attention is closely focused on the task in hand. Variations of this might combine daydreaming with free association (see Section 8, 'Visualisation'), or with making specific links between randomly chosen ideas ('Link-it', below), or as a way of brainstorming a spray of ideas from an initial stimulus ('What Could This Be?' and 'What If?')

33

	1	2	3	4	5	6
1	hand	fog	vegetable	hair	sword	target
2	funhouse	heart	treadmill	circle	flower	horseshoe
3	fountain	foam	colour	chorus	gate	library
4	crown	floor	needle	bait	tapestry	pool
5	smoke	forest	bomb	sponge	shaft	fire
6	detour	partner	planet	camera	boobytrap	song

◆ Link-it

This activity makes use of a 6 x 6 grid so that dice-rolls can be incorporated to choose the words. However, smaller grids can be utilised as appropriate. In this case each word is numbered. Write the numbers on bits of paper and put them in a bag. Ask children to draw out two numbers and to make links between the corresponding words. Encourage 'spontaneous speech' and point out that no ideas will be wrong; even 'silly' ideas are acceptable if the link between the words can be explained.

A sample 6 x 6 template is given below, but children can make their own by choosing words randomly from books or from a word bank prepared earlier. Keywords pertinent to a particular story (or subject area) can also be cross-linked in this brainstorming way, often with interesting results.

As with every 'without-trying' game, once the initial wave of ideas had peaked, move on to another stimulus. Once children begin trying hard to have ideas, the links will become more artificial, the flow of the game will become stilted, and the fun factor will plummet.

Link-It variations

- If you find that the game is too loose and open (too much lee-way can inhibit children's thinking), fill the grid with words related to a particular genre (see Section 5, 'Genre').

- Ask children to select two or more words according to a simple mathematical pattern; every third word, say, or according to the 4x table – choose word 4, 8, 12, 16, 20, etc.

- Ask children to pick out groups of words which are similar in some way, such as having the same number of syllables, the same first letter, the fact that they refer to living things, etc.

- Fill the grid with the names of the children in the class (hopefully you won't need a bigger grid than 6 x 6!). Roll dice to select pairs and have them talk about what they have in common/what books they like/what story they're working on now.

- Fill the grid with characters from a story (choosing the grid size to suit the number of characters, or filling up remaining space with the names of children in the class). Randomly select two characters and have children imagine/write out a scene or conversation featuring them. Or match a real child with a story book character to be interviewed.

- See also *Self-Intelligence* pp. 200-205 for ways of using a grid template to invent characters, choose locations for a story, break down a narrative into manageable chunks (see also 'Chunk Me', below), and investigate emotions.

Link-it using side bars

Flexible formatting of text is discussed elsewhere in the book, but in the context of the 'Link-It' game, use wide borders in your students' notebooks and fill them with words or visuals which you invite the children to link. Begin by asking for simple associations, although you might find children get carried away in their thinking. This activity provides a useful opportunity for Pole-bridging (see above).

A	Link A & B in each case. (in note form or in a sentence)	B
floor	The autumn leaves were scattered across the floor…	
	Bright, fiery, comet, shooting-star, space, freedom, speed… Treadmill – routine, drudgery, boredom, obedience… I know how I like to make stories!	treadmill
hair	I was walking into town to have a haircut when suddenly this great big object landed in the middle of the street. There was a lot of smoke and confusion, and I was forced to take a detour… I think I'll call this story 'Bad Hair Day'.	detour
		camera
song		fountain

◆ The ethos of intuition – diffusions, downtime and attention skills

In a very important sense, whenever we are awake we are 'paying attention' to something. The term is usually intended to mean focusing our concentration on some external stimulus (although it may not in fact stimulate!), in order to retain and remember, link ideas together or otherwise manipulate the material on offer. Retaining and remembering information in the form in which it was given is actually a fairly low-level skill – and sometimes a tedious one, as any child or adult can attest. Being invited to make links and manipulate ideas is far more active, interesting and involving, and employs a range of higher-level skills such as observation, deduction, speculation, analysis and others, often including specific strategies for recall.

When our attention wanders, for instance when we daydream, it doesn't go away; it wanders to some other place – it internalises. Daydreaming combines conscious passivity with more or less focused concentration upon internal ideas, memories, anticipations and the links between these, although often the thoughts that rise up during daydreaming are fleeting and disconnected: we may notice or construct associations, however, in which case we follow a train of thought for a short way before some other notion drifts into our quietly idling field of consciousness.

Paying attention in the narrow sense has always been valued, indeed demanded, in the classroom, while daydreaming has usually been frowned upon. And yet both are capabilities of the mind that can be utilised and exploited in a variety of ways to facilitate learning.

In *The ALPS Approach* the point is made that 'we tune in and out naturally', and in accordance not just with our immediate environment but also in line with numerous other factors such as intake of food and water, recent experiences, and cycles such as the 90-minute ultradian rhythm that runs through our lives (Ernest Lawrence Rossi, *The Psychobiology of Mind–Body Healing* – see Bibliography). Our attention moves in subtle and complex ways across the field of consciousness, creating a state that may be external or internal, vigilant or relaxed (active/passive):

external	vigilant
internal	relaxed

When attention is externalised and vigilant or focused, concentration peaks quickly and tails off more slowly. In other words, in traditional classrooms the attentive state is expected, but in all children it changes inevitably, and attention wanders. One way of maintaining concentration is to break the state deliberately just as concentration tails away, and/or allow 'downtime' or diffusions where a different mental-physiological state is not only allowed, but built in to the learning programme.

In Alistair Smith's books and in other books on accelerated learning listed in the Bibliography, much more information is to be found on listening and attention skills, diffusions and downtime. For our purposes here we can mention some strategies in passing:

- diverting the attention, however briefly, constitutes a 'break state'. the diversion can be towards something else that's external ('Oh, I can smell lunch cooking!'/'Just listen to those seagulls outside!'/'And as you can see from the poster on the back wall...'), or towards the child's internal world, making use of 'easy recollection' or active imagination ('And I wonder how much *you* remember now about your last holiday...?'/'So imagine what the world would be like if *everyone* could turn invisible whenever they wanted to!').

- changing the physiology changes the mental state. Something as simple as breathing differently allows children to relax, and thereby refreshes the concentration (See *Self-Intelligence*, 'Utilising Relaxation and Break States'). Another technique is to ask children to notice various groups of muscles and consciously relax them. Many of the exercises in Brain Gym and educational kinesiology serve the purpose (among others) of giving learners a break from concentrating through diverting the attention and physical movement.

- visualisations (see the section on visualisations later in this book) deliberately and systematically direct the attention inwardly, while exploiting the mind's ability to construct scenarios consciously (internal-vigilant) and 'notice effortlessly' more-or-less assimilated information coming from the subconscious (internal-relaxed). This process, in which we become aware of stuff that we didn't know we knew, is the essence of creative thinking. Simply put it amounts to intuition – inner tuition, by which we recognise meaningful clusters of associations through sequences of illuminated moments.

All of the above mental skills can be developed through stories in the reading, writing and telling. The formatting of text in stories tends to remain constant and conventional (although designers are paid sums of money to decide on font, point size and other attributes of text). And if the stories are good, they will involve readers for extended periods of time. Using illustrations diverts attention, breaks the 'reading state' and adds information visually to the child's perception of the world of the story. Utilising wide borders ('side bars' – see the section on flexible text formats) with instructions, questions, icons and other visual prompts, diverts the attention and evokes active imagination and subconscious preprocessing. The advent of books in electronic format (e-books) is opening up the field of possibilities for interactive text whereby reading, writing and telling can blend into a rich experience which will be both entertaining and instructional (the two things actually go hand in hand).

Storytelling demands a section of its own (Section 9). It is sufficient to say here that people are never too old to listen to a story, while learning storytelling skills boosts confidence, stimulates creative thinking and opens the doors to a range of educational opportunities. If you choose to learn those skills for yourself, it is highly recommended that you teach them to your children. Storytime should not always be a time of the teacher telling and the children listening quietly!

◆ Questioneering

'Question' and 'quest' share the same root – to seek. Intuitions, self-listening, quiet reflection, all allow a learner to seek and find out by looking in. Indeed, most novelists would tell you that a story evolves through the asking of hundreds or thousands of questions, and then listening patiently to the answers that pop into mind. The writer Douglas Hill begins his story-making with the fundamental question, 'What's the problem?' that his characters must face. This stimulates the quest for the answers that inform the writing of his story.

'Questioneering' is the art of systematic, ongoing questioning, driven by curiosity, taking into account information gleaned through previous enquiry. It is a term that applies equally to the scientific method and the creation and study of stories. Questioneering is a skill *underpinned by an attitude* that is as profound and important as literacy or numeracy to the developing mind. Throughout this book it is defined, explained and developed through a range of techniques.

We have already seen how creative thinking is stimulated by asking open questions, admitting all responses in a non-judgemental way (the evaluation and verification comes later). This kind of questioneering leads to the subsequent manipulation of ideas; notions are associated, they evolve, they often consolidate into a deeper understanding. And the tendency is for the 'questioneer' to become more independent, flexible and yet discriminating and incisive in the questions she asks. She will also be increasingly prepared to speculate wildly and think radically, realising that taking these routes is not frivolous, but may lead to some startling and useful new insights…

'What If?' is a brainstorming game which stimulates spontaneous generation of ideas (See *Imagine That…* p.86). It's a great group game which allows all children to become involved and to develop their confidence in having ideas while also having fun. On one occasion when I played the game I asked, 'What if people began shrinking once they reached middle-age, so that pensioners were only one inch tall?' The usual rush of ideas came along, some outrageous and mischievous ('Steve, we could keep Miss Brown in a jam jar!'), some considered and practical ('Older people could live in doll's houses'), others refreshingly innovative ('Steve, kids could buy a family pack – a kind of rucksack with different-sized pouches for parents and grandparents. That way the kids could carry the adults around easily'). Another bonus, which became clearer as the game went on, was that some children were basing their ideas on themes related to issues. One little boy, for instance, was quite concerned that old people, being tiny and vulnerable, should be adequately protected in society. He suggested special walkways covered over with tough transparent plastic, where older people could walk in safety. This led other children to talk about miniaturised railway systems and underground tube transport in cities and towns; specially trained 'guide rats' to act as pack animals and protectors for pensioners; houses-on-stilts so that old people could still lean over their garden fence and talk eye-to-eye with younger folks…

It hardly needs pointing out a) that the group ended up talking about real-life issues to do with special provision for minority groups (although most of the kids thought they were still just playing a game) and b) that out of this great seethe of vigorous ideas, something truly original and useful could easily emerge, for, as the saying goes, 'Voyages of discovery consist not of going to new lands, but seeing with new eyes.'

It is worth mentioning here that many scientific and technological innovations came about through what-if type questions, seeing with new eyes, recognising the potential behind a supposed mistake or failure. Einstein asked himself, 'What if I could ride on a light beam? What would the universe look like?' This and other 'thought experiments' allowed him to conceptualise and develop his ideas on relativity.

The German chemist August Kekule describes in his notebooks how his researches into the class of chemicals called benzenes was hindered by his ignorance of their molecular structure. He writes that one evening as he dozed in a half-sleep in front of his fire, he dreamed of snakes writhing at his feet. One snake curled itself round and put its tail in its mouth – and Kekule woke with the certainty that the benzene molecule was a ring shape. This 'factless knowledge', visual, representational and accompanied by 'just knowing it was right' had been assimilated subconsciously and projected into consciousness leading, to a moment of illumination. Kekule's subsequent experiments verified his insight.

One also recalls that sticky notelets came about because a batch of adhesive had not been correctly formulated; that velcro was developed after someone noticed how teazle heads snagged in clothing; that a huge leap forward in holographic technology occurred when a technician dropped a glass holographic plate and noticed that the entire image was reproduced within every fragment. The history of science is littered with similar stories, where the principles of creativity and thinking skills outlined here, driven by curiosity, led to breakthroughs and quantum jumps in understanding.

The activities presented in *Alps StoryMaker* and the broader field of a child's engagement with and interest in stories offers a range of wonderful opportunities to hone skills pertinent to 'the real world' in any number of ways. To be sure, skills development is almost a subsidiary aspect of one's love of stories and adventure, the feeding of one's sense of wonder of the world, and that profound and sometimes blissful realisation that the author of a story has had the same kinds of experiences and ideas as the reader, and has here articulated them perfectly in a way that warms the heart. Ezra Pound said that 'A book is a ball of light in one's hands', while Einstein maintained that 'Imagination is more important than knowledge'. A story is the realm where these wisdoms meet, and where children can come to know the true meaning of Education – to draw out one's understanding of the world so that others may know what you mean.

◆ Meaning-making

This term, coined by Neil Postman and Charles Weingartner in *Teaching as a Subversive Activity*, sums up the basis of all learning in all people. We need to make sense of the world in order to survive and flourish in it. If our life was bereft of meanings, one way or another we wouldn't last long. As our brains develop, we come to understand the world in more detail – and vice versa, for as we make meanings based on experience (through imitation, trial-and-error and insight) the neurons in the brain wire up to reflect our growing understandings.

This neurological configuration is reflected in what has already been called the 'map of reality'. It is our mindscape, a mental landscape of memories, beliefs, attitudes, values, opinions and ideas existing largely at a subconscious level, but expressing itself consciously through thoughts, emotions, physiological states and language.

What we say and how we say it – our 'wordscape' – offers clues to the deep structure of our understandings. Jean Paul Sartre said that words are loaded pistols. They are also powerful tools to help accelerate learning.

◆ Challenging the language

Human beings are creatures of habit, and that includes habits and patterns of language. Steve recalls a neighbour he would often meet outside the sub-post office and grocery store at the end of the street. Habitually he would mention the weather and the neighbour would equally automatically reply, 'Well at least it's dry.' One rainy day they encountered each other again, both hurrying to escape the heavy downpour. 'Awful weather we're having today,' Steve said, to which the neighbour replied, 'Well at least it's dry.'

Although language patterns give clues to deep understandings, and although in one sense we're (usually) conscious when we speak, we're not always fully aware of what we say. Nor, indeed, are our listeners fully cognizant of what we mean – the cause of many an argument, no doubt, since everything that goes into their heads is filtered and interpreted through *their* understandings of life. One of Steve's tutors had a big sign above his chair which said, 'I am responsible for what I say, but not for what you hear.' Wise words, although we can ponder how responsible we really are if we are not fully aware of what we are saying.

One aspect of this is 'limiting language' or language which reflects limiting beliefs. How often have you asked a child to carry out a task, only to be met with, 'But I can't, it's too hard'? Or 'I'm no good at doing things like that'? Or 'Yes, but can't I do such-and-such instead'? Once you become aware of such language in particular children, which is often habitual in them, you can begin to intervene to change it.

A useful starting-point is to realise that individuals weren't born with the beliefs echoed in what they say. 'I can't, it's too hard' expresses a belief which has been constructed, and like a wall made of bricks it can be dismantled and rebuilt to a different design. This may not happen swiftly or radically – indeed there might be very little change within the span of your working relationship with the child – but simply to make the child aware of other possibilities can be very liberating for that person and set them on a new and positive path.

An intervention should not amount to a flat disagreement. 'I can't do that' is not best modified by replying, 'Well of course you can.' That response simply isn't congruent with what the child believes. One approach asks precise questions to retrieve precise information: ' What exactly is it (about the task) that you find hard?' Or 'What exactly stops you from going ahead?'

The 'can't' bit of the belief is a closed door barring the way. Challenge that by saying something like, 'How exactly do you know that you can't?' Or, 'What are you feeling that tells you that you can't?' What you're asking for here is for the child to become aware of physiology and emotions, and then you can work to modify them (see, for example, 'Personifying emotions', p.190). Precise questioning for the retrieval of detailed information makes use of the 'meta model', a derivative of work within the field of neuro-linguistic programming (NLP). NLP literature is extensive, but a good place to start to find out more is *Introducing Neuro-Linguistic Programming* by Joseph O'Connor and John Seymour.

Another handy intervention puts a different frame around the child's limiting belief so when she says, 'I can't do this,' say, 'Well pretend you can, and let me know when you've done it.' This simple and elegant response serves several purposes. It does not deny, judge or criticise the child's belief, it evokes the idea of 'pretend': in other words, the child is not doing the hard task for real and so there's no reason to fear failure. The world of pretend is the world of make-believe (making beliefs!). The child can do the task safely. The use of 'when' subtly presupposes success, and you can elaborate on that by saying, 'You might not have many ideas, perhaps only five or six – or maybe many more.' That puts a lower limit of five or six ideas on the outcome of the task. And your pupil will go away and pretend she can have that many ideas, and she'll let you know when she's done it!

◆ Connective prompts

The use of connective prompts, like employing the meta model, seeks more detailed information about a block to progress. The tool is best used when the child feels comfortable and safe, and has some experience of playing the Without-Trying Game. Connective prompts are words which connect ideas in a sequence and prompt the respondent to follow that sequence. Good prompt words are: because, while, before, after, when.

Child:	I can't do this.
You:	You can't do this because?
Child:	I can't do this because it's hard.
You:	It's hard because?
Child:	It's hard because I don't understand it.
You:	You don't understand it because?
Child:	I don't understand it because I'm no good at spelling.
You:	You're no good at spelling because?
Child:	I'm no good at spelling because I can't remember the letters.
You:	You can't remember the letters because?
Child:	I can't remember the letters because I can't see them in my head...

And so on. This is an idealised example, but it illustrates the point that when the questionee is prepared to admit (to let into conscious awareness) 'the reasons behind the reasons' you can soon get to the heart of the matter and suggest resolutions of the issue. In this case, the child does not have an effective strategy for spelling – and to find out about some great ones, see *Dynamic Learning* by Robert Dilts and Todd Epstein.

Incidentally, connective prompts can be used powerfully in connection with 'Context Sentences' for plotting (see *Imagine That* p.90).

◆ Many endings

A related activity which exploits a child's ability to have many ideas puts gentle pressure on her to explore reasons for the difficulty. Again, the child needs to feel safe and assume the state of relaxed alertness that will allow information to flow easily into consciousness.

Child:	I can't do this because it's hard.
You:	Put another ending on it: I can't do this because –
Child:	I can't do this because I'll feel foolish.
You:	Put another ending on it: I can't do this because –
Child:	I can't do this because kids will laugh at me.
You:	Put another ending on it: I can't do this because –
Child:	I can't do this because Mr Simms used to shout at me.

Again with the 'Many Endings' technique you can quickly find the heart of the matter as memories and significance emerge. (See *Self-Intelligence* p.182.) The technique is also used in conjunction with 'Story Tree', p.139.

◆ Menu of options

Sometimes children find tasks difficult because it's the only way they've ever been shown of achieving something (learning spellings is a clear example of this). In light of this it is important to offer a menu of options which cater to the wide range of learning styles and preferences you'll find among your students. This is not just a matter of differentiation of materials, but showing children different strategies to achieve the fixed goal of succeeding in the task.

Child:	It's no good, I can't think of ideas for stories. It's too hard.
You:	I understand what you're saying, so I wonder if you'd investigate something for me? I've got some games for story-making here and I'd like to know how easy you find them. Would you run them through and give them a difficulty rating out of ten?
Child:	Well...
You:	This one for instance asks you to roll a dice to give a character a one-to-six score for intelligence, strength, evil, and so on. This one, called 'Think Bubbles', asks you to decide what characters are thinking (p.181). This one asks you to pretend you're Anthony out of the Double Dare Gang and decide what you'd do in certain situations ('Getting to Know You' p.168). I mean, there are lots of games here. Pick whichever appeal to you and let me know when you've done them.

Child:	The dice one sounds all right.
You:	Are you going to start with that one, then?
Child:	OK then.

◆ Models and metaphors

The world of the story is itself a powerful arena within which meanings can be made. In the same way that we build into our own persona traits from people we like and admire in 'real life', so we may model behaviours we find in the characters who populate stories. People have said to me often that they're sorry to reach the end of a book because it's like saying goodbye to old friends. In one sense it is, but in another we carry with us the characters we met and sometimes – in a very literal way – we embody what they were like.

Some stories, via their themes and motifs and other elements, communicate directly to the subconscious mind through metaphor. One reason why myths and legends and fairytales resonate so powerfully in our minds is because, however fantastical they appear, at their core they contain truth. Well written stories of science fiction, fantasy and horror perform the same function: these genres especially articulate meanings of great importance, frequently through metaphorical reference we might not consciously appreciate at the time. For more information on this idea, and used in a therapeutic context, listen to *How Stories Heal* by Pat Williams (see Bibliography).

T. S. Eliot said that poetry communicates before it is understood. The same is surely true of the best stories, which speak to us at many levels. Children will draw meaning from such tales. They might not understand why a story made such a lasting impression on them, but they will usually have a sense of its significance anchored in vivid impressions and strong emotions. Similarly, perhaps as part of the 'hidden curriculum', you will run StoryMaker activities in the knowledge that any constituent feature of a story a child is making can possess a metaphorical aspect which touches upon the life-themes and ongoing concerns of the writer. This point will be raised again and explored elsewhere in the book – for now it is enough to plant the seed of the idea and allow it to grow as we move on to other things.

◆ Wordplay

Creative thinking, and therefore effective learning, is characterised by curiosity and also by a great sense of fun. Neil Postman maintains that playing with language is an important means of making discoveries. Within the world of StoryMaker, it is an essential prerequisite.

Wordplay can take many forms. Here are a few ideas

- Take words to bits and put them together again, perhaps with a few small amendments: 'in-formation/quest-I('m)-on/now-here/in(ner)-tuition/under(where I'm)-standing/in-sight/out-come/imag(e)-nation'.

- Look at the etymology of words and review and refresh definitions:
    - education – Latin: *educare*, to draw out.
    - emotion – French: *emouvoir*, move, motion.
    - story – Latin: *historia*, history (his-story!).
    - legend – Greek: to gather, say, akin to *logos* (logic), speech, word, reason.
    - character: Greek: *charakter* from *charassein* to scratch, engrave.
    - narrate – Latin: *gnarus*, knowing, from *noscere*, to come to know.

- 'Flip the Coin'. State the opposite of something said:
    - I'm not so bad – you are so good.
    - At least it's dry – at most it's wet.
    - The glass is half full – the glass is not half empty.
    - There's life in the old dog yet – there's death in the young cat yet.

    (*Note*: This is more of a habit to get into rather than a game to play in any formal or structured sense. It can bring up some startlingly fresh ideas, but can be very irritating if you do it too much!)

- Spoonerisms and variants: transposing letpers or whole words can be great fun. Again, encourage children to try it out 'without trying' as they go through their day…
    - Don't cross the road until you see the mean gran.
    - Would you like some keys and parrots with your dinner?
    - That was a clever answer – you're as mean as custard.

- See also 'Playing with prefixes and suffixes' (p.217); 'What's in a name?' (p.209); *The Oxford Book of Word Games* by Tony Augarde.

◆ Representing the knowledge

A listair Smith and Nicola Call assert that 'We know people truly understand when they can represent the knowledge in more than one way.' One of the aims of StoryMaker is not only to offer children a menu of options for achieving success in story-making according to their own needs and requirements, but to allow them to represent their learning and understanding in a variety of ways. So, for instance, you'll find these activities elsewhere in the book which give children the chance to express and explain their thinking about plot:

- **Story Map** caters to visual and holistic (Big Picture) learners.
- **Story Tree** satisfies sequential thinkers while opening out possibilities.

- **Story Tray** offers kinaesthetically-oriented children the chance to move stuff about as they consolidate their ideas.
- **Retelling** allows children to review and assimilate their thinking while building confidence through mastering storytelling skills – How do I know what I think until I hear what I say?
- **Embellishing** allows children to practise free-association within a framework of understanding.
- **Restructuring**, for example using **Story Path**, gives children the opportunity to manipulate ideas and discover new possibilities through trying out different sequences of ideas.

These are truly 'different doors into the same house', and as such you should encourage children to take an eclectic approach to their learning: give them lots of options and allow them to use what works well for them.

Someone who carries his
own lantern has no need
to fear the dark.

Traditional

Section Two

The story process

... But now, like the click of some small switch which starts a great machine in operation, it proved to be the jog which awoke his mind to action.

L.T. More describing Newton's insight into gravitation

Section 2 : The story process

Page	Topic/activity	Story element covered	Accelerated learning link
51	The story process		Personalisation of knowledge
52	Story overview		Preview-do-review process / inspiration and reflection
52	Top down, bottom up	*Layers and levels in story-making*	Chunking up and down/flexibility of strategies
53	Outcomes thinking	*Planning at all levels, from themes to descriptive details*	Thinking across the span and through the layers of a story – a story as a structure for information
54	Blurb it!	*Summary/persuasive and emotive language*	Categorisation of information / templates as structures for the organisation of ideas
59	Keywork	*Analysis of text / identification of key ideas / personal response to text/exploration of ideas through questioning and speculation*	Learning styles and the assimilation of information – 'meaning-making'
62	Quality questions	*Exploration of text at all levels*	Questioning as a tool for generating information and analysis of text / selection and prioritisation of information
63	Embedded questions and instructions	*Generating ideas at all levels*	Preprocessing/ nonconscious learning/elegant structuring of the linguistic environment in the classroom
64	Chunk me	*Awareness of the 'chunk size' and layers within a story*	Chunking as an organisational device / planning/decision-making
66	The tale unfolds	*Visual mapping of story constituents*	Learning styles/the big picture
70	Off the top of your head	*Generating ideas at all levels*	Brainstorming/association of ideas / VAK/visualisation across the sensory modes
72	Help me to write a story	*Intentionality in writing / planning strategies*	Anticipation of outcomes/success thinking
75	Countdown to a story	*Intentionality in writing / planning strategies in detail*	Elaboration of preview–do–review process/prioritisation of information
80	Countdown to a story circle-time	*Intentionality in writing / planning as group work*	Circle time/development of social skills and the personal intelligences
82	Strategy cards	*Incorporating ideas into an individual plan*	Prioritisation of information / awareness of strategies / personalisation of ideas/goal-setting
83	Countdown grid	*Story planning*	Incorporating feedback into an individual planning strategy/decision-making/development of self-esteem and independence of judgement
83	Reflective dialogue	*Review of story elements*	Development of self-assessment skills / consolidation of learning/synthesis of information/strategic thinking
85	Get an attitude!	*All elements*	Affirmations and success thinking / recognition of links between attitude and outcome/target- and goal-setting
87	What have I done?	*Review of writing*	Development of self-assessment skills / understanding and use of feedback / development of self-esteem

89	The self-assembling curry	*Use of metaphor in planning*	Consolidation of thinking tools / balance between conscious and subconscious abilities
90	Consider your audience	*Planning with reference to audience*	Development of interpersonal intelligence/visualisation skills / planning and purpose
93	Grading and assessment	*All elements*	Development of critiquing skills / elegant use of feedback/awareness of 'the 5rs'
94	The contrast-comparison grid	*Review of story elements*	Development of critiquing skills / elegant use of feedback/awareness of VAK in writing
95	Writing blocks	*All elements*	Awareness of limiting beliefs / development of problem-solving strategies/development of intrapersonal skills
98	Rapport	*All elements – the writer–reader link*	Development of self-esteem and the personal intelligences
99	Tips for good practice	*All elements*	Consolidation of the above

If you want creative
workers, give them
enough time to play.

John Cleese

Section Two

The story process

If students are to become better thinkers – to learn meaningfully, to think flexibly and to make reasoned judgements – then they must be taught explicitly how to do it.

Carol McGuinness, DFEE Research Report 1999 *(quoted in* The ALPS Approach *p. 97)*

The central premise of ALPS StoryMaker is that fiction can be used to make students 'better thinkers' by raising their awareness of the kinds of thinking that are possible (i.e .using the full range of thinking tools) and the circumstances in which different thinking skills are most appropriate. Virtually all the kinds of thinking that children will be required to do in schools generally (and some that they may never be required to do!) can be practised within the rich and engaging world of stories. Flexible thinking (of which 'making reasoned judgements' is one outcome) is a natural consequence of story-making – a complex of skills which can then be applied to the study of other fiction and non-fiction work.

'Learning meaningfully' is a more loaded and controversial idea – learn meaningfully by whose judgement, standards and criteria? The point has already been made that we all learn anyway: we absorb the world, we soak it up by virtue of the fact that we are alive. Everything has meaning and significance in our lives, whether we are aware of it or not. And, as the subconscious agenda builds within our minds (creating the 'bundles of contradictions' that we call human beings), patterns of thought, emotion and physical response appear as a consequence of the lessons we learn from the world and the beliefs those lessons define. A balance must always be borne in mind, therefore: meaningful learning is a compromise between what is personally significant to every individual, and what can be measured by the gamut of tests and assessments that help to form the assault course of the current educational system – which is to say that children must prove they have learnt meaningfully by reproducing the right answers. The old wisdom says that we should 'include the knower in the known'. Above and beyond test results (which admittedly are important to many children) we should encourage children to ponder ideas like: What does this mean to me? What else could it mean? How can I use my understanding most effectively? All of the activities in StoryMaker support these primary questions.

◆ Story overview

Stories are complex structures. Often the study of text deconstructs stories to the Nth degree, which is fine if one holds on to the idea that the whole is more than the sum of the parts – knowing precisely how a sports car is put together does not amount to the thrill of a fast ride! Creating stories, however, can be systematic only up to a certain point. Despite all that has been said about the subconscious resource and 'reigning in the muse', space should always be left for the magic to flow throughout the three main stages of the story-making process: the thinking time (preview/preparation), the writing time (action/reaction) and the looking back time (review/reflection).

A corollary to that idea is that no writer can tell you 'how to do it', but only how they do it. Similarly, no technique offered in a book such as this will suit all learners. Therefore, children should be guided within an environment that allows them to feel confident enough to discard techniques that don't suit them, and to adapt those others in which they see some potential. Doing it by the book is ultimately limiting because it's someone else's book. The trick is to create a book of your own.

◆ Top down, bottom up:

Stories are multi-layered structures, a bit like people. The processes of story-making and story study both take account of these layers, which can be approached from the top downwards or from the bottom upwards.

The layers of a story:

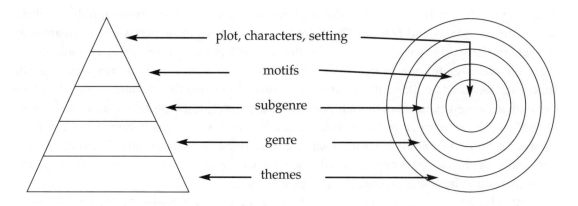

Each of these sections will be explored more closely later. The top-down approach to story construction begins with an idea that might have come 'out of the blue', or which has derived from one of the StoryMaker games (coming systematically out of the blue!). Often such an idea is plot-related: 'What if this happened one day?' More experienced writers are likely also to have character-centred ideas as a starting-point, or ones based on the precepts and conventions of a genre, or maybe ideas where the setting/location/background is central to the logic of the story.

Once the initial idea exists, story-making activities allow plot, characters and setting to be developed. The 'world of the story' will begin to be fleshed out. As this occurs, the motifs – constituent features or 'ingredients' of the story – become more clearly defined and their significance more deeply appreciated. Many children enjoy writing genre fiction, and soon come to see if/how their evolving ideas fit within the landscape of any particular genre. ('Sub-genres' are smaller areas in the overall territory of the genre.) By this point, and throughout the writing and 'looking back time', an awareness will be growing of the themes that underpin the story (and which may link many of that writer's stories and the issues that occur in her life).

The bottom-up approach to story-making starts with a theme or with several themes interlinked. The writer then moves up through the levels, considering how those themes are pertinent to one or more genres. This will confer significance upon the story's motifs as they come to mind, together with insights about plot, character and setting. At any point along this bottom-up journey, what we recognise as an idea for a story can appear and unfold in the writer's mind.

What has been said so far might sound abstract or vague. Further specific activities will clarify the process. In the same way that a circle can be measured by starting anywhere, so a story can grow from any beginning. Creativity is messy, and children empowered by curiosity and confidence will spray out ideas that pay no heed to top-down or bottom-up or any other approaches you've shown them! That's fine, although do take the opportunity to examine a child's story-making strategy; work out how and why it works, and then have that student explain her process to others for them to use if they wish.

◆ Outcomes thinking

Whatever approach to story-making a child uses, it is helpful to encourage the writer to think about the outcome of the work as a whole and during each stage of its construction. Outcomes thinking might be described as 'auto feedback', reflections in the form of questions applied at any point and with reference to any level of the story.

The writing process:

	beginning	middle	end
character	1		
setting		2	
plot			
motifs	3		
genre	4		
themes			5

General outcomes-thinking questions look like this:

- What will the finished piece of work be like (form, style, length, appearance, etc)?
- How will I know within myself if the work is successful?
- How will I know based on feedback from other people that the work is successful?
- How might I feel about their comments?
- What might I have learned from completing this piece of work that will help me to do the next one more effectively and successfully?

Questions can also relate to specific levels or aspects of the story anywhere along the 'time line' of thinking–writing–looking back. So:

1 What effect do I want my main character to have on readers when I first introduce her?

2 How am I going to let readers know that the action jumps to another setting and a week later at the start of Chapter Three, without saying so in so many words?

3 What might be the best way of linking the meeting in Mr Lee's Magic Shop (end of Chapter One) with the theme of the story, which is trickery?

4 How closely do I need to link the idea of masks and tricks (and the time of year, Halloween) with the horror genre? Does that fact that Anthony is (probably) going to get flung on the bonfire turn it into a horror story?

5 How much emphasis should I put on the idea that the boys now, for the first time, realise that Anna is a girl with her own sexuality? How far should this change of balance affect the later stories?

Outcomes thinking, whether in the context of story-making or in any area of the curriculum, or life, proceeds from the stage of 'conscious incompetence', where we try hard and deliberately and obtain less effective results, to 'nonconscious competence', where the process happens automatically and with elegance.

◆ Blurb it!

It has been said that the best way to learn something is to teach it to somebody else. Nearly as good is to tell it to somebody else. Book blurbs are carefully and concisely written text 'bites' designed to make the maximum impact in the minimum space. Encouraging children to write their own story blurbs allows them to review the work and consider language that is to have a particular effect upon the reader. A sample blurb (from Steve's short story collection *Catch*) is given below. The use of templates makes it easier to chunk down the blurb into separate elements, each with its particular job to do.

Hook – intriguing questions or exclamatory statements	What dreadful secret is the new girl in school keeping from her friends? How does a shy, quiet boy deal with the bullying he suffers? Who lives alone at the heart of a mysterious stretch of woodland? Why does a normal, ordinary kid go fishing in a dark room in a tumbledown old house?
Category of story	Tales of horror, fantasy and science fiction all come together in this collection of short stories by –
Information about author	Steve Bowkett – author of *Dreamcastle* (from Orion's popular Web series), *Roy Kane – TV Detective* (A&C Black's Graffix series), *Horror At Halloween*, and the forthcoming SF/Fantasy trilogy *The Wintering* .
Quotes and testimonials	'Steve Bowkett has a rare flair for creating an atmosphere of fear and horror out of the most prosaic of situations' – *Junior Bookshelf* 'Steve Bowkett's writing catches the stuff of adolescence' - *The Observer* 'Steve Bowkett proves in this collection that Horror fiction need not be gratuitous, but can have an important message at its heart' – Ben Leech, horror writer

Have children study other blurbs to notice patterns of language and organisation that they can incorporate into different templates. Use this opportunity to raise awareness of emotive language, cliché and over-writing, and encourage writers to obtain 'real' quotes from other people, and to develop a healthy and realistic attitude when bad crits come along!

Suggested blurb templates for use with Steve's books *Dreamcatcher*, *The Planet Machine* and *Roy Kane – TV Detective* follow:

Logo for story or series	
Hook line	
Three or four short statements elaborating on hook line	
Brief paragraph outlining story scenario	
'Punch' line articulating theme of book or series	

From Steve's book *Dreamcatcher* from Orion's Dreamtime Series

Exciting bit of dialogue from the story		(Half-page illustration from story)
Brief paragraph outlining plot		
Hook line common to all stories in the series	Head-and-shoulders of character with speech bubble	

From Steve's *The Planet Machine* from A & C Black's Comix series.

Banner hook line common to all books in the series		
Cropped image from cover art		Brief 'teaser' about the opening of the story
		Short paragraph overview of story
		Info. on cover art, illustrations
		Series logo

From Steve's *Roy Kane – TV Detective*, A&C Black's Graffix series

◆ Keywork

This activity makes use of a template that involves children directly and immediately in 'making meaning' of the stories they read. Conventionally fiction is presented as solid text written on both left- and right-hand pages. The ethos implicit in ALPS StoryMaker encourages text to be presented in a variety of ways, depending upon the learning needs and requirements of the reader.

The following Keywork template reflects the important accelerated learning principle that different people's brains prefer to absorb and assimilate information in different ways. Children will have diverse ideas/questions/responses to the fiction they read. The template makes allowances for this and respects the differences.

In the case of fiction already published, the text comes first and the key ideas, questions and task-symbols are added later. With children's own writing, the ideas, questions and tasks act as a 'preprocessing preliminary' to confident writing.

With reference to key ideas, children are encouraged to note down what they think is important to them, as well as speculating on the author's intentions. This is emphatically not a game of 'guess the right answer'. Questions can be asked freely and openly in the accelerated learning environment without the fear of accusations of ignorance. The task-symbol code could be standard, or might be invented by children themselves as part of their learning about punctuation marks and signs and symbols in general.

Text	Key ideas	Key questions	Task symbols
You could smell the apples, sweet and tempting, in the still September air. We were crouched down behind clumps of willow-herb overlooking the allotments. The purply-pink flowers had withered and died, and by Christmas the patch would be nothing more than dried sticks, giving no cover at all. But for now we were camouflaged, hidden from everyone except a small terrier who came and sniffed at us before Brian scooted him on his way.	*time of year*	*Why mention the 'purply-pink' flowers?*	*[I like this bit of description]*
	everything lives and dies	*Why does the author pick Christmas, in particular?*	
	comic relief to ease the tension		" "
'OK,' said Nige in brisk, military style. 'We go in just there, to the side of that black shed. A piece of the chain-link fencing has come loose; it'll be easy for Bri to ease it away enough for us to slip through...'	*characteristic of Nigel*	*Why do they want to steal the fruit anyway?*	*[I've told this part to a friend]*
	stealing fruit		

Text	Key ideas	Key questions	Task symbols

◆ Quality questions

The importance of asking questions has already been mentioned ('Questioneering', p.38–9) and the distinction made between closed and open questions. Closed questions are intended to retrieve precise pieces of information, which is fine if the circumstances are conducive to further learning. There is a world of difference between playing the 'guess-the-right-answer game', and a child initiating a closed question with the aim of finding a specific answer.

Let's suppose that a young writer wants to describe the colour of the sky as part of a description of place. If he uses the VAK-Splat technique (p.27), he will likely want to do more than write about the blue sky or even the light blue sky. You might direct him to notice the number of shades of blue visible right now in the classroom, and perhaps he should go look at the real sky for some further insights. Maybe (with your prompting, or perhaps on his own initiative) he will want to compare the sky with, say, a blue egg to capture the essence of the sky's colour and create an impression of texture and curvature. So his closed question would be: What sort of bird's egg most closely matches the colour of the sky I have in mind?

Reaching that point-of-questioning has already involved visualisation, with reference to submodalities (see p.192, noticing, discrimination (between colours), insight into simile/metaphor. Finding the answer could necessitate IT skills, or library skills, including understanding the Dewey (or whatever) referencing system, using an index, browsing, and decision-making when a number of alternatives have been gathered.

All of this comes about within an environment where the child is encouraged to ask the questions and find the answers, with more or less help from a teacher. It is of course important that all students are made aware of the nature and purpose of the questions they can ask, together with the range of skills the questioning process incorporates.

Questions, then, can be closed or open. 'Tightly' closed questions would have one answer. The question about the colour of the sky could have a number of possible answers, which need to be gathered and assessed. Wide open questions are the 'what if?' type questions mentioned earlier, which evoke a world of possibilities and speculation.

Questions also have scale, and what might be called direction. The blue bird's egg question is small-scale and directed towards outside resources. Look back to the key questions on the Keywork template (p.60).

- Why mention the purply-pink flowers?
This is small-scale and moderately closed, and is a 'mind-reading' type question where the reader speculates about the author's motives. Such interpretation of intention ultimately directs the reader's attention back inside herself: unless the author is there in person to supply the answer, the reader must reason or intuit an answer.

- Why does the author pick Christmas in particular?

Similar to the above, but it has a larger scale relating to timespan and the thematic underpinning of the book. This becomes more significant as the reader proceeds and realises the stories are presented chronologically within a four-month period from early September to late December. The seasons and their changes also carry an implicit symbolic and thematic meaning: summer and the long holiday are over – the landscape changes and becomes bleaker – darkness becomes more apparent, and evil shows itself in a number of ways (see the section on themes, p.229).

- Why do they [the Double Dare Gang] want to steal the fruit anyway?

Initially this seems like a small-scale question, but further thought or discussion uncovers the 'ethos' of the group and touches upon the motives of certain characters such as Nigel, whose intrepid attitude feeds his need to be the boss. The question also directs the reader's attention inward to an examination of her own feelings and actions if she were placed in a similar situation.

Understanding the nature and purposes of questioning is a higher-level skill that children will come to master if they are allowed to practise in an environment that encourages and celebrates the process. Invite students to think about the questions they intend to ask:

- What is the question?
- How else could I ask it?
- How would that change the answers?
- Are there any other questions arising from my first question?
- What do I intend to gain from this question?
- Is it closed or open? Small- or large-scale?
- Where are the resources that will allow me to answer the question?
- How will I know when my question has been answered?
- How can I use the answers?

◆ Embedded questions and instructions

Explicit questions tend to activate conscious thinking tools to answer them. We try hard and/or logically to remember or work out what the answer might be. Embedding or 'burying' questions or instructions inside longer statements stands a greater chance of bypassing the intellectual, evaluative, critical aspects of the conscious mind and appealing more to the subconscious, which is more associative and holistic in its processing.

Saying something like, 'I wonder what it would be like when, by the end of the lesson (book, term, etc.), we understand why the Double Dare Gang stories take place from September to December?' triggers the search for meaning at various levels. Consciously we might perceive it as a rhetorical question ('I wonder why Steve's wondering that?'). But the subconscious sees the

Chunk Me Template

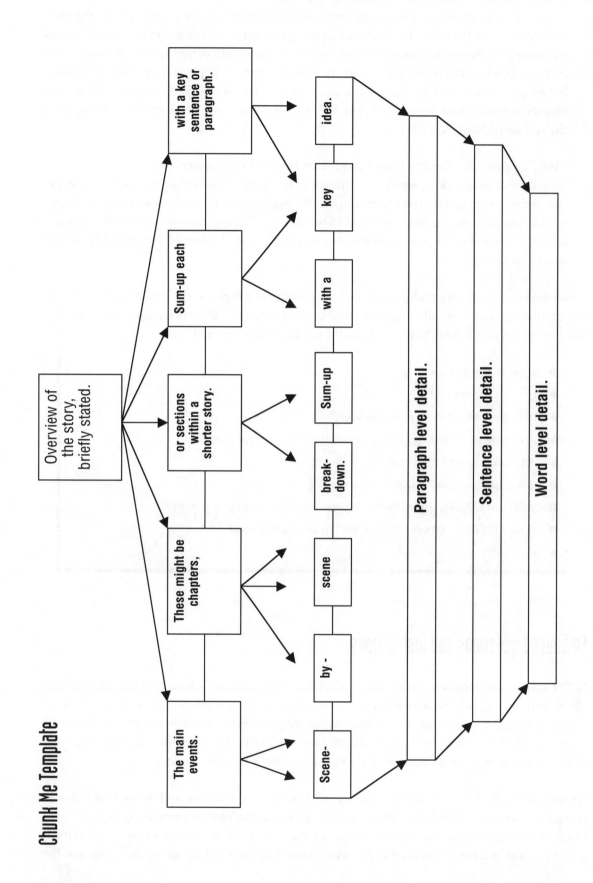

The main events.

These might be chapters,

Overview of the story, briefly stated.

or sections within a shorter story.

Sum-up each

with a key sentence or paragraph.

Scene-

by -

scene

break-down.

Sum-up

with a

key

idea.

Paragraph level detail.

Sentence level detail.

Word level detail.

instruction hidden there – 'By the end of the lesson we understand why...' and begins to gather up information to achieve that embedded goal. The question 'I wonder what it would be like when...' also stimulates 'preprocessing', which is a deep-level search for one or more answers.

Embedding questions and instructions can become an elegantly useful part of the linguistic environment of the classroom. You can also – explicitly – teach children to embed questions for themselves and their peers as they think around various aspects of their own and others' stories.

- It's really interesting to wonder why Nigel started the Double Dare Gang.

- Wouldn't you like to ask Steve why he jumped across the garage roofs even though he was frightened?

- If Old Man Jones walked in here right now I wonder which three questions out of all the ones I can think of I'd like to ask him?

◆ Chunk Me

One approach to both story-making and the study of text is to break it down into smaller chunks. A number of story-making activities make use of this idea and represent it in various ways. Chunking down serves several purposes:

- It allows learners to realise that stories are layered and operate across several scales (though with the proviso that the whole is more than the sum of the parts!).

- Children understand how the story components link logically together. This allows writers to model the format they've noticed in extant text when composing their own work.

- Working with bite-size pieces is more effective when you have an overview of the entire project. Similarly, understanding the Big Picture is easier when you can see how it has been put together.

- A chunked-down map of the whole story allows writers to work out how small changes at any point can ripple through the whole structure. Consequences become more easily observable.

- Breaking a large project down into manageable pieces helps overcome 'stuckness' and any sense of helplessness or being overwhelmed, and boosts confidence. It's harder to feel lost when you have the map in front of you.

Practise chunking-down with short, easy stories to begin with – the Double Dare Gang tales might suit your purpose. Follow the template suggested overleaf, or one similar. You might work with a whole class or smaller groups. Have them write out key ideas on file cards and configure them on a tabletop or the floor. See 'Story Track' (p.118) for more ideas on how to use this technique.

Remind children that effective writers make hundreds of decisions in the course of writing a story. Every element of the story is intended to serve at least one purpose, so the central question to keep in mind is 'What does this chunk of the story do?'

◆ The tale unfolds

'Deconstruction' is a term often used to explain the process of critical analysis or literary criticism of a text. It suggests a mechanical and systematic approach accomplished through cold logic, when in fact finding out more about a story through discussion, questioneering, speculation and insight can and should be a sparkling and enjoyable experience – as enjoyable as writing stories for oneself.

For this reason the technique of discovering how a story has been put together and why will be called 'unfolding', reflecting the gentler and more organic process of exploration we wish our students to undertake. Once children are adept at unfolding other people's stories, they can apply the same strategy to their own work as part of the looking back/review stage of writing. This will inform their more effective writing of the next tale. It must also be kept in mind that while the purpose of many of the story's elements will be obvious or clear, there are times when the writer herself cannot say for sure (at least consciously) why she chose such-and-such a word, or a particular sentence structure or sequence of events. The essence of a story is that it delivers an experience to the reader. Analysis of 'how it was done' might be useful, but should never take precedence over the experience itself.

Broadly speaking, a story has an internal structure and an episodic structure. These correspond to the ingredients of a meal and the process of creating it. The two structures interweave and are complementary. Unfolding which focuses on the ingredients will cast light on the episodic structure. (One way of doing this follows.) A technique that emphasises the process of creation (such as the 'Chunk Me' activity) will of course draw out the range and uses of the story's ingredients. Another way to think of the episodic structure is as the way in which resources are processed; how raw data becomes information, which in turn becomes understanding expressed through writing. In that sense, within our heads we carry an internal and an episodic set of resources for use as part of our meaning-making imperative.

Review the 'Layers of a Story' diagram on p.52. The same basic template is used to unfold for ingredients. Draw five concentric circles on the board and point out the purpose of each:

- innermost circle – for ideas about *character and setting*

- next, observations about *relationships* between characters and the setting (interpreted as broadly as you like)

- then ideas relating to the nature and rationales of the *genre* being used (again interpreted loosely to include 'action', 'adventure', 'comedy', etc.)

- next, observations and insights about the *motifs* found in the tale. (Motifs are the constituent features of a story and may refer to character types, dialogue, typical scenes, settings and sequences of events, set pieces typical of the genre, etc.)

- finally, encompassing all, are the *themes* on which the story is built. (Read more about themes on p.229). This circle might also accommodate ideas about how these themes thread through other stories and/or the children's own life experiences.

A partly worked example for the Double Dare Gang story *The Gift* follows. Think about what else you/your students could add. There are some further ideas three pages on.

◆ The Tale Unfolds – 'The Gift'

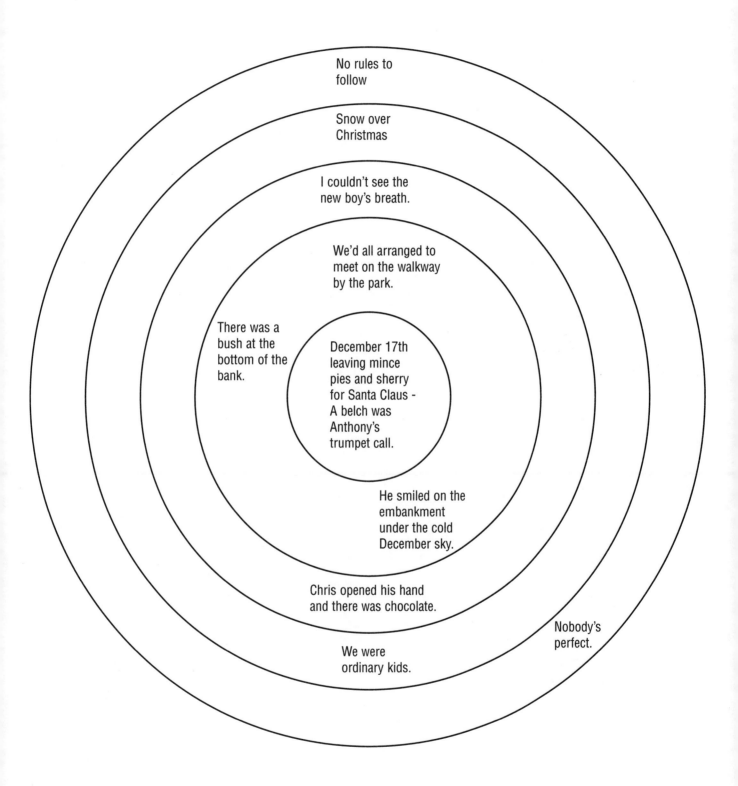

No rules to
follow

Snow over
Christmas

I couldn't see the
new boy's breath.

We'd all arranged to
meet on the walkway
by the park.

There was a
bush at the
bottom of the
bank.

December 17th
leaving mince
pies and sherry
for Santa Claus -
A belch was
Anthony's
trumpet call.

He smiled on the
embankment
under the cold
December sky.

Chris opened his hand
and there was chocolate.

Nobody's
perfect.

We were
ordinary kids.

67

◆ The Tale Unfolds

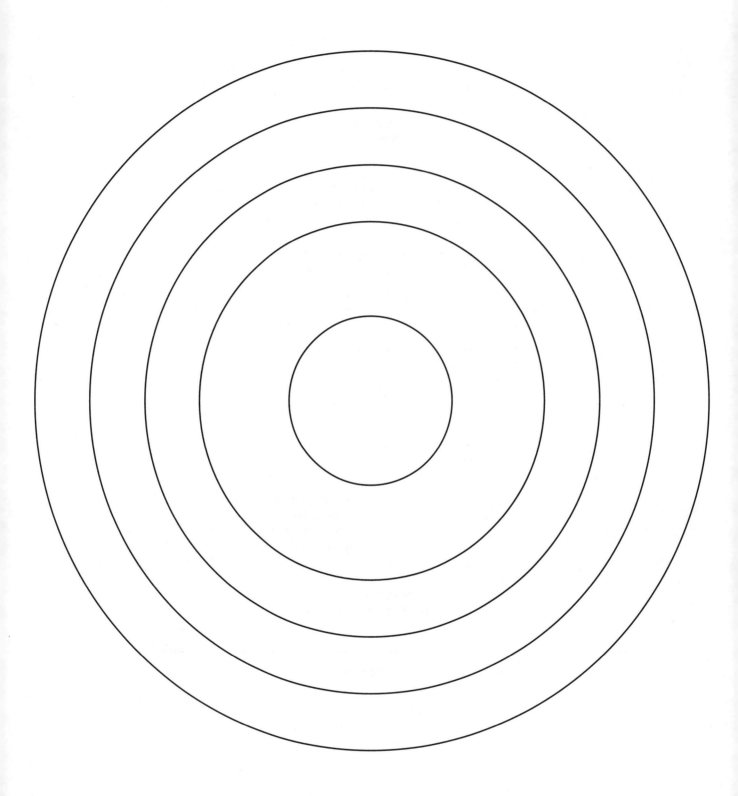

◆ 'The Gift' unfolded

◆1 character and setting:

- The church spire stuck up like a dark icicle.
- Brian came lumbering over with a big square grin on his face.
- 'Maybe the new boy's from the Travellers' camp up the road.'
- Kev and his father and Mr O'Connor, who was a policeman in the town, came scuffling down towards us.
- A faint freezing mist hung in the air around us.

◆2 relationship between character and setting :

- There was a bush at the bottom of the bank and you had to jink sideways to avoid it.
- The kid was standing there like a white smudge made out of the pale frost itself.
- The strange thin boy just looked back at us and the sky grew a little darker.
- We stood like shadowy cardboard cutouts in the dark.
- Mr O'Connor dragged Chris along like a sack of potatoes, up the bank towards the back gardens beyond.

◆3 genre:

- I offered the sweets round to everyone. Odd though, but when I was done there seemed to be just as many in the bag. If not more…
- His hands opened and closed and gifts spilled from them like rain…
- We watched Chris fade like a faint pencil sketch on the misty paper of the night; becoming a blur, a memory, and then nothing at all.

◆4 motifs:

- The frost was already forming on the ground again, even though the sun had just gone down behind the houses.
- Brian glanced suspiciously at his balloon that showed our twisted reflections.
- 'Oh just do it, Neil,' Nigel said impatiently. ' The game's nearly over.'
- He reminded me of one of the urchins you find in Charles Dickens stories.
- 'Give me a Christmas tree,' Nigel grinned wickedly. 'With plenty of lights flashing on and off.'
- Quite soon Mr Hughes the Headmaster arrived, and Mrs Porter-Smith, who was the Mayor of the town.
- 'Good – God – ' The Reverend breathed the words and made the sign of the cross.
- There were too many people between us and the door. I searched madly for a way out.
- So we went our own ways.

◆ **69**

⑤ themes:

- 'There was a balloon man handing balloons out in the mall.' (See e e cummings' poem *in Just-spring* [also called *The Balloon Man* and *Chanson Innocente*]): evil in disguise.

- He played as though he meant it, as though the whole world and its winter had been made just for him to enjoy himself tonight as though nothing else mattered: seize the moment. 'Look, you've been really kind, and I want to give you something in return': giving and taking; you get nothing for nothing.

- Chris looked up and his eyes were filled with an innocent light: innocence and experience.

See also *Self-Intelligence* pp 178-9 for notes on how the same technique can be used for dealing directly with children's emotions and issues.

◆ Off the Top of Your Head

This activity combines the notion of spontaneous ideas (see 'The Without-trying Game', p.33) with focusing-in on one particular level of a story. 'Off the Top of Your Head' is a typical brainstorming game where all ideas are encouraged, and no evaluation or judgement takes place at that time.

You might begin with a warm-up activity such as this – Give your group a time limit of one or two minutes. Hold up a black dot drawn on card and say, 'What could this be? What does this remind you of?'

You are likely to be astonished by the range of associations the class hurls at you! Once the children are 'in the mood' to spray out ideas, make the task more challenging. Having selected the level and part of the story you wish to focus on, ask the group to tell you what comes to mind as they think of it.

So (all items are taken from 'The Gift'):

- **sentence level/setting/visual**: The sunset was orange through the trees. Anthony came trotting across the park (What does the park look like?).

- **sentence level/motif/visual and kinaesthetic**: Kev had a posh hand-made sled. (What does it look like and feel like?).

- **paragraph level/character and setting/multisensory**: What feelings does Brian experience as he sledges? What colours do you notice – clothing, the scenery around, the frost? What sounds do you imagine as Brian sledges down the bank and hits Neil?

> Bri dived on his surfboard-like rectangle of plastic sheeting and skimmed down the bank like a big square torpedo, deliberately sideswiping Neil and knocking him right off his feet. Neil dropped like a felled tree. But Bri, out of control himself, hit a tuft of grass that spun him sideways and tipped the sled over. He went tumbling in a spray of frost-smoke with his arms and legs flailing.

- **paragraph level/motif/multisensory**: Notice the gifts spilling from Chris's hands. What do they look like? Hold one and describe its shape, texture and weight. What sounds do these objects make?

> Chris's hands opened and closed and gifts spilled from them like rain; coins and jewels, meaningless bits of plastic, things we couldn't identify, pieces of electrical circuitry, sweets and stones, eggs and living creatures, counters and dice, treasures and worthless toys.

- **Word level/theme/multisensory**: What ideas come to mind as you hear the word 'innocence'?

71

◆ Help me to write a story

Children write most effectively when they have a support structure that allows them to do it well. Initially this can mean more experienced and confident writers offering sustained advice and guidance. The point has already been made that successful writing is *intentioned* writing: decisions are made all the way down the line from the first idea to the final full stop. Giving less developed writers the benefits of these insights can be extremely valuable. There are a number of ways of achieving this.

Use a template such as the following, where portions of the finished story alternate with 'gaps' where there is no text. In parallel, the author supplies a commentary describing his intentions, the effects he wanted to create, and other insights. The reader is invited to fill in the gaps to link up the already written portions of the story.

I wanted **The Gift** to be an atmospheric story where the cold frosty weather added to the magic. Nigel jumps up and down to emphasise how cold it is. He's also impatient to get sledging!

I've always loved describing colourful skies. Being quite visual, I notice details like that. I mention the moon and stars to bring out the idea of 'the heavens', to give a sense of huge things existing around the little world of the children's play.

Then I wanted to change the mood and bring in some 'light relief'…

We waited for a while until the others arrived. Nige started jumping up and down, flapping his arms around himself to keep warm. I stood away from him and stared at the sky...
It was orange through the trees, turning to green and then purple as you went higher. The church spire stuck up like a dark icicle. Further round, hanging low over the nearby roofs, hung the moon and a really bright star, very close together. In another half an hour or so, all of the stars would be out and it would probably be too dark to bother. I wished the others would hurry up...
A loud belch echoed across the park.

The commentary continues and the reader is invited to suggest ideas…

I want to say a bit more about Anthony and mention a past incident about his super-loud belch –

Nigel and Steve watch him running across the park, leaving footprints in the grass. I wonder what ideas you'll have to make that impression really vivid? -

I want a change of mood now, and to illustrate that Anthony has a wacky sense of humour. He's carrying a tin-tray sled. I also want to have the characters interacting as they meet -

Notice how the writer states his intention and gives bits of information to work on. In this case, he also embeds a question and presupposes more than one idea to solve the problem. It's not vitally important to supply the missing text, but it does satisfy curiosity, and it's interesting to compare different versions of the scene...

'Anthony's here,' Nige said with a silly twisted grin. A belch was Anthony's trumpet call, and a speciality. Once he did it so loudly in the playground that Mr Hughes had heard him from his office. Gemma Freed told on him, and Anthony had to stand in the corridor outside the Head's office all that afternoon for being rude.
He came trotting across the park leaving a trail of dark footprints in the just-frost on the grass. As he reached the bottom of the bank, he whirled his round plastic tray up at us like a giant Frisbee: it sailed close over our heads and vanished into a patch of bramble on the other side.
'Missed us both - useless shot!' Nige called.
Anthony burped again and scrambled past us to retrieve the tray.
We spotted Kev almost immediately afterwards...

The example given operates on the paragraph/sentence level. The author has already written the story and has therefore explored the world of it in great detail. The technique also works earlier in the writing process and on a larger scale. Here, the author states broad intentions scene by scene and seeks more general ideas...

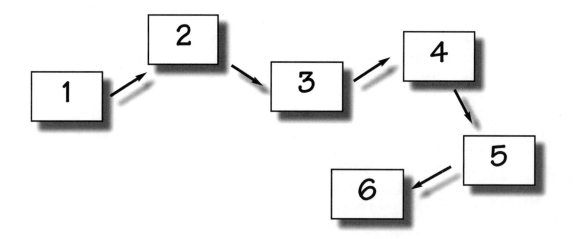

1 In this scene I want to establish the time of year – just over a week to go to Christmas – and have some main characters in school; excited, impatient for term to end. They are doing typically seasonal things. Writing a lesson to Santa introduces an important theme of 'gifts and giving', tied in with the idea of wanting and materialism.

2 The scene changes. It's after school. The kids meet to play sledging. I want to describe the setting and how cold and frosty it is. The characters have different kinds of sleds. The smarter ones can make a couple of the gang envious.

3 They play on the embankment, and for a short time they forget about what they want and what they've got. They are just innocent children again.

4 Something is added. The new boy, Chris, arrives. He is thin and pathetic-looking. A couple of the boys are aggressive towards him. Steve and Anna are more understanding and try to include him in the game. I want to introduce the idea that there is something mysterious about Chris.

5 Chris has a go on the sled. He is more childlike in his playing than the others, and one or two tease him about it. He offers something in return for the children's kindness. This is the pivot of the story, where an ordinary day turns into something astonishing. I don't want to overdo the fantasy elements. I want the magic to be simple, almost like a conjuring trick at first, open to scepticism and doubt.

6 Chris does his 'bit of trickery' and a couple of the kids – Nigel maybe and Kevin – tease him further and challenge him. He responds with startling power, still carrying his innocence. But the tale takes a dark turn here. We see greed appear for the first time, and at least one of the children grows frightened. This opens the way for adult involvement, which could prove disastrous because adult greed is much more dangerous…

Having children write commentaries on their stories for the benefit of others allows them to clarify their own intentions. The activity also evokes the 'How do I know what I think until I see what I say?' principle. Teaching someone else how you wrote or want to write your story encourages you to have further insights into your own process. Note that this activity is emphatically not a game of 'guess-the-right-answer'!

Children will come up with a range of ideas as they flesh out the bones of a story. In this way they come to understand that although a finished story has a linear, logical structure, a writer can take any number of alternative paths. This allows children to tackle more challenging and ambitious activities.

Countdown to a story

This is a checklist most usefully employed towards the end of the 'thinking time' when the writing is about to begin. It allows children to consolidate their planning and reminds them of any aspects they may have forgotten. After the writing, the list helps children to 'look back' and use the information they glean to inform the planning of their next project. This is not necessarily an exhaustive list. You may want to add, delete or alter items to suit the particular requirements of your group.

17 **What themes does my story explore?**	*Themes are 'big ideas' or broad subjects often concerned with 'the human condition' and the way people live their lives. One or more themes form the platform on which a story is built.*	
16 **Does my story fit into any particular genre? If so, where within the 'territory' of the genre would my story be located (see subgenres, p.220)**	*Genres define and describe story types. They are 'landscapes' where particular kinds of plot, characters and setting are to be found.*	
15 **– if using genre: Have I thought enough about how the plot, characters and setting can be used metaphorically, perhaps to comment upon things that happen in 'real life'? (See 'Structure and function', p.224 and 'Story Symbols', p.264.)**	*Many aspects of genre stories comment on people and situations found in society today, like distorting mirrors reflecting and interpreting aspects of the modern world.*	
14 **Broadly speaking, what do I hope to achieve in this story a) for myself as a writer, b) for my readers?**	*Every piece of writing helps to develop that writer's skills. The process works best when you have thought about the purposes behind the story. That allows you the flexibility to sharpen up, alter or add to those purposes.*	

13	Has the basic idea of my story been done before? By whom? How? What is my reaction?	Your writing needs to be informed by a knowledge of what else has been done within your area of interest. 'Knowing the territory' helps you to avoid writing stuff that's been done many times before: it helps you to avoid cliché and lets you take a fresher, more original approach.	
12	Am I using motifs deliberately? To what effect? (see 'Motifs', p.229.)	Motifs are the 'ingredients' of a story. They can be characters, objects, locations, bits of dialogue, even stylistic devices like short sentences for pace. If you are making soup, for example, every ingredient and the amount of it you add has an effect on the final flavour. So it should be with motifs within a story.	
11	Do I know enough about my characters? If someone asked me any question about any character, would I at least have an insight into the answer?	A writer needs to know more about her characters than she ever puts into the story. When you have thought enough about them, you can make an informed guess about any aspect of your characters and their lives.	
10	Have I imagined the setting of my story clearly enough?	A setting – the place where the events of the story occur – is more than just stage scenery. The best settings actually contribute to the vividness of the characters and the power of the plot. If it seems that your story could take place more or less anywhere, then you haven't thought enough about your setting and how it interacts with the other elements of the story.	
9	Is the storyline mapped out clearly?	A storyline is like a route map that leads you to a destination. You need a plan, even if you choose a different route once you have started on the journey.	

8	Do I have some alternative routes if I need them (even if these haven't been planned in detail)?	Having a range of options gives you flexibility during the writing. You have already admitted the possibility that there can be several directions the story could take. As you write, you'll know by instinct which is the best direction.	
7	Do I have an idea of how long my story will be?	This seems to be every schoolkid's concern – 'Please Miss, how long does it have to be?' Every idea has its own size and shape. By this stage, you should know whether your story will be a few pages long, or twenty, or a hundred. Mapping out the story idea automatically allows you to explore its boundaries.	
6	Do I have a structure in terms of chapters or scenes?	Some writers like to plan in this amount of detail before they begin. Others don't. As you become more experienced, you'll come to realise what works best for you. In the beginning, it's probably better to plan more rather than less.	
5	Whose point-of-view will I take?	You can write the story in the third person (the it/he/she person). The advantage of this is that you maintain a 'narrator's overview' of everything that's going on, and can jump about in time and space. You can write in the first person (I-voice). The advantage is that you have insight inside a character's head and can describe the story through his or her eyes. You can write the story in the second person ('you'). This approach isn't used much now but the advantage is that you talk directly to the reader, which can involve him/her very powerfully.	

4	**Do I feel confident that I can write this story well?**	*If you do, anchor that feeling (see 'Anchors', p.xxx). If not, what exactly prevents you from writing this story well? What strategies do you have to allow you to overcome your difficulties now?*	
3	**Do I have a strong first sentence/paragraph/scene?**	*A newspaper headline hooks a reader's attention and attracts him into the story. A punchy story opening does the same. No need to go over the top. Strong openings often take the form of questions, or statements that beg lots of questions (see 'Context Sentences', Imagine That p.90), where you hit the reader with an unexpected change of direction.*	
2	**Do I have a final scene/paragraph/sentence in mind?**	*As we said before, you need to have a route map with an end in sight and a destination. You can of course change your destination – that is, your final scene, etc. – but to have one in mind at the outset helps to keep you fixed on your goal and writing to the point.*	
1	**Am I ready to begin?**	*Having reviewed all of the above, is there anything now preventing you from making a start? If so, what strategies do you have to overcome the difficulty? (If you don't have strategies, consider where you will find them).* *If more than one thing is blocking you, write down all of the obstacles. Put them in order of priority for dealing with them. Break each obstacle down into the smallest bits you possibly can, and set about solving each bit with determination and confidence.*	
Now write your story!		

The same technique can be used to look back on what you've written in preparation for your next project. Maybe we should call this 'Count up from a Story'...

1	**Am I broadly happy with the outcome?**	*If yes, list what you feel you've done right to achieve that outcome. If no, list your points or areas of dissatisfaction. Put them in the order in which you'll deal with them. Find the strategies you'll use to deal with them and take action.*	
2	**Are there any ways I can improve upon my story through a further drafting?**	*Arthur C. Clarke says that stories are never finished, only abandoned. The law of diminishing returns means that the amount of effort you put into making a story better produces smaller and smaller improvements. But it is worth combing through your work to see if it would benefit immediately from any alterations.*	
3	**Am I particularly satisfied with certain scenes, paragraphs or sentences in the story?**	*Allow yourself the pleasure of knowing you did something well. Notice the details of your work. Enjoy your accomplishments and use them to inform your next project – and your positive attitude towards it!*	
4	**What precisely can I take from this story to use in my next piece(s) of writing?**	*Your 'resources' might include a strong character or character type, a setting that works particularly well, further ideas for new plots, motifs that you can recycle, and aspects of your attitude, approach and writing routine. All of this is your stuff – use whatever is effective to improve what you do.*	
5	**Can I repackage this idea in other ways?**	*A story is the form in which you've expressed your idea. Could the idea be morphed to make a poem, a play, a longer or a shorter story, a fictional diary or sequence of letters? 'Squeeze the orange' to get the last drop of juice from your thinking.*	

6	What have I learned about my characters, settings, plotting, genre and writing techniques from this project?	*Look at these different aspects of your story to double-check that you've gleaned the most benefit from what you've done.*	
7	Is the presentation of the work up to my best standards?	*Presentation counts. You don't need to be too concerned as you write your first draft, but during redrafting and editing you should pay attention to how the work looks. Taking time to get small details just right creates a good impression, and helps you to maintain standards on a larger scale.*	
8	What is my next project?	*Their attitude as well as their standards of performance define 'professionals'. A professional is driven to write and always has ideas coming to fruition. Take time now to gather up ideas for your next piece of work – if you haven't already done so. Go back to the top of the 'Countdown' list...*	

◆ 'Countdown to a story' circle-time

'Countdown to a Story' can be used by individual pupils as a personal checklist. Or you might want to do it as a group activity. In this case supply the group with a large sheet of paper. Draw five concentric circles to represent character and setting/relationships/genre/motifs/themes (see 'The tale unfolds', p.66).

Nominate a group leader to work down the countdown list. As each question is read out, invite the other group members to come up with their ideas. Record these in some way – tape them, take notes, etc. – then subsequently write them down on cards and place them on the appropriate circle. You now have a rich but not yet fully organised resource for creating a story. Once organisation has been imposed on the ideas, you have something much more effective: you have a strategy.

Countdown to a Story

◆ Strategy cards

Again in this activity, children might want to work alone or perhaps in pairs. The most useful strategies (at least in this context) are the ones that are individualised – the tasks and techniques that fit most comfortably with each individual student.

Ask each student or pair to work through the ideas generated in the previous activity. These ideas are written on cards and broadly organised into the five categories represented by the five circles. Children work from the outermost circle (themes) towards the centre, selecting those ideas/responses which seem most helpful. Note that a child is as likely to pick someone else's ideas as she is her own. Very soon the student/pair will have five sets of 'most useful' ideas, which they now lay out in five rows.

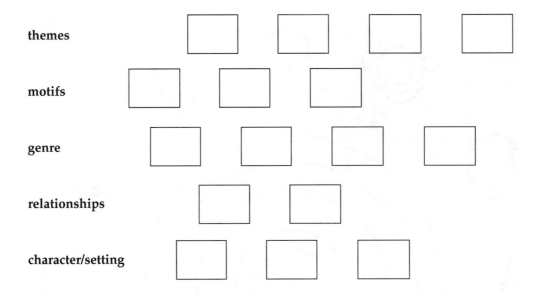

themes

motifs

genre

relationships

character/setting

Now have each child organise the cards into an order of priority *that suits her best*. If there are two people in the group, have each child go through this stage separately. This is a further refinement of organisation, another level of personalising the subsequent action.

Every child now has a list of things to do or think about that 'feels right', and in order of action. You can represent this stage of planning thus:

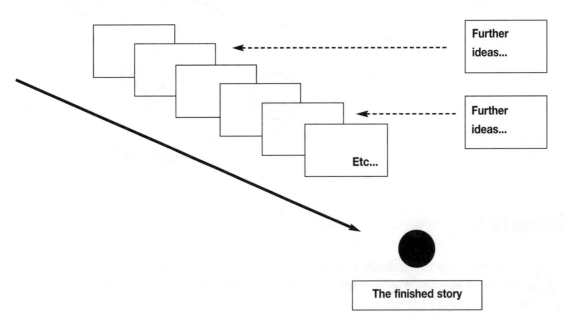

As children carry out the actions on the cards, they may have further ideas that need to be slotted in to the sequence. Or you might find that an activity suggested by one card needs to be chunked down into smaller bits. This is to be encouraged in line with the 'how-do-you-eat-an-elephant' principle (a little bit at a time). Remember that strategies are flexible, whereas the goal remains fixed. A corollary of that is that the strategies described in *ALPS StoryMaker* are flexible – change them however you like to suit your needs and requirements!

◆ Countdown grid

The countdown checklist can also be used with a grid template. This could be made into a wall display. Children could add their ideas – and other suitable feedback – in the appropriate box at any time during the course of the Countdown activity.

What themes does my story explore?	I like the idea that 'big things can come from little beginnings.' Xander	I want to write about the idea of someone who is an 'outsider' - and so she can see things from a different perspective. Cordelia	(What you two have said made me think about something that happ ened to me once. I'm going to write about it in my journal. Thanks guys). Faith	
Does my story fit into any particular genre?	I like Science Fiction. I'll write about what computers might be like in 2050 – very realistic virtual reality! Ramesh	I found this image on a clipart CD and will base my story around it. I'm not sure yet if it fits a genre – but I get impressions of romance and secrecy. I'll keep you posted. Carol	I can get a story out of this stuff too – a fantasy but set in our world, modern day. Faith	I'm not bothered about genre stuff. I just want my story to have plenty of action, and I'm interested in the idea of 'blind authority' (I guess that's a theme). Paul

As you see, the countdown grid display can almost become a 'work-in-progress' chart. The entries are informal but contain useful information and offer good feedback.

◆ Reflective dialogue

Reflective dialogue happens during the 'looking back' phase of story-making and is a way of gathering up the benefits of the writing experience. Ideas are reviewed at all levels in an atmosphere of support and mutual respect. It is a world away from competitive criticism, corrective marking or negative judgement. Participants are fellow writers, walkers along the same road, not critics or reviewers in the conventional sense. The aim of reflective dialogue is to provide positive, educative feedback for the benefit of both students and teacher.

Thc elements of reflective dialogue include:

- highlighting particular qualities of a piece of work
- pinpointing areas for improvement. (Be selective. We can all improve in our creative writing, but specific advice and insight are better than any general invocation to try harder/do better.)
- developing independence of judgement linked with training in self-assessment
- articulating insights and understandings – how do I know what I think until I hear what I say?
- consolidating new learnings into the web of earlier understanding
- learning to use open questioning as a way of 'surfing possibilities' with ease and elegance
- creating a context for insights and further ideas through the use of specific activities and exercises.

The practice of reflective dialogue builds a sound and positive attitude towards creative writing – and therefore towards learning itself – which underpins the development of literacy and its network of interrelated skills. Practically speaking, link reflective dialogue with 'Countdown to a Story' (or rather count up to a new story!), and be sensitive to the level addressed by the question/exploration. Do you want students to offer general comments about the large-scale structure of their stories, or specific ideas and opinions at the sentence or word level of the work? Aim for flexibility within the framework of an organised feedback session. So, using 'The Allotment Ghost' as an example:

- What do you think works well in this story to make it an effective piece of children's adventure?
- Notice the main chunks of the story: Deciding on the dare/Steve's agonising over the challenge/The gang meeting and learning of the old man's (supposed) death/Entering the allotment/Being surprised by old Man Jones/The aftermath... What happens in each of these chunks that supports the story as far as you're concerned? Do any scenes or episodes in the story slow it down or seem unnecessary to you?
- The story begins with kinaesthetic details. How effectively did these work in allowing you to enter the story? If they weren't effective, what details would you prefer to have at the opening of 'The Allotment Ghost'?

Note that these questions endeavour to open out the dialogue and invite personal opinion and subjective impressions from the reader. They are emphatically not seeking a 'right answer' and encourage the students to begin to verify their judgements by supplying their own alternatives. The movement of reflective dialogue is from observation through comprehension towards greater insight.

◆ Get an attitude!

Attitude underpins performance. Exploring the story-making activities instils 'the write stuff' non-consciously in children (and, we anticipate, in teachers), but a practical and positive stance can also be made more explicit through the handy tool of affirmations. Affirmations begin as statements of intent swiftly embodied (literally) in patterns of thought, feeling and behaviour. Their charge of energy has nothing to do with hope but everything to do with anticipation, action and pride-in-achievement. Affirmations properly used become *reaffirmations*, which swiftly establish a powerful feedback loop where attitude manifests in action, and attainment of one's goals allows the underpinning attitude to flourish.

Affirmations need to be:

- positive
- present-tense
- personal
- particular
- precise.

Emile Coué's famous 'Every day in every way I am getting better and better' may stimulate subconscious preprocessing in a general way, but has little effect on precision goal-setting and gathering up the exact resources you need to get there. Consciously one needs to frame the affirmation and then employ the 'as if' principle by behaving as if it had already been realised. Since subconscious action follows conscious decision, swift and powerful shifts in attitude can then occur.

Target affirmations to apply to the different stages of the writing process – the table offers suggestions. Construct them carefully and with precise emphasis. Use one or two affirmations at any time, and when you notice the changes they produce, move on to others that build upon the good work already done.

Affirmations are like little self-contained treasures (pearls of wisdom, if you like) that can be used in conjunction with future-basing techniques (see p.132) to great effect. Imagine framing an affirmation, travelling forward in time in your imagination, anchoring the attitude and then returning in the knowledge that it is already having an influence.

Similarly, affirmations can be taken back through internal, subjective time and planted in the past. This encourages a beneficial reconfiguration of the map of reality, accelerating current positive change. See the section on visualisation to learn more.

Thinking time	Writing time	Looking back time
I am excited about all the ideas I'm having for this story.	I write with pleasure and an effortless flow of moment-by-moment ideas. Writing is always fun to do.	I enjoy learning how to write more effectively from the story I've completed.
I have ideas often and know at once how they fit together.	I enjoy watching sentences form and feel pleased with my ongoing achievement in storymaking.	I feel a great sense of achievement in having made this story from scratch.
I write ideas down straight away and I'm delighted at how they build into a story that works.	I feel good to realise that my conscious and subconscious work together as an effective team.	I am eager to keep writing and feel excited about my next story.
I wake up with insights into how my story will work out.	I enjoy framing my ideas in clear language. The right words come to me easily and naturally.	I feel strong in knowing that I have done my best.
I notice details of other people's appearance and behaviour and apply these easily and naturally to the characters in my story.	I am glad I notice my own feelings and reactions as I write. I am a good judge of my own work.	I am happy to hear people's opinions about my story and allow their remarks to work for my greatest good.
I am amazed at how I apply what I've learned from my earlier writing in my present work.	The characters in my story are my friends. I learn from them constantly.	I realise that all the writing I have done makes me a more accomplished and effective writer.

◆ What have I done?

Effective writing unites honesty and sincerity with determination and hard work (which is not the same as 'trying hard'), thus allowing the best to be achieved. This combination of attributes applies with equal importance at the review stage of the process. Looking back at work done is as much about noticing areas for improvement as it is about enjoying the accomplishment of having finished. Remember that in one sense a story that's been completed is but one step forward in the preparation of the next piece of work.

It pays, therefore, to he open, honest and systematic in evaluating one's own work, and in reviewing the work of others (See also 'Grading and assessment' p.93). Use the following template or a similar one to categorise and consolidate feedback.

Focus of comment	My ideas	Reader A: Gareth	Reader B: Sue
Plot (general)	I think there was too much description in the middle of the story. (But I can use some of the descriptive details in my next one!)	The story started off really well. I thought the first few paragraphs were the best. A bit slow later on, but I realised that Steve was trying to develop the atmosphere here.	I liked the flashback idea, and saying 'A week went by' on page nine stopped the story from sagging.
Main character	The character of Eleanor was strong and clear in my mind. I will use her as a character type in future stories. The crippled arm she had in this story provided the imperfection I wanted her to see in herself, although I think I'll use something less obvious from now on.	Eleanor was a brilliant character, although I thought the withered arm idea was a bit over-the-top. I liked the way she needed a crisis in her life to see how strong she really was. I thought she put herself down too much.	I liked Eleanor generally, except she put herself down too much - there was a real danger she'd turn into a 'poor me'. (I think you avoided that, just about.) She seemed realistic and natural: you must have spoken to real-life girls to get your insights for Eleanor!

And so on. A variation of the idea is to import the text into such a template and have the writer/readers comment on a sentence-by-sentence basis.

87

Text:	Author comments:	Reader A	Reader B	Action Plan
I walked between two tall rows of bean canes, coming at last to the stand of gooseberry bushes at the far side of the allotment. I glanced round to spot the others, but they were invisible in the night. I couldn't even hear the sound of apples being picked from the tree, or rhubarb stalks being snapped off at ground level… Most gooseberries when you pick them are not quite ripe; they're hard and crunchy and very sour, and the stiff hairs prickle in your mouth. But as my hand ruffled about among the leaves searching for the fruit, I felt one big goosegog that *was* ripe, just soft enough to give a little between my finger and thumb. I knew it would have a wonderful fruity mellow taste and a tangy, delicious flesh. *I'm going to eat you,* thought. *I'm going to eat you before I do anything else, so that I can honour the memory of Old Man Jones.*	I wonder if I should just mention the silence, rather than sounds I'd expect to hear but don't? Do these details slow up the action – or increase the tension? I like this – it echoes back to the smell / touch details at the start of the story. The gooseberry is forbidden fruit – like the app le in Eden.	I think you should say 'coming soon' – 'at last' makes it sound like you took ages. I like these details. They really make you feel like you're there. I imagined this so clearly my face *did* scrunch up!	The darkness and silence make for a scary atmosphere. You can't snap rhubarb at ground level, can you? Would you 'ruffle' about among leaves? Never heard the word 'goosegog' before. I'm not sure the DDG know what honour means!	Keep 'at last'. The walk seems long to Steve. Keep the details in. I'll check to see if you can snap rhubarb at ground level. Keep the details. They contrast with the ripe gooseberry which is important in the story. Check 'ruffle'. The meaning of 'goosegog' is clear and it makes the story sound more ordinary. Read on!

The activity works best and generates the most useful outcomes when the ethos of the commentary is clear in children's minds. Emphasise that they are not to be critical in any petty or negative way. The point of their remarks is to support the writer in his process of making the best story he can. This assumes a growing awareness that everything contained in the story is there for a reason. (See 'Intention – output – effect', p.20)

Practically speaking, many writers often won't have reasons behind the details of what they write – at least not consciously. Careful and positive reflection tends to draw out supportive reasoning, or else gently forces change to details which are frivolous or gratuitous (This principle becomes very important in random-answer activities such as 'Dicework' (p.107): 'Yes, Wayne, but why *does* your character have to be a zombie serial killer with two heads?')

Vary the template to suit your purposes. You may want only the author's commentary and one other, for instance. Be aware also that what the readers say provides useful feedback for you as a teacher. In the example above, Reader A responds in a kinaesthetic way to the description of being in the allotment. Reader B is more interested in atmosphere and tends to pick up more on the meanings of individual words. The author in his action plan treats his readers' ideas with respect, but shows a certain independence of judgement when reacting to them. One definition of a story is an organisation of ideas supported by hundreds of decisions. The action plan not only gives direction to the final polishing of a story, but also primes the writer to be aware of similar details when planning the next story.

'What have I done?' works well as a computer-based activity where text can be imported straight into the template and comments typed directly onto the screen. Alternatively, templates can be photocopied or easily drawn into notebooks.

◆ The Self-assembling Curry

When all's said and done, the best writing happens when a writer is 'in the flow' of the work, enjoying a state of relaxed alertness as ideas rise easily from the subconscious and are only lightly evaluated consciously before they reach the page. This state occurs most readily when preparation has been thorough and when the immediate point of the work is enjoyment and the adventure of exploration. Trying consciously to follow too many rules at the point of application hinders the creative process and leads to stilted, artificial and unsatisfying output. Adherence to rules should grow out of a state of subconscious competence – so that a writer may notice a word 'doesn't look quite right', or that a sentence 'isn't properly balanced', or that a certain character 'wouldn't behave in exactly that way'. Gut reactions, hunches and subtle intuitions play a vital role in the creation of effective writing. They are easily stifled if the writer is worrying about dotting i's and crossing t's at that moment.

A useful strategy is to introduce a rule, practise it a little and then forget about it. Allow the writing to happen, *then* look back to see if or how well the rule has been applied. Consolidate the learning of a number of rules by playing the game of 'The Self-assembling Curry'.

Think of the finished story as the cooked curry, a delicious concoction of subtle flavours and textures. Something wonderful has happened to the raw ingredients during that slow simmering process. Everything has blended to make the whole more than the sum of the parts. And as all good curry cooks know, there *is* no hard and fast rule for producing the final unique flavour people will travel miles to taste.

Take:

- two kilos of action
- a generous measure of excitement
- a level spoonful of horror
- a handful of humour
- a liberal sprinkling of dialogue
- the tiniest pinch of sadness
- a twist of irony...
- simmer gently until the ingredients are well blended, keeping half an eye on neatness and punctuation. When the dish is ready (you'll know when that is), leave to cool and then sample to see if any final touches are needed. Add your name with a flourish and serve with pride. This dish goes well with good company and an expectant silence.

A variation of this activity is to match story ingredients with actual items of food. Collect a wide range of pictures of foodstuffs and decide beforehand which story elements you wish to concentrate on. Discuss which element can be matched with which kind of food:

- potatoes with pace, because it's a staple ingredient
- peas with dialogue, because you can scatter them over the plate
- asparagus tips with exclamation marks, because they should be a rare treat
- hot sauce with violence, because it should be used sparingly and with good reason.

And so on. Visual displays of 'story meals' help children to remember a range of elements and allow them to understand that ingredients can be 'mixed to taste' – although certain conventions are followed. Food symbols drawn or stuck into notebooks also allow you to mark correlatively yet in a subtle way, and without the bad connotations of a X.

◆ Consider your audience

Writing is not usually a totally private and personal affair. Perhaps we might keep a diary for our eyes only, or occasionally pen a letter we have no intention of sending, but by and large we write for an audience other than ourselves – often knowing the work is to be judged, marked, compared and returned. And as most professional authors will tell you, the dread of the rejection letter or unfavourable evaluation still looms large, even after a writer has had books published. Steve recalls the time when an editor returned a children's play he'd written with more editorial blue pencil scribbled over the manuscript than there was text. The editor (who shall remain nameless) ended by saying, 'I hope these comments will be useful to you.' Of course they weren't, because the only thing that lingered was the negative emotional impact of having gotten it so wrong so effectively (as far as *that* editor was concerned).

At school children write almost exclusively for their teachers, and as such you have a responsibility a) to let them know just what you expect and b) to encourage them to pretend they're writing for other audiences also.

One helpful strategy is to target one or two story elements and mark only for those. You might choose character development and pace, or VAK descriptions and economy of language, or dialogue with a particular emphasis on effective punctuation. It doesn't matter which ingredients you select; the fact remains that some of the pressure will be taken off children's shoulders, allowing them to write more naturally, while encouraging them to focus their attention – during preview, writing and review – on specific story elements. And if you thought ahead and displayed your intentions on a class planner, you would be engaging the preprocessing abilities of your students' minds while defusing any tendency to worry.

Another strategy is to reframe the notion of marking. Most teachers and children still regard marking as a comparative evaluation of work which frequently (or always!) includes corrective elements. Why not consider:

- abandoning marking for a time and replacing it with a 'raising awareness' week. If you focus on spelling, discuss and practise various spelling strategies instead of doing spelling exercises. If you wish to emphasise verbs, play appropriate word games and gather your feedback on children's understanding by your observations of how they play.

- marking what's right in a story rather than what's wrong. Indicate only work well done without even suggesting that children should look again at the unmarked areas. (They'll probably do this anyway out of curiosity.)

- marking a child's work in comparison with his previous pieces, rather than against the work of others or some general (politically imposed) standard. 'You have really grasped the idea of dialogue and now use it effectively' is so much uplifting than 'Well done, Jason, you've reached level four.'

Encouraging an awareness of other audiences also helps children to become more effective in their planning and writing, since they become more sensitive to what their readers are like and what they expect. One way of approaching this matter is to have children create a 'typical' reader for whom they will write. So you might discuss, for example, what the typical ten-year-old female reader of fantasy stories might be like, or how a nine-year-old male SF fan might behave, and what kind of 'ingredients' he'd prefer to see in a tale of space adventure. The point should be made that the idea of a typical reader is a generalisation used for convenience – although it is the case that publishers use more sophisticated versions of the idea to target their audiences, which in turn helps to mould their list and series and titles within that list.

The 'typical reader' activity creates an opportunity for children to articulate their own reading preferences and why they enjoy those types of stories.

A variation on this theme would be to write for one of the characters within a story. Such characters might be the children's own creations, or well-known characters from already published material. Discussing, for instance, what Nigel or Anna or Kevin from the Double Dare Gang might enjoy reading will give extra insights into these characters.

Giving thought to your audience highlights the principle of 'intention – output – effect' (see p.20) and helps to emphasise the importance of purpose (discrimination, judgement and decision) through all the stages of the writing process. 'Teasing out' the purposes behind the writing of a story clarifies intention and informs preparation. It also makes for a more transparent agenda as far as assessment is concerned. See the following table.

Audience/reader(s)	Purpose(s) for writing
Teacher Purposes should be prioritised and explained to children beforehand. Starred items (*) are those which will be marked for.	• to practise creative writing skills previously learned • to introduce and extend the new idea of genre and the use of motifs found in specific genres. • to check understanding of the use and layout of dialogue • to prepare for the introduction and development of storytelling techniques
Peers Children can decide for and amongst themselves why they are writing a particular piece for an audience of classmates.	• I'm writing this story because we began it as a whole class Story Map and I'm interested to see how my ideas are different from my friends'. • I'm writing this story because Ramesh and Carl said they liked the way I describe things clearly. I will pay extra attention to my descriptions. • I'm writing this story because Julie and Carina want to write a sequel.
Oneself Personal purposes for writing can remain private if this is appropriate.	• I'm writing this story because I love science fiction. • I'm writing this story because I'm excited by the Star Wars movie I saw at the weekend. • I'm writing this story because my teacher said she thinks I'm really good at writing action scenes. • I'm writing this story because I get good marks in English and that makes me feel good!

Postman and Weingartner maintain that 'One becomes fastidious about method only when one has no story to tell.' If you find that you or your students struggle to identify purposes for writing beyond practising the technical aspects of grammar and syntax, then you might choose to ask some precise and searching questions such as those below, or you might just decide to have children write for the sheer joy of it, which is how the best stories are usually produced.

● Who are you writing for principally?

● What exactly does that person expect from the finished work?

● Why are you writing this above and beyond what your main audience wants and expects?

● How do these answers affect what you will write?

● How would your writing be different if you were doing it completely for yourself?

◆ Grading and assessment

> God created the writer, then took a handful of the scraps that were left and made three critics.
>
> *T. J. Thomas*

This is a complex and sometimes contentious issue, since any meaningful assessment of creative writing involves judgements of an entirely subjective nature. Ultimately – within the context of story-making anyway – a personal response is more valuable, since in a very real sense the meaning of a story is the behaviour it elicits. Clearly you will want and need to know how your students are progressing in relation to their previous performance (in a variety of areas), the achievements of their peers, and according to the criteria of nationally defined standards. But these things are different from a heartfelt reaction to a heartfelt creation.

Critiquing work is an art in itself. While a detailed exploration of this is beyond the scope of this book, perhaps you'll find the following pointers of use:

- Decide exactly what you are grading, and what you are grading for.
- Bear in mind that standards for learning are not the same as standards for grading. A child might achieve 7/10 (whatever that means) for use of adjectives, but actually could have learned a huge amount more about the art of creative writing and the attitude that best underpins it – elegantly summarised by Alistair Smith's 'Five Rs':
  - Responsible
  - Resourceful
  - Resilient
  - Reasoned
  - Reflective-reflexive
- ' Include the knower in the known.' Ask the writer how well she feels she's achieved her own and your objectives.
- Generally speaking, offer three positive responses and then highlight one area for improvement.
- Avoid 'pseudo exactness' in commenting upon children's achievements. Steve once had a story returned with the comment, 'We like this story, but we can't publish it because we feel you're only 87% of the way there.' Note also the use of the royal 'we' (safety in numbers).
- Similarly, avoid vagueness. If you have a point to make, make it clearly and in a no-nonsense way. Another of Steve's returned stories carried the highly valuable tip that 'We enjoyed this story, but we thought it lacked that certain something.'
- Remember always that a story is a person's heart in another person's hands.

◆ The contrast—comparison grid

Creative comparisons are as much a part of skill development as quantitative assessments. The use of a contrast-comparison (C-C) grid brings together a range of items which can be directly compared and contrasted, and can be a very flexible tool.

Example 1: Steve's story starter

Text

Even what happened with Old Man Jones didn't put us off ghost stories. If the weather was bad, or if we were In the mood, we'd meet at DDG Headquarters and tell each other scary tales.

Our headquarters was Nigel's Dad's shed at the bottom of the garden. The Lloyd family lived in Bowden, a village that was now separated from Kenniston only by the open space of the Rec. They had a huge back garden, and the shed was lost among trees and ancient lilac bushes. Nigel's Dad had used it as his potting shed, but since he'd lost interest in gardening a couple of years ago, Nige said, he never bothered coming down here, and so the place was exclusively ours.

Opening paragraph	• gets straight into the story • mentions 'ghosts' and so engages the interest • introduces the idea of DDG Headquarters • prepares the reader to hear scary tales • assumes you've read the previous story
Descriptive details	• clear sense of location • brief background on Nigel's family • use of the word 'lost' creates impression of overgrown garden • 'back story' details tend to slow pace
Use of language	• contractions ('he'd', 'Nige', 'Rec', etc.) give a sense of familiarity and an ease of telling. • choice of first person narrator 'welcomes' the reader into the gang • the conversational use of ordinary language builds a frame of believability ready for the scary tales to follow

Example 2: Opening sentences

Points of comparison ——————————————————→
Items to be compared

	'Hook'	VAK detail	Language
'I did the last clap yesterday,' Anthony announced proudly as we sat finishing our sandwiches.	*Readers are intrigued to know what the 'last clap' might be.*	Vague impression of sandwiches (maybe more detail needed?).	• *Opening with dialogue gives a sense of being immediately there.* • *announced' proudly declares Anthony's sense of achievement.*
I tried hard not to think of the afternoon growing darker outside.	*Sense of menace implied by the narrator's unease.*	Visual impression of fading light.	• *Use of first person 'personalises' the menace of the dark. We are in there with him.* • *Stating the negative – 'I tried hard not to think' - suggests he failed and is even more frightened.*
We were ordinary kids from an ordinary town, and there was no reason at all why it should have happ-ened to us in particular.	*The reader is intrigued by what 'it' might be.*	No details (Check if you have some VAK impressions in the following sentences).	• *The mystery of 'it' contrasts with the fact that the kids and their town were ordinary.* • *The long second clause creates a sense of 'nervous rambling' because 'it' goes beyond reason.*

The C-C grid can be set up to compare and contrast any story element against any combination of criteria. The grid format serves to 'chunk down' one's impressions of the story, focuses the attention on those smaller pieces, and allows impressions to be located within a larger 'map' of commentary.

◆ Writing blocks

Writing blocks come in all shapes and sizes. Sometimes young writers (and adult authors too) know exactly why they feel they cannot begin, sustain or finish a story. At other times the origins of the block are entirely subconscious. Or the problem may be partly on the surface and partly outside conscious awareness. One cornerstone of ALPS StoryMaker is the creation of a safe environment where children feel at ease in generating ideas and have access to a menu of techniques for organising the material in clear, logical and effective ways. Allowing young authors to feel safe and confident in the craft as they play with ideas and language will steadily and surely remove the vast majority of the blocks to successful writing.

If any blocks remain, a general formula for resolving them is:

$$\text{awareness} \longrightarrow \text{understanding} \longrightarrow \text{control}$$

Raising awareness of the issue leads to a greater understanding of it. Understanding the issue informs the use of strategies to control it. And control, of course, implies resolution.

Blocks to writing might originate within the writer, within the writing task, or both. And they may be due to a lack of information, a lack of organisation and/or (in the writer or teacher) limiting beliefs that inhibit success.

	Lack of information	Lack of organisation	Limiting beliefs within the writer	Limiting beliefs within the teacher
Writer		• *I don't know how I'm going to finish this story by Thursday.* • *I can't find my story plan!*	• *I'm no good at writing.* • *I'm never happy with my stories because my spelling is so bad.*	• *I just know Set Four will struggle with the concept of motifs.* • *Steve can't string sentences together to save his life!* • *We'll never cover all these points by half term.* • *How will these kids cope when I can't write a decent short story myself?*
Task	• *I don't know how long the story has to be.* • *I'm not sure what the teacher will be marking for.* • *I'm still not clear about how to use apostrophes.* • *I don't really know what 'genre' means.*	• *I can't work out how to use all my character details in such a short story.* • *I can't remember what VAK means or how I should use it.*	• *I'll never understand how paragraphs work.* • *I'm hopeless at thinking of good dialogue.*	

A flexible and highly effective strategy for overcoming blocks might be termed 'self-noticing', which is the habit of being aware of what you are thinking as you think it. This very act of self-awareness allows you to realise that what you are thinking is a powerful determinant of outcomes. Awareness of a lack of information immediately supplies the solution – just ask. Awareness of a lack of organisation is followed by the direct, positive action of seeking out organisational strategies. Awareness of the patterns of thought which reflect and help to define limiting beliefs offer directions for change and resolution.

It must be pointed out that limiting beliefs within the teacher (about her own capabilities or the potential of her students) will have a profound influence on how those students perform and what they achieve. Steve was once told by a teacher who had invited him in for a storytelling session that the class 'were incapable of listening for more than a few minutes at a time'. This belief was likely to be reflected in the children's behaviour. (A similar though subtler variation is that any child's attention span in minutes equals her chronological age plus two. Really…?) Since Steve's unshakable belief is that all children have imaginations and can be enthused – and because he had some cracking good stories to tell! – the class sat and listened for an hour, entranced by the magic of the tales.

Limiting beliefs in children can be regarded as the outcome of what is often a long process of indoctrination. Many beliefs are absorbed nonconsciously; facial expressions, sarcastic remarks, a general atmosphere of intimidation or simply lack of confidence in children may be absorbed by young minds and woven in to their maps of reality. More direct negative comments – ' How are we ever going to get anything through that thick skull of yours, Steve!' – of course take their toll.

Educating children frequently involves re-educating them into a state of greater self-esteem and self-confidence. (See *Self-Intelligence* for ways of achieving this.) A good ploy is to invoke the 'salesman' metaphor. Point out to your group that a suggestion, idea or opinion is like an item being peddled by a travelling salesman. He knocks on your door and tries to persuade you to take his wares. Make this your plan:

- examine the goods carefully to check for flaws
- ask precise questions about anything you don't understand
- question the salesman if you can about why he is trying to sell you this stuff
- make a definite and determined decision as to your action. You can:
  - buy the goods wholesale and you will own them (and they can come to own you)
  - take the item for use on a trial basis with the proviso that you can return it later
  - say politely, ' No thank you, I'm not buying this.' And firmly close the door.

An alternative technique is simply to regard writer's block as an illusion, pretend you can do whatever you set your heart to do – and get on and do it.

◆ Rapport

R apport defines an effective relationship between people – effective in the sense that communication at all levels is meaningful and beneficial. Rapport involves mutual interest, trust, attention, understanding and even empathy, and in that vital sense it both necessitates and enhances a high degree of 'emotional intelligence' within and between its participants.

Rapport forms an essential part of the story process. It is a powerful force when you are establishing the optimal environment for writing within the classroom, and beyond, when children take their skills and their attitude out into the wider world. It exists between the children themselves as they work collaboratively on story-making and as they practise their story telling skills. Rapport also establishes a beneficial link between a writer and the characters she creates, since ultimately every component of a story represents some aspect of the author's own psyche. Thus rapport between a writer and the world of her story defines and develops the subtle but profoundly useful skill of intrapersonal (self-)intelligence: knowing one's own emotional landscape and drawing from it the resources one needs to behave appropriately and capably.

It is a cliché that writing is a lonely occupation. This is not an entirely accurate view, since a writer engaging with her characters and their experiences remains too busy and interested to be lonely! In any case, story-making can be a very social and sociable process where the elements of rapport are picked up both nonconsciously and explicitly within the safe framework of the story-making activity and the world of the story so created.

The handy equation of awareness – understanding – control applies here. As children write and talk about their stories, notice their facial expressions, postures and the little patterns that run through their language. All of these provide clues about the deeper structure of their thinking and emotions. If you notice indications of difficulty or uncertainty, raise the issue as appropriate with the child concerned and apply suitable strategies for resolving it. (See 'Writing blocks' above, and *Self Intelligence* [see Bibliography]).

Rapport can also exist in marking, grading and assessment. These are elements of the larger relationship between pupil and teacher. Be sensitive to what the writer is trying to achieve, given his current capabilities, over and above what you as a teacher have been endeavouring to allow him to learn.

◆ Be a writer yourself

Perhaps most importantly, *be the writer* you would like the children to aspire to be. Practise what you preach, at least in terms of the personal qualities you advocate with regard to writing, language and creativity. When the children write, take the opportunity to write for yourself and enjoy the bonus of being a powerful and positive role model for your students. Successful authorship is not necessarily publishing a best-seller, but producing work on an ongoing basis; which is to say, achieving the goals you set for yourself in your endeavours. Your professionalism is your attitude. George Bernard Shaw said that he was not a teacher, 'only a fellow traveller of whom you asked the way'. All writers travel that same path. The best of them don't follow in the footsteps of the wise, but make footsteps of their own as they seek what the wise themselves are seeking.

Tips for good practice

- write regularly. Fifteen minutes a day is better than a couple of hours on a Sunday afternoon.

- always carry a notepad and pen to scribble down ideas as they come to mind. Anticipate that you will enjoy a steady flow of ideas, and thank yourself and be quietly pleased when they arrive.

- devise a practical filing system for the spray of ideas you'll generate. Don't let odd scraps of paper accumulate randomly in an overstuffed desk drawer. Be systematic.

- things happen for reasons. When you do things well, reflect on what you did and deliberately build those procedures into your ongoing approach. Similarly, if you have difficulties, explore their context and devise strategies for their resolution. Despondency is the handmaiden of defeat. Every writer has struggled on the road to success.

- adopt an eclectic approach. Experts don't tell you how to do it, only how *they* do it. Have the courage to take what works for you and adapt techniques to be the most useful tools as far as you're concerned. Discard what doesn't feel right.

- life itself is a story which isn't over till it's over. In a most important sense we are always in the process of becoming writers along an endless, wonderful soaring learning curve.

- everything is material. Whatever happens in your life can be used to express through your stories how you feel and what it means to be truly human and alive.

6

The best way to explain it is to do it.

Rudyard Kipling

Section Three

 # Plotting

Let us learn to dream, gentlemen.
Then perhaps we shall find the truth.

Friedrich August Kekule, chemist

Section 3 – Plotting

Page	Topic/activity	Story element covered	Accelerated learning link
105	Use anything!	*Multisensory input for generating plots*	Awareness of VAK/development of other learning styles/stream-of-consciousness generation of ideas
107	Dicework	*Random selection of plot elements*	Generation and discrimination of options/purposeful questioning / decision-making
109	Spinners	*Random selection of plot elements*	Generation and discrimination of options/purposeful questioning / decision making/circle time group work
113	Maps and tracks	*Consolidation of ideas about theme, genre, setting and character*	VAK-ability/story mapping as an application of Mind Mapping® chunking/purposeful questioning
120	Catch me!		Review of information / development of social skills
122	Story profile	*All elements*	Decision making/evaluation techniques/feedback strategies
122	Hot buttons	*All elements*	Rapport/linguistic awareness
123	Cliffhanger cards	*Pace and tension*	Linguistic awareness/analysis of information/anticipation of outcome
125	Keyword work	*Vocabulary*	Linguistic awareness including VAK details
128	With good reason	*Elaboration of ideas at all levels*	Anticipation of outcomes / reflection
129	Predictions	*Elaboration of ideas at all levels*	Anticipation of outcomes / awareness of timeline techniques
132	Time spans	*Awareness of time in narrative*	Awareness of timeline techniques / awareness of subjective time / development of time management skills
133	The video remote game	*Awareness of time and examination of detail in narrative*	Visualisation skills/awareness of variable point-of-view as a strategy for establishing rapport and understanding
135	Along the track	*Awareness of narrative structure and pace*	Development of time management and organisational skills
137	Touching base	*Sub-plotting/character development through time*	Development on interpersonal skills through the analogy of the 'life path'
138	Many endings	*Conclusions/generation of multiple story endings*	Decision making/awareness of multiple options
139	Story tree	*Generation of multiple options throughout the story*	Decision making/awareness of multiple options as a strategy for the resolution of difficulties/goal and target setting
140	Looking at the gaps	*Elaboration of any story element/subplots*	Development of the personal intelligences/speculation as a thinking skill
143	Proof reading	*Review of text for technical accuracy / editing skills*	Development of concentration / development of technical competence/evaluation of text

145	Connective prompts revisited	*Development of plot through character*	Development of empathy and self-knowledge/access to an allowance of subconscious information/practice of group work through circle time
146	The meanwhile game	*Narrative overview*	Group work skills/feedback / point-of-view skills
147	Stepping stars	*First person writing*	Development of empathy/point-of-view/association-dissociation skills
150	Story circle	*Narrative overview , time spans and pace/self-evaluation of work*	Awareness of the Big Picture/the clock face as an organisational device/time management skills
154	Treasure mapping	*Review of story elements*	Awareness of metaphor / nonconscious learning/gathering personal resources/modelling behaviour
154	Story box	*Generation and elaboration of ideas through random stimulus*	Awareness of metaphor / nonconscious learning/gathering personal resources/lateral thinking skills
157	My favourite story	*Awareness of story elements*	Awareness of metaphor / gathering personal resources
160	Story trees revisited	*Generation of multiple options throughout the story*	Decision making/awareness of multiple options as a strategy for the resolution of difficulties/goal and target setting

Life is either a daring
adventure
or it is nothing.

Helen Keller

Section Three

 Plotting

◆ Use anything!

Authors are frequently asked where they get their ideas from, as though having ideas was a mysterious random process beyond the control of the will. Actually, once a creative attitude has been established, the flow of ideas is ongoing in the form of new connections and how those connections build towards a 'bigger picture'. Creative thinking becomes a habit – a state of subconscious competence and conscious effortlessness.

The creative habit lies at the heart of *ALPS StoryMaker* and is implicit in all of the activities in this book. Specific techniques highlight and help to define certain aspects of creative thinking, but beneath lies the ethos that soaks into the bones. And so if you wish to allow young writers to have lots of ideas, encourage them to use anything, because everything is material for creative thought.

- Select a piece of instrumental music. Ask the children to imagine the music is a person. Have them write down any ideas about that person as the music plays. Then split the class into groups. Each group is to focus on one aspect of the person as the music plays again:
  - the music tells you what the person looks like
  - the music tells you about the moods and emotions this person has
  - the music tells you about this person's background and past experiences
  - the music tells you about this person's future.

- Instead of a character, suggest that the music to be played represents a place. You might use the two-stage process of listen and listen again, or split the class into groups at the outset and have them listen selectively to imagine various aspects of the place.
  - the music tells you about the layout and/or architecture of the place
  - the music tells you about the climate and weather you find there
  - the music tells you about the history of the place
  - the music tells you about the kind of people/animals/plants that live there.

● Take any object to hand and ask the children what it reminds them of. Use a tape recorder to capture the surge of ideas, or maybe spidergram their thoughts. For example:

- On my desk as I write I have a pocket-watch on a chain. This reminds me of time... We carry our time around with us... We keep time in mind... We might not be able to let go of it... The watch has a chain... Time is chained – it is chained to me... I hook it on to my jacket... I wind the watch... I need to make an effort to keep time running to time... If the watch speeds up or falls behind it is 'wrong', it is 'broken'... The bits of the watch are put together in a silver case... Time is constructed, it is contained and has boundaries... I put boundaries around my time... And in this silver case time is only the sum of the parts... If I took apart those parts time would have no meaning... I watch the watch. (So that's why it's called a watch!)... I must not let go of the steady tick of time...

Several things become apparent from this short extract of 'stream of consciousness' writing. Firstly, it feels more like a 'stream of *sub*consciousness' flow: how do I know what I think until I see what I say? Little insights and realisations pepper the fragments. Secondly, when you and your children let go of the formal constraints of the writing process, you will notice that the ideas come along with ease. The metaphor of flowing/water/stream is an apt one. Thirdly, and especially if you maintain the intention to discover ways of organising your ideas, you will notice connections between the fragments which will lead you towards a plot – particularly if you are thinking on the level of themes (see p.229) or within a genre (Section 5).

● A similar outcome of such going-with-the-flow thinking occurs through using aromas. The olfactory nerve connects directly with the limbic system in our brains, which is the seat of our emotions, particularly aggression and sex (which is why perfumes and colognes can be so powerfully evocative). Aromas stir emotions, and if we are not instantly reminded of something by a particular smell, the meaning-making function of our minds mobilises to make sense of the experience. Aromatherapy oils and spices work well for this activity. Select an aroma:

- ask children what the smell reminds them of (stream-of-consciousness writing)

- suggest that the smell is a person/place/event, and note ideas down

- ask children what colour the smell reminds them of

- ask children what kind of music the smell reminds them of

- ask children how the smell reminds them of any story they have read, or seen on TV, etc.

● Take a picture. Have children describe what they see. Then ask them to imagine what sounds are in the picture, what they imagine beyond the frame, how the world-in-the-picture looked five minutes earlier, how it might look in a day's time, etc. (See *Imagine That*, p.19).

One interesting and important element of the activities above is that they encourage young writers to represent one idea in terms of another (metaphorical thinking), and/or describe impressions from one sense in terms of another sense. This phenomenon, when such trans-sensory impressions are fully experienced, is called synaesthesia. Susan Greenfield (in *The Human Brain: A Guided Tour*) asserts that synaesthesia is more common as a natural process in children (as opposed to a dysfunction in adults suffering from schizophrenia or under the influence of hallucinogenic drugs). This is perhaps because children's minds are more flexible in their interpretations of reality and do not yet suffer from the 'hardening of the categories' which characterises the mindsets of most grown-ups.

For the purposes of storymaking, trans-sensory or multisensory impressions are to be valued, since they stimulate creative thought processes (indeed are the result of them) and add weight to the aphorism that 'Voyages of discovery consist not of going to new worlds, but seeing with new eyes.'

◆ Dicework

Authors are nosy. Their curiosity drives them on to find out more. They notice things. They ask questions. They speculate and daydream about what was and what might be… This is systematic daydreaming of course, part of the process leading to the fixed goal of story's end.

Using a dice, coin, spinner or any other method of generating random answers satisfies a young writer's thirst to know more and keeps the thinking fresh. Using the simplest method – tossing a coin, where heads = 'yes' and tails = 'no' – ask ten questions about an imaginary character. For example: Is this person male? Is this person an adult? Is this person tall? Is this person kind? Is this person sly?…

Although these are closed questions, they are generalised enough to keep options open. Asking if the person was actually a famous pop star would end the game if the answer were 'yes'. Also, notice that later questions are informed and directed by the earlier ones. Knowing that the character was sly might lead you to ask: Is this person a criminal? Has this person already been caught? Is this person under investigation by the FBI? etc. Storylines are suggested very quickly by asking simple questions about characters. In fact, asking questions about any major aspect of a story – plot, characters or background – generates information about the others.

An implicit element of this activity (although you can make the point to your students if you wish) is that the questioner is responsible for the answers she gets. Silly questions generate silly answers: Is this person covered in purple spots? A 'yes' answer raises a chuckle, but leaves you with a character covered in purple spots. If necessary, remind children about intention and purpose. What purpose does a purple-spotted character serve in your 'proto-story'? If the questioner can persuade you of one, then perhaps you'll allow the character to remain!

If the game is teacher-led you can elegantly maintain control if (when?) children attempt to subvert it. Whenever an unsuitable question is asked, you might let the coin/dice (Steve calls it 'the boss') decide: is Dean allowed to ask the question he's just mentioned? Using a coin, Dean has a 50/50 chance of getting his own way. Using dice gives you the advantage – 'OK Dean, if you roll a six you can ask that question.' Refreshingly, children rarely argue with 'the boss's' decision.

Generating random answers also helps combat the 'and then' syndrome. Children often try to make up stories by leap-frogging in a linear way from one idea to the next. These chains of ideas are frequently derivative and predictable, and are sometimes accompanied by a failure of the imagination – 'and then they woke up and it had all been a dream'. Tossing coins and rolling dice causes the questioner to think again and explore other lines of enquiry when the expected answer is not forthcoming.

Another powerful aspect of dicework is that you can introduce increasingly sophisticated versions of the game. Initially a coin gives you 'yes/no' responses, as does a dice if you specify that, say, 1–3 = 'yes' and 4–6 = 'no'. Once children are familiar with that idea, incorporate more elegant variations:

- use the dice on a 1–6 sliding scale, where 1 = low/not much and 6 = high/a great deal. This allows for questions such as: how popular is my character? How resourceful is my character? etc.

- use one or more dice to generate pure numbers. So: how many close friends does my character have? How many problems will my character face in this story?

- attach an idea to the numbers on a dice as children explore story scenarios.

  1 – meet an ally

  2 – face sudden danger

  3 – lose a valuable item

  4 – gain an advantage

  5 – confront an enemy

  6 – move in an unexpected direction

Or the numbers could simply refer to items you might find in a story: a car, a key, a weapon, money, a document, a rail ticket... Their unexpected appearance stimulates children to find a purpose for them as their ideas weave into a coherent scenario.

- A more elaborate version of the above uses a 6 x 6 grid. Two rolls of the dice locates any box, which you might fill with story motifs, keywords and other prompts. Roll the dice first to tell you how many boxes you will visit. You can assemble 'story resources' before you begin plotting, or during planning or first-drafting to freshen up your thinking. (See 6 x 6 grid template on p.34)

- Wean children off the dice by instructing them to alternate dice-rolls with decision-making. So: is my character a criminal? (Yes.) But he's trying to make amends. Are the police hunting my character? (Yes.) And he must avoid being caught until he finds proof he is innocent. How many other people know he is innocent? (Three.) And he must find them to clear his name... Suggest to children that they use the dice less and less often as they become increasingly capable in making their own decisions. Eventually the coin or dice will act as an occasional stimulus for thought if writers get 'stuck' and can't see their way out of a situation.

For further ideas about using dice and coins in this way see Imagine That p.177, and *What's The Story?* A & C Black, 2001. Consider using dicework with other storymaking techniques to explore plot, characters and setting.

◆ Spinners

Using a spinner is another way of generating random elements for storymaking. The advantage of this device is that any number of different base cards can be used: the spinner is placed in the middle, the pointer is spun and the selection is made in a second.

Base card displaying words, numbers or visuals

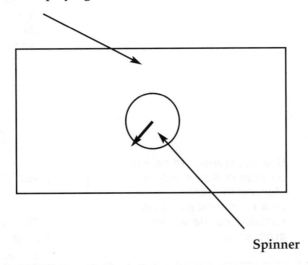

Spinner

Base cards are quick and easy to make. If exploring genre, for example, use suitable clipart images arranged around the borders of the sheet and have children select some as a stimulus for storymaking. Other images and keywords can be used to choose characters, locations, methods of transport, weapons or whatever other elements children wish to select randomly for their stories. Example templates are given below, but the range is enormous.

◆ Base card for a mystery story

Jones lay
slumped on
the sofa

There was a
sudden flash of
light in the
darkness. He fell
with a groan...

**Use the spinner to select
a range of items before
starting the story and/or
pick individual items as a
stimulus as the writing
proceeds...**

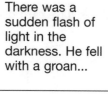

He had only one
chance - and that
was a slim one.

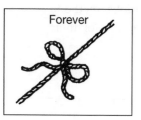

The car skidded
off the road with a
screech of brakes
and overturned
into the ditch

Forever

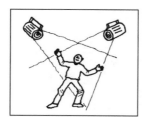

Now there were
only two things
standing between
her and success –
but one of them
was deadly...

◆ Base card for selecting degrees in a story element:

No danger.
Continue normally.

A hint of danger. You may get some small sense of difficulty ahead.

There is a small chance of risk to you and your friends. Faint but definite signs of danger.

Extreme danger. Risk of death. You may be forced to abandon your adventure.

You suspect there will be problems ahead. As yet you are not sure what they might be.

The danger level is high. Great risk to you and your adventure is likely.

Use the spinner to select a degree of – danger, speed, progress, state of the weather, injury after an incident, etc... The example given is for danger.

Danger signs are few and far between, but quite definite. You will need to plan for trouble.

The danger is moderate-to-severe. There is quite a great risk of injury.

There are fairly clear warnings of difficulty ahead. Some aspects of the danger are predictable.

The degree of danger is forcing you to change your plans. You may have to abandon some of your possessions.

You know more clearly the danger you face. You are actively thinking about how to avoid it.

The danger is obvious and is causing you some worry. Risk of injury or loss is moderate.

The first effects of the danger are affecting you. Some delay and difficulty will be experienced.

The danger is very close now. You know it will hinder you but can't yet work out how risky the situation might be.

ALPS STORYMAKER — USING FICTION AS A RESOURCE FOR ACCELERATED LEARNING

◆ Base card for a story:

Use the spinner to select a range of items before starting the story and/or pick individual items as a stimulus as the writing proceeds...

◆ Maps and tracks

Stories can begin anywhere and can be generated out of nothing. All of us, including the children we teach, already have an enormous amount of material stored away at a subconscious level. Storymaking encourages access to the subconscious map, stimulates the free flow of ideas, and helps develop selection and consolidation of those ideas using conscious thinking tools.

Story mapping is an ideal activity for getting children started on a story. It can be used with a range of other techniques to be found in this book, and lends itself to the use of dice, coins or spinners for generating random answers. What's important is that children associate with the world of the story, jump in, see what's there, listen to the sounds, get a hands-on impression of the place, talk to the people, find out more, *experience the world they are creating*.

Details of basic story mapping can be found in Steve's *Imagine That* and *What's The Story?* Once a setting has been created and the children have some idea of the genre, and perhaps the themes, they wish to work with, the adventure can begin…

Refer to the story map template on p.117. One option would be to send groups to explore different areas of the map, and even places beyond what is shown there. Equip the groups with specific tasks and the means of completing those tasks well. So:

- **Themes**: Forbidden lands/Events have consequences.
- **Genre**: High fantasy (although characters and locations from our world may feature).

† **Group A**: Go north-east to the mountains known as the Three Sisters. Legend tells of a creature there called the Wight. He owns a weapon of great power. With its help we may be able to defeat the evil King Boreas. You may ask the Wight up to ten questions, using a coin to find out his answers. Bring those answers back, together with a report of the land through which you have travelled.

† **Group B**: Go west through the endless lightning storm to the city of Mondas. Before you get there you will encounter three things. Use the 6 x 6 story box and rolls of the dice to find out what they are. You may choose any, all or none of them to help you on your way. Once you arrive in Mondas, prepare a description of this most astonishing place. Find the mage known as Tenumbriel. He will give you music which hints at the meaning of the dream he had, which can save our world. Select a suitable piece of music, listen to it and write down impressions from Tenumbriel's Dream.

† **Group C**: In the depths of the Primeval Forest to the north there is said to be a doorway leading to another world. In our ancient stories the world is called Erth. It is a very different world from ours, and yet startlingly similar in a number of ways. Find the doorway. Go to Erth and enlist the help of four people whose hearts are strong and whose minds are open to wonder. During your journey you will meet danger three times. Use the spinner with a 'Danger' base card to assess the risk you face. How do you overcome those threats to your safety? Once you have located your four helpers, find out what strengths they possess.

Prepare a brief report on each character and send your findings back to me – the Dragon Helcyrian will carry your documents safely home.

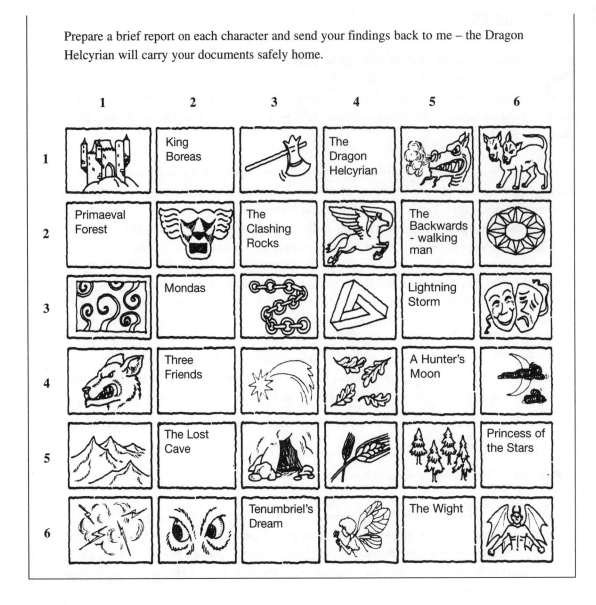

Use the map to develop other skills too:

- Fine-focus questioning. Select a feature from the map, for example the house on the hill. Say to children:
    - What can you actually see?
    - What sounds do you imagine as you approach the house?
    - When you arrive at the house, touch its walls and describe what you feel.
    - Go into the house. What's there? What distinctive smells are you aware of as you move among its rooms?
    - Notice the strangely beautiful decorations. Describe them.
    - Walk through the house and give a commentary as you do so of anything you notice…

● This last activity paves the way for a technique called 'Pole-bridging'. Pole-bridging is also known as 'muttering your understanding', and is the process of talking something through as you think it or do it. You may recognise that effective Pole-bridging requires the now familiar process of allowing the free flow of thoughts and insights without conscious effort to retrieve or associate them – 'How do I know what I think until I hear what I say?' In this case, Pole-bridging is coupled with a sustained visualisation of the mysterious house (which you can map as the children mutter their understanding). If you come across the 'I can't' syndrome, say to the child,'Well, just pretend you can and notice how many ideas come into your mind.' This simple trick of 'let's pretend' can work wonders!

Story Tracks are predetermined routes through a map that has already been wholly or partially created. A track makes use of ideas already generated, but 'chunks down' the process of plotting into more easily manageable steps. There are several ways of using the technique.

● Create a track which 'tours' the map. Include a manageable number of steps as far as your children are concerned. More experienced writers will appreciate more steps along the track.

  - You can give children a general instruction such as, 'What happens at each step in your story?' and allow them to use dice, etc., as well as discussion and negotiation to generate a storyline.

  - You can create a key that indicates the kind of thing that might happen at each step. The group then works out the details, using techniques with which they are familiar. A sample key is given below; see Story Map 2 as an example of its use.

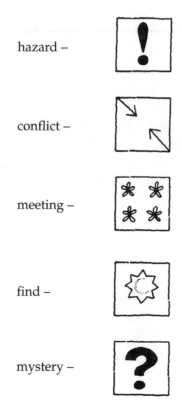

You can use clipart as appropriate to introduce characters and events, and to enable children to become familiar with signs and symbols – and if you wish to be more prescriptive about what certain steps of the story will contain.

this happens here

introduce this
character

● Create a network of story steps allowing children free choice as to which route they take (See Story Map 3). They could use coins or dice to pick their route randomly, and a spinner and base card or 6 x 6 story box to flesh out the scenes within the narrative. The story step network gives children working in a group the opportunity to strike off by themselves and investigate different parts of the map. Each child then becomes an authority on his or her particular area and can report back snippets of useful information to the others. The network also gives writers the chance to 'recycle the material', using the same settings and company of characters again, in a different narrative.

● Use the map in conjunction with a network of steps and an 'envelope of ingredients'. Such an envelope contains items of clipart, key words, instructions and questions on separate pieces of paper. As children work their way along a story track, they can delve into the envelope as they need or according to your instructions.

   Tip: Laminate story maps to turn them into a durable and reusable resource.
   Print story tracks onto OHP film to use as overlays.

● Story maps can be created based on previously published stories. One story track can reiterate the plot of the book. Different tracks encourage children to explore other aspects of the story, which the author may not have developed. This activity allows children to review texts and gives them the opportunity to manipulate the ideas they find there.

◆ Story Map template

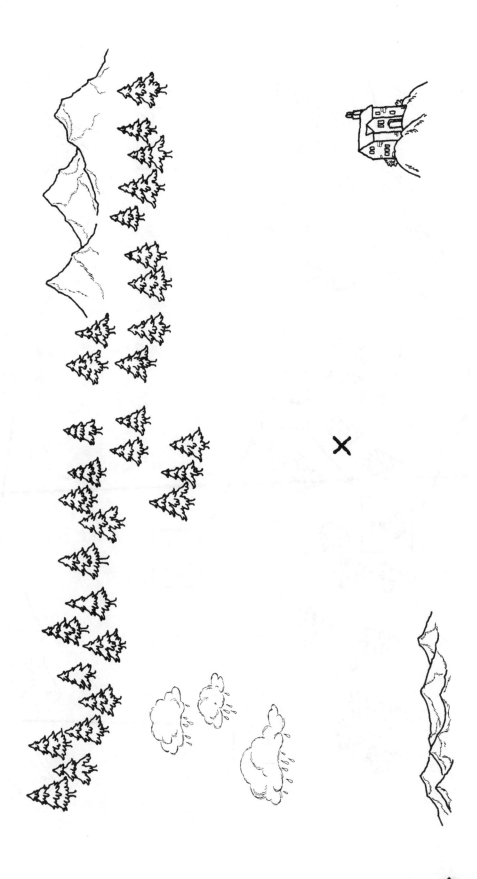

ALPS STORYMAKER — USING FICTION AS A RESOURCE FOR ACCELERATED LEARNING

◆ Story Map 2 showing story track

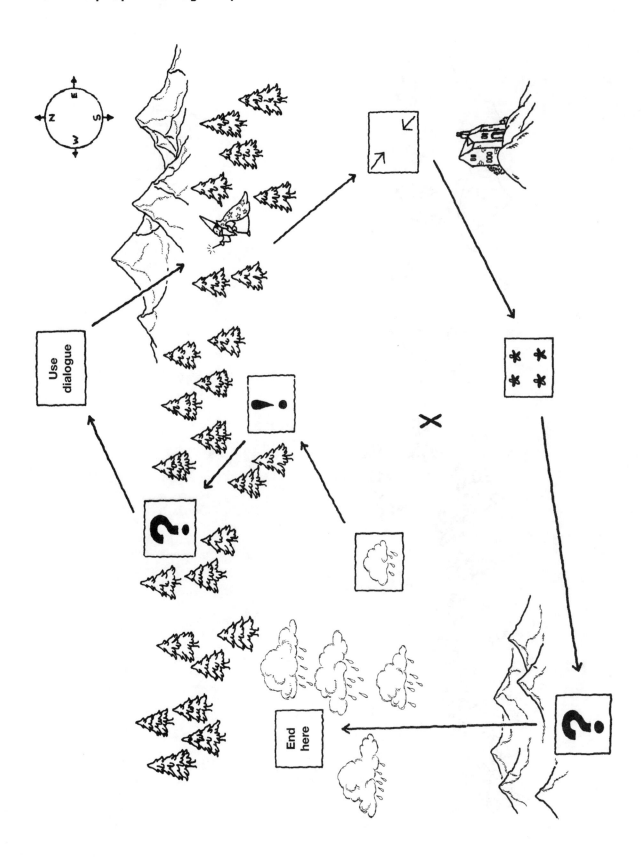

◆ Story Map 3

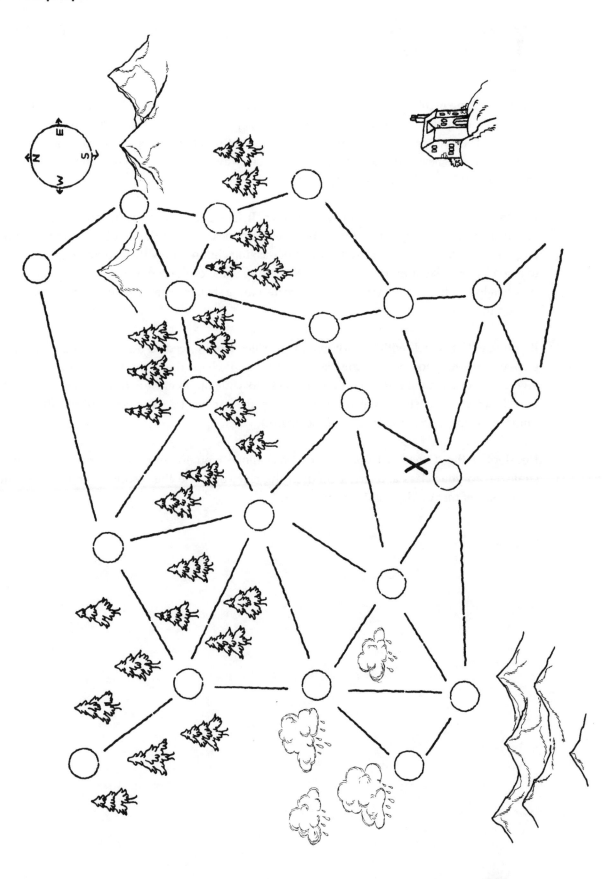

◆ Catch me!

This little game uses the story step network template and can be used with or without a story map or other accoutrements.

The basic game involves two players, each represented by a different coloured counter. Players start as far away from each other on the network as possible. One is the catcher, the other is the 'catchee'. The catcher rolls a dice first and moves that number of steps towards his opponent. The catchee rolls next and moves that number of steps away from the catcher. The game of chase continues until the catcher catches his opponent.

Children will find 'Catch me!' brisk and brief. It is a good warm-up to other storymaking activities, or a refreshing 'brain break' between activities. Clearly, the game lasts longer with a larger playing board and more steps. Consider asking children how they could adapt the game to extend it or make it more interesting. (Removing some of the connecting lines is an obvious ploy.) Help children to invent rules which create a more structured and sophisticated framework around the activity.

If you use 'Catch me!' with a story map, then rules would need to be formulated which give players something to do when they land on a circle. Perhaps they'll find a treasure which will give them an advantage (e.g. you are invisible to your opponent for three turns). Or maybe they'll bypass an obstacle which could trip up the catcher (if the catcher dice-rolls an odd number she must go to the far end of the board.)

Developing the 'Catch me!' game over time allows you to introduce various groupwork strategies to your class and gives children the chance to use the resources and practise the techniques of the *ALPS StoryMaker* approach.

◆ 'Catch me!' template

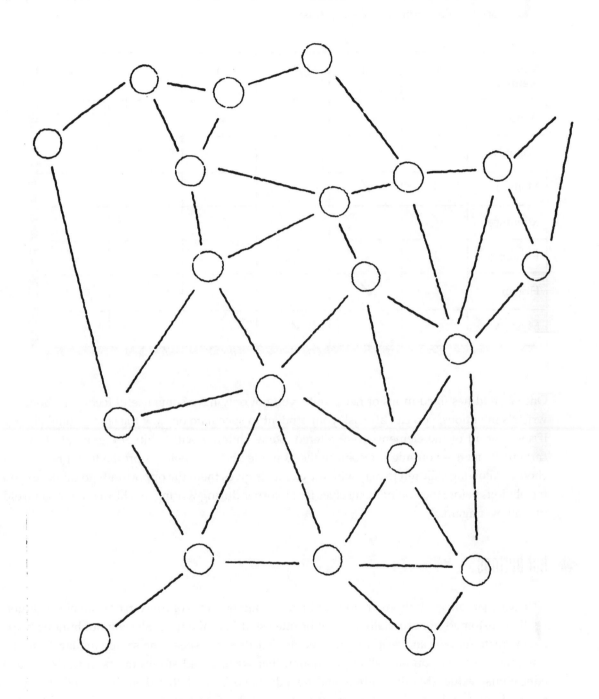

◆ Story profile

This technique extends and formalises the 'Self-assembling curry' activity (p.89) It can be used at any stage of planning, and acts to codify and formalise story elements. A typical story profile template looks like this:

Story element	1	2	3	4	5	6
Action				✓		
Comedy	✓					
Menace		✓				
Romance	✓					
Excitement						✓
Horror		✓				
Mystery			✓			

Once a child has filled in his or her profile, you not only have some useful feedback about the writer's intentions; you can also ask your student to speculate on how the story would change if some or all of the elements were altered. Some children will habitually gravitate towards certain elements – you might recognise the example above as being a profile that a boy might choose. Allowing children to play with the elements gives them the opportunity to think beyond the obvious before they paint themselves into a corner during writing, or churn out the same old plot all over again.

◆ Hot buttons

In sales jargon, hot buttons are ideas, phrases, fashions, areas of concern or even bits of jargon that customers are especially fond of or interested in at the time. Sharing hot buttons helps to create rapport and reaffirms for people that they all 'speak the same language'. In one sense, as a teacher you are selling the notion that writing and stories are both fun and have educational value. (Many children will already have bought this deal, but some still need persuading!) Similarly, all writers endeavour to get their readers to buy into the world of the story. Within the context of StoryMaker, where story reviews and commentaries are part of the collaborative process of storymaking, mirroring the characteristics of the writer's language forges a bond between the writer and reviewers, letting everyone know that you are all walking the same road together.

As a writer, look back at your work and identify the ideas, words, phrases, settings, character types and situations that particularly excite you. Explore why this should be so – why does a certain set piece of action feel so satisfying to write about? Tease out the elements that make aspects of your work come alive and sparkle. Check out your own hot buttons and use them to boost your positive attitude to even greater heights.

What are your hot buttons?

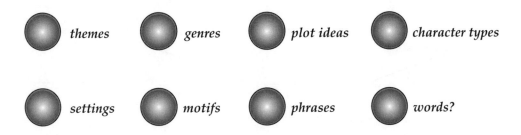

themes   genres   plot ideas   character types

settings   motifs   phrases   words?

◆ Cliffhanger cards

> The storm howled overhead as Kane clung desperately to the roof of the runaway truck. Lightning flashed across the clouds. In the sudden flickers of illumination Kane saw the sharp bend up ahead and the flimsy wooden fence marking out the cliff edge. He imagined the awful drop to the river far below as the truck careered on; fifty yards from sure destruction – forty – twenty – ten…

The author Ian Fleming was once asked why his books were so successful. He replied that his primary concern was to make the reader turn the page. Indeed, we describe thrilling stories as 'page turners' and many of us have enjoyed the experience of not wanting a story to end because it is so exciting.

Compelling your reader to read on is not just a question of creating a swift pace. *Variety of pace* is more effective. Just as a runner paces himself over the distance of a race, so should a writer map out the route a story is to take and aim to create an elegant blend of fast action and more leisurely description and evocation of atmosphere. Success in this is a matter of practice, but young writers can begin by using the technique of cliffhanger cards…

◆ 123

Cliffhanger cards can be written in advance. Have children create thrilling scenarios like the one above, ending at an especially tense moment. Use them in various ways:

● **Look at the situation itself and 'tease out' what's in there to create the excitement**

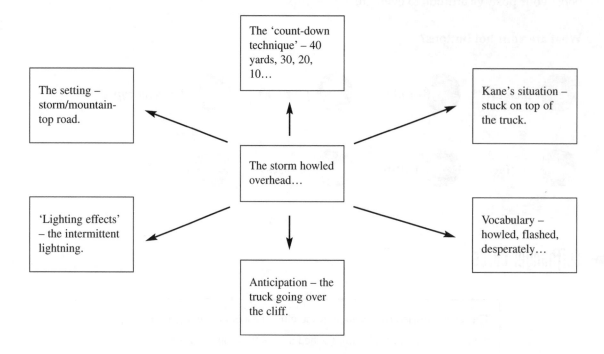

● **Look back and think about what led up to the cliffhanger situation**

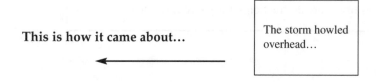

● **Brainstorm a number of 'What happened next' scenarios**

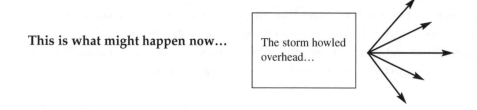

● Look at a number of cliffhanger cards to see what common elements exist between them

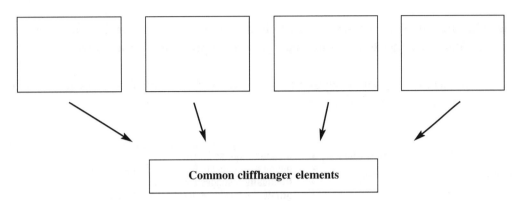

● Use these elements as you plot a story to create cliffhanger moments at the ends of scenes or chapters

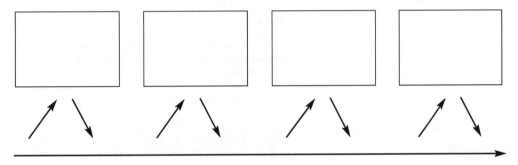

Creating interest and curiosity is not just a question of managing pace. Posing a question which will be answered later draws the reader on – *What was it about the truck that set Kane's nerves tingling?* Using a subtext sentence encourages pre-processing of answers in the reader's mind – *Kane looked inside and realised that the owner of the truck just had to be caught.* Sprinkling the narrative with intriguing and carefully chosen details gives texture to the story (see 'One unique detail', p.181) – *Kane noticed that the boy's face was deathly pale, bloodless. But his eyes sparkled with a fierce light of anger.*

◆ Keyword work

Jean Paul Sartre said that words are loaded pistols. Certainly words are powerful and can be used either positively or negatively. Raising awareness of the meanings of words leads young writers to understand how influential language can be and gives them greater control over what they say and write, how they say it, and what effects they aim to achieve.

Words work in combination, of course. A story is an elegantly woven complex of interlinked meanings. It has an overall effect, but within that 'zone of influence' certain scenes, paragraphs and sentences stand out. The informed choice of one word over others can make all the difference between a story that is merely competent and one that leaves a lasting emotional impression.

Working with individual words sensitises children to the power of language and how that power is determined by choice. There are many ways of approaching keyword work:

● Take a piece of writing and suggest alternative keywords. Think about how this changes the meaning and effect of the sentence.

The storm **howled** overhead as Kane clung **desperately** to the roof of the runaway truck.	• **raged** – suggests anger as well as wildness • **moaned** – not as fierce • **boomed** – suggests thunder and deafening wind • **frantically** – suggests Kane's in a panic • **grimly** – suggests determination and purpose • **recklessly** – suggests Kane's wild and devil-may-care attitude to life
Lightning **flashed** across the **clouds.**	• **blazed** – suggests sheet lightning rather than fork lightning, and evokes the colours of flames • **flickered** – indicates rapid flashing (would need to change 'flickers' later on) • **jabbed** – suggests menace and the fork-like quality of the lightning • **sky** – is vaguer than clouds and suggests wider horizons • **heavens** – more majestic than clouds, but may contribute to over-writing
… Kane saw the **sharp** bend up ahead and the **flimsy** wooden fence…	• **ninety-degree** – more precise, but longer-winded description • **tight** – suggests difficulty of taking the bend • **rickety** – emphasises the weakness and age of the fence • **broken** – suggests past accidents at that point

● Use keywords in conjunction with a story map (see p.117). Ask children to visualise certain parts of the map and suggest keywords that vividly describe that place.

Visual: gloomy, dense, dark, shadowed, vast

Auditory: hushed, soundless, silent, whisperings

Feeling: lonely, isolated, uneasy mysterious

Gustatory: loamy, pine-scented, earthy

Kinaesthetic: damp, dank, cold. Rough bark, prickly needles

● Take the whole map. Plan a route. Stop at certain points and have children describe what they see, hear, feel, etc. Gather up the words they use and discuss the effect and effectiveness of the language.

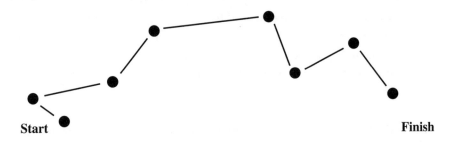

Start   Finish

● Follow the 'name it – describe it – give it an action' pattern in conjunction with a story map or any picture. This produces basic sentences that children will soon 'outgrow' as they realise what combinations of words work more effectively. So:

Basic pattern: noun / adjective / verb	The trees are tall and blow in the wind.	What did you do? *
Make it better:	The tall trees blow wildly in the wind.	I put the description before the name and added a word to describe the action.
Make it better:	The tall pines blow wildly in the roaring wind.	I changed the name to give a clearer picture of the trees. I added a word to describe the wind.
Make it better:	The tall pines blew wildly in the roaring wind that had been growing stronger all day.	I changed the sentence to the past. I added a bit of description about the wind blowing. This helps you to imagine the storm and to think it might get worse!
Make it better:	The tall pines blew wildly in the roaring wind. The storm had been growing stronger all day.	I turned the one long sentence into two shorter ones because it sounds better. Andy

* As children become familiar with the parts of speech they can include these in their sentence review.

Obviously you would not ask children to do this activity for every sentence in a story! Those children who pick up the idea swiftly will naturally begin to incorporate the 'make it better' concept naturally as they write. Those who struggle can be gently encouraged to comb through certain sentences or parts of their story to make some changes.

Notice that as Andy becomes more confident in the process of refining his sentences he begins to add reasons for the changes. This principle can be extended through the storymaking process and can operate at any level…

◆ With good reason

The point of this activity is to let children practise the art of doing things in their writing for reasons they have considered. Generally speaking, this does not happen. When most children are questioned about some element of their work, responses tend to be along the lines of 'I don't know', or 'Just because I wanted to', or 'Well, I like (violence, monsters, car chases, teddy bears, etc.)'. Including ingredients that you enjoy writing about is fine as far as it goes, but if their contribution and effect beyond that have not been planned and judged, then the story remains more or less gratuitous.

As with keyword work, challenging young writers to examine their reasons is not something to be laboured. Tread lightly, for you tread on their dreams. Decide on the level at which you wish to work, how far you will press children for reasons, and be prepared to help them with a bagful of off-the-peg reasons they can adopt if they want to.

The examples here are taken from the Double Dare Gang story 'The Gift'.

Level	Elements	Reasons for use	Further thinking
Themes	Innocence, greed, childhood's end, there's always a price to pay	*I wanted to write a Christmas story and I wanted it to be magical and yet dark. It angers me that Christmas so often seems to be about having things – the TV ad campaign starts at the end of October!*	I had ideas for a few different endings for this story (in one of them, Chris dies.) But I chose something upbeat. Also, I wanted the character Steve to know that innocence and wonder still exist in the world.
Location	An ordinary town, mention of the shopping mall, the embankment where the kids play	*Kenniston is my 'typical town'. I wanted an ordinary place where extraordinary things could happen. The shopping mall symbolises the compulsion of society to consume – it's a glittering shop window. The embankment is an out-of-the-way playing place.*	The embankment is a place where children can play freely and naturally. In a number of stories and traditions, waste ground is where different worlds meet.
Characters	The regular gang, plus Chris the newcomer, plus various adults	*In this story, the kids in the gang represent different aspects of 'the child': there's suspicion, hostility, understanding, compassion, excitement, greed, etc. Chris is Christ-mas, and the spirit of innocence and giving freely. The adults are icons representing human greed hiding behind facades of respectability.*	There's a bit of a clutter of characters. I could probably do with one less.

Level	Elements	Reasons for use	Further thinking
Scene	The moment where Chris offers his first gifts to the children.	*I wanted this to be a magical moment, something mysterious and a bit scary as the children's wish for more and more things starts to take over – the magic goes completely out of control when the adults dredge up their darkest wishes later on.*	In another version of the story, the children's scepticism lasts longer. They think it's a conjuring trick. On the other hand, I think their swift acceptance of the magic is more appropriate. They still carry innocence in their hearts.
Sentence	Chris opened his right hand and a rosebud lay in his palm: opened his left hand and a butterfly flew away: his right hand again, and there was a gold pocketwatch: left hand, and a fancy ring just like the vicar was wearing.	*The objects themselves:* • *rosebud – out of season, something about to unfold, William Blake's poem 'The Sick Rose'* • *butterfly – the mystery of life remains a mystery!* • *the watch – gold represents the goal of greed, the watch represents time/timelessness* • *fancy ring – the vicar's ring is just another thing. But possessions can come to possess you.* *Sentence structure:* • *I wanted a long sentence chopped into phrases to suggest a smooth and seamless act of bringing-into-being. I wanted the sense of a magician effortlessly doing wonderful tricks.*	When I wrote this I was really in the flow of the story. At the time I didn't think about the objects Chris created. He begins by choosing what comes into existence, but increasingly the dark dreams of the adults dictate what appears – it starts to run out of control until a monster is made. The details of it remain vague, so that the reader can conjour a dark imagining!

An important point to bear in mind is that focusing a writer's attention in this way will allow him to have further insights into why he wrote what he did. At the time, the reasoning and choices may have been subconscious. Revisiting the story allows more ideas to come to light.

◆ Predictions

In this activity, children discuss what might happen later in a story that they are reading, based on what they already know. Such a habit of looking ahead will transfer naturally to their own writing and operate largely at a subconscious level. There are a number of ways of using the technique:

● **Straight predictions at various points in the text, and at various levels of detail**

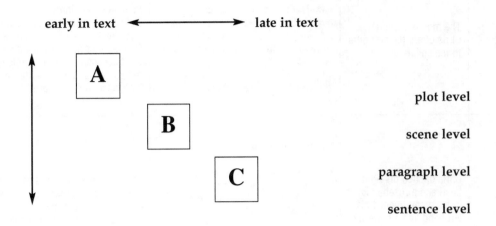

A   The Double Dare Gang plan to raid Old Man Jones's allotment and steal some fruit. Shortly before they do… (what might happen?)

B   I reached the end of Auriga Street and hurried along the walkway until the allotments came into sight. I spotted the patch of willow herb where the others would be waiting, although there was absolutely no sign of them from the path. In the allotments themselves, a couple of old guys were tidying up at the end of the day, cleaning off their tools and locking up their sheds before going home to a late tea. In a few minutes, the ground would be deserted… (What might happen now?)

C

● I walked between two tall rows of bean canes, coming at last to …

● I glanced round to spot the others, but …

● I couldn't even hear the sound of …

(What might happen next in each case?)

Guide the kind of predictions the children make by focusing their attention in different ways.

● **Choose a sense to focus on**

I walked between two tall rows of bean canes, coming at last to … (What do you smell? Reach out and touch what's around you: what do you feel? What sounds do you hear? List them in order of quietness.)

● **Be one of the characters**

Decide exactly where you are and what you are doing at this point in the story; then answer the following questions…

> … We all fell silent, hunkered down in the shadows and the growing gloom. There was a green smell in the air. A green, sweet, incredibly tempting smell - of apples and plums, leaves, grass and rich, healthy soil. The woodsmoke smell was there too like a delicate perfume. The whole world was sinking into darkness as the sky turned purple at the edges and deep, deep blue right above. One or two of the very brightest stars were out and twinkling.
>
> 'OK now...' Nige's voice was a whisper. 'Give yourself five minutes. Stuff as much in the bag as you can, then we leg it out of here... But take your time. Don't panic. If somebody comes along, just freeze. No-one can see us in the shadows. OK?'
>
> 'A-OK Nige,' Anthony said smartly, like a soldier.
>
> 'Five minutes,' Nige repeated. 'Let's do it!'
>
> We went our separate ways…

- Past
  - Who do you like most/least in the Double Dare Gang, and why?
  - Why were you attracted to the gang in the first place?
  - What do you think the other members of the gang feel about you?

- Present
  - What are you wearing?
  - What have you got in your pockets?
  - Look around (even though it's dark!) – what five colours can you see?
  - Listen – what sounds do you hear?
  - What are you thinking right now?
  - How do you feel at this moment?

- Future
  - What do you think will be the consequences of what you're doing?
  - What do you think you'll be doing in 1 year/5 years/20 years?
  - How do you think you will have changed over that time?
  - What do you suppose will become of the other kids in the Double Dare Gang?

Emphasise to your group that getting the 'right answer' isn't important. The author herself will probably have considered a number of scenarios based on questions like those above – and may not even have thought of all the options. What matters is that children use the information they already have about the story to think beyond the present frame.

◆ Time-spans

The time-span of a story is an important element within the storymaking process. Many inexperienced writers* give little thought to 'in-story' time, and either incorporate no sense of time passing, or else let it 'take care of itself' with minimal deliberate manipulation of minutes, hours and days.

Raising children's awareness of time-spans allows them to use some elegant tricks in the telling of the tale. What they learn can also be used more or less overtly in the context of time management and goal setting in their own lives. The internal organisation of time inside people's minds is a rich and fascinating area of interest: to learn more read Tad James's work on time-line therapy (see Bibliography).

A first step in raising awareness of time-spans is to review stories previously read with the explicit purpose in mind of noticing how much time passes within the tale. Follow this up by combing through the text for time related references. Look for flashbacks, 'flash forwards' ('A week went by', etc.); events occurring simultaneously in time ('Meanwhile, just at that moment, on the other side of town…'); accelerated time where plenty happens in a few instants ('All of this seemed to happen in the blink of an eye'); slow time where events seem to unfold in slow motion ('It felt like a minute passed by between tripping over and hitting the ground'); and frozen time ('The children held their breath and the world seemed to stand still.'). Look also at the total time-span of events within the narrative.

Example: 'The Allotment Ghost'

- opening scene – real-time events taking 10–15 minutes
- accelerated time – 'For most nights that week I was haunted by dreams of Jones.'
- flash forward – 'By Friday morning I was all set to pull out of the deal.'
- flash forward to teatime on Friday afternoon. 'Mini flash-forward' in this scene – 'Five minutes later I went into the lounge…'
- real-time events as Steve races up to meet the rest of the gang, and the ensuing conversation (about 30 minutes)
- real-time events as the gang creep through the allotment (about 10 minutes)
- accelerated time as Steve sees the light come on in the shed ('A swarm of thoughts filled my head about how a light might have come on by itself…')
- frozen time as Steve watches Jones casting about for the kids ('I was frozen… I could hear him breathing.')
- flash forward to Steve arriving home and the aftermath of the raid

* Inexperienced writers are those who have either written very little creative fiction, or whose writing occurs without reference to the elements of storymaking explored in the ALPS StoryMaker materials. Much school-based creative writing focuses on surface features such as technical accuracy within a competitive/comparative frame, while the supposed mystique of creativity and having ideas is maintained through lack of systematic investigation and training.

- flash forward to the following Monday at school
- total time-span of the story – about one week

A variation of the technique uses annotated notebooks for children to remind themselves, or be reminded, of subjective time passing at different rates in the story.

Annotated page	Text page
First scene - real time, 15 mins	The story will be written here
Flash forward – 5 days	
Frozen time as Brian trips over ...	
Flashback as Brian lies stunned in the street	

◆ The video remote game

Learning to organise time inside a story (and by implication learning to organise time subjectively inside your own head) can benefit from a study of film and TV narratives. Scenes are often elegantly composed with no wasted words or details, and link together in a variety of ways that make full use of 'time manipulation techniques': cut, fade, whip, pan, cut away, mix, etc., all describe ways of moving through time and space within a story. Study TV dramas with your group and have them notice how time-spans are used and how these tricks help to maintain the pace and interest in a story. Use time manipulation terms or icons on bookmarks or as margin reminders in annotated notebooks to help children become familiar with them. Playing the 'Video remote game' also achieves this and helps develop powers of visualisation.

Start with a sample of text. This extract is from the Double Dare Gang story 'Wise Guy':

- visualise the scene and 'freeze frame' it at an interesting point – just imagine you've pressed the pause button on your internal video. With everything absolutely still and crystal clear, notice other details now and note them down.
- imagine the action happening in slow motion. Notice new details of facial expression, body posture, etc. Focus on one particular detail (for example, a single match spinning to the ground) and write a brief description of its movement.
- draw the scene as a map. Include the main features and the positions of the characters. Imagine you are filming this scene for a TV drama. You have three cameras. Where do

133

you position them? How do they move through and around the action? At what points do you cut (or fade, etc.) from one camera to another?

● (if you are feeling ambitious) Rewrite the scene in film or TV format. There are plenty of books around to help you.

● in TV serials at the start of an episode there is often a brief resumé of what happened in the previous episode. This usually takes the form of a voice-over and very short intercut scenes from that part of the story. Read Wise Guy and write such a resumé to prepare the reader for the action that follows.

● play with visuals. In your mind, run the action backwards and at double speed and notice the effect. Change gravity – double it or halve it and be aware of how that changes the scene.*

We all broke into a run and started howling at the tops of our voices. It was like a snapshot had been taken. Henderson and his gang were standing there, frozen in surprise, with silly expressions on their faces.

Clive Henderson, who was our age, had an open box of matches in his hands. I leaped towards him and did my best karate kick, knocking the matches flying before he could light any of them.

That broke the spell. A really nasty expression darkened Henderson's face. He bunched his fists and came at me. So did this other kid.

Neil came in from the side and crashed into the other kid, knocking him over and falling down on top of him, squashing him to the ground. Brian was busy fighting off three other boys who were climbing all over him, and Kev was doing some fancy kung-fu dancing around the group without getting too close to any of them.

I got ready to defend myself. Nige flew at Henderson, who grabbed his arms, swung him round and flipped him over the picket fence into the woodpile. Nige disappeared amidst a crackling of sticks and a small avalanche of boxes.

'You – are – history!' Henderson said as he squared up to me. He was bigger than I was, about three years older, and was known to be one of the hardest kids in the town. I thought about what he'd said, and decided to believe him.

Even so, I wasn't about to turn around and run. I was one of the Double Dare Gang, and it was all for one and one for all.

So I clenched my fists and dared myself to face up to Henderson without trembling.

In the distance, I heard the shrill whoop-whoop of a police siren. It seemed to give Brian extra strength. With a roar he flung off the kids clinging on to him. Kev tried to kung-fu kick one of them, missed and fell to the ground.

Nige was struggling to free himself from the bonfire, and Neil had now got off the boy who was pressed down into the mud.

Henderson realised he was beaten.

'I'll get my own back,' he spat, glaring at me, and turned to run for it -

That's when Anthony decided to come to life. He jerked like a robot that had just been switched on, rose slowly out of the buggy with his eyes glowing and came tottering towards Henderson, arms outstretched, going 'Whoooooooooo!!!'

---

* Note that in the field of communication known as Neuro Linguistic Programming – NLP – visualisations of this kind are used therapeutically, and within an educational context for removing learning blocks, modifying unhelpful behaviours, gathering internal resources and for other purposes. See Bibliography for further reading.

◆ Along the track

Consciously we perceive time in a linear way. The spotlight of our conscious attention shines on the here-and-now. That's what's real to us. And we tend to orient time so that the future is in front of us (we often say how we look forward to something) and the past is behind us (we look back on things that have been). Finished stories take the same form, with a beginning, a middle and an end (or, as a critic might say in an unfavourable review, a beginning, a muddle and an end).

Practising the skills of moving backwards and forwards along the track of a story helps children to become more capable and versatile in their planning and writing. The skills are also transferable within the context of goal setting, and across subject boundaries.

The basic activity takes the form of representing the story as a line. All major events are added if you wanted to use this method to preview or review the story with your group.

'Wise Guy'

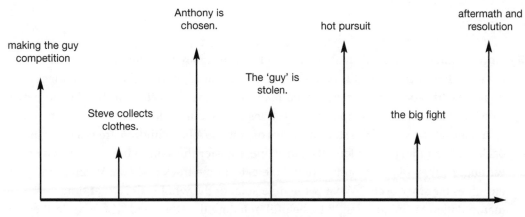

time-span – over a single evening

Variations of the activity include:

- Translate the tale into a story map/story track (see pp.117–8) where the narrative is represented 'holistically' as a Big Picture.
- Show children the first part of the story line and ask them what could happen next (gather a range of ideas).

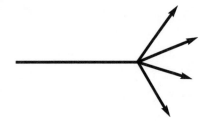

● Have children speculate beyond the time-span of the story. What other adventures might the Double Dare Gang have around the time of Guy Fawkes?

● The Double Dare Gang stories follow a sequence that starts in September (after the long summer vacation) and ends around a week before Christmas. Have children come up with story lines that 'fit between the gaps' of the DDG tales, or story sequences that make deliberate use of other times of the year.

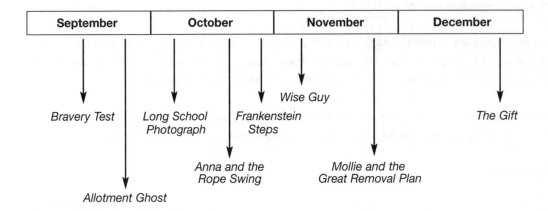

September	October	November	December

Bravery Test

Long School Photograph

Frankenstein Steps

Wise Guy

The Gift

Anna and the Rope Swing

Mollie and the Great Removal Plan

Allotment Ghost

● Once children are familiar with a story and its time-span, have them move freely along the story line both ways. If they are moving to an earlier part of the tale, ask them to imagine what good advice they would take back to the characters. If they intend moving forward, have them make up some questions they would ask of the older-wiser characters at the end of the story or series of stories. When children are easy moving backwards and forwards along the story line, transfer the skill to the children's own writing. As they plan, encourage them to create a time track early on. When in the year, etc., does the story occur? What is the time-span of the whole tale? What time manipulation techniques might be helpful in telling the story, and where could they effectively be used? Generally speaking (at first), what do the characters learn through their experiences? How do they change as a consequence? If they knew at the start what they know at the end, what good advice could they give to their younger selves?

● Transfer the skill to the children's own experience of goal-setting and time management. Through the process of story-making they will already understand ideas like 'What do I need to know?' 'How do I find out what I need to know?' 'In what order will I need to do things?' 'How long do I intend to take in completing these tasks?' Encourage your group to draw time tracks relevant to their own agenda. Encourage them to think of all the tasks they need to do within a time-span, and then prioritise them along the line.

◆ Touching base

Most of us like to keep in touch with friends and acquaintances and catch up on news and gossip the next time we meet. In the world of the story, characters have lives too, even when they aren't in each other's company. It is a good tip that a writer should know more about his characters than he puts into the tale. That sound base of knowledge informs the character details that are used.

'Touching base' draws attention to this idea. Running the activity through can also allow the writer further insight into a character's makeup and motivation. In the diagram below, each line represents a character's 'life path' across the time-span of a story. Where the lines cross is where the characters meet in a tale.

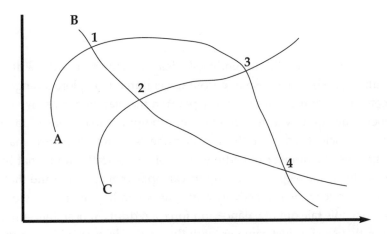

In this scenario, three characters and four meetings are involved. Characters A and B are introduced at the start of the story, while character C appears a little later. The first meeting is between characters A and B: the second involves B and C: the third involves A and C, and the fourth meeting takes place between B and C again. (Other scenarios are possible of course.)

Already there are some interesting reference points to work on, and almost automatically we begin wondering what those meetings were about. When you have reached this point, you may find it helpful to run the activity in conjunction with others:

- combine 'Touching base' with a story map, where characters meet in a physical locality which has a bearing on the reason for their meeting. (You may need several copies of the map to accommodate meetings through the time-span of the story.)
- use 'Touching base' with a theme (see p.229). The theme you choose will provide the reasons why the characters meet, and will allow insights about what they do in the meantime.
- imagine that the 'Touching base' template is part of a genre story. What could be going on if the example above were a murder mystery? Or a science fiction tale? Or a romance? Lensing the activity (see p. 228) allows you to use one template to generate several sets of ideas.
- use the template with a proverb – why did the four meetings take place based on 'Faint heart never won fair lady'? Now do it again using 'As well be hanged for a sheep as a lamb'.

- instead of drawing it on paper, use a corkboard, pins and coloured thread to make the template. This not only makes the activity more tactile, but allows children to explore various combinations of meetings between characters.

- investigate what happens to a character in between meetings. You may gather only minor details, but consider how they could play a significant part in the major events of the story.

- having constructed a template and gained an idea of why the characters meet, speculate about how the story would change if one meeting took place a little earlier or later in the tale; or if, say, A met C instead of B at point 1.

- use a story that's already written and construct a 'Touching base' template based on the meetings the characters have. Extend the lines beyond the time-span of the tale: what happens to the characters now? What other meetings do they have? What have they learned from their experiences in the story?

◆ Many endings

We have already come across the 'Many endings' idea in connection with writing blocks and difficulties (p.95). Use it also to encourage children to explore a range of options for the conclusion of their stories at any point in the planning. Even when a young writer has only a general idea of how a story might run, prompt her to consider a range of scenarios, in line with the ancient wisdom 'In the beginner's mind there are many possibilities'. As a story progresses, the number of endings that follow logically from what has already occurred will diminish. Even so, suggest that insights can appear at any time and that a writer should be open to them – indeed, he can actively anticipate them happening. At worst, such a revelation can throw the whole tale out of balance and force a redraft. At best, the 'eureka moment' convinces the author that she has just come up with the best ending possible, one that was waiting there in the back of her mind all along.

Similarly, using a story that's already written, have children come up with other endings. Take *Little Red Riding Hood* as an example:

- the wolf eats both Grandma and Little Red Riding Hood (this was the original ending of the tale as collected by the brothers Grimm)

- Red Riding Hood arrives before Grandma is eaten and persuades the wolf to show compassion

- the wolf is beguiled by Red Riding Hood when he meets her on the path and abandons his plan to go to Grandma's house

- the wolf wants to eat Grandma because he is starving. Red Riding Hood shares the food she is taking to Grandma

- the woodsman deliberately encouraged the wolf to attack Grandma and Red Riding Hood so he could play the hero

- Grandma is tougher than she looks and defeats the wolf in hand-to-paw combat

- and so on!

◆ Story tree

This is a decision-making device but also one that allows for the exploration of many possibilities (See *Imagine That*, p.168 and *What's The Story?*)

- start with a simple scenario or premise: three friends note that a new kid at school is a little unusual. This is the 'first shoot' of the story tree, and becomes its supporting trunk.
- ask 'What happens now?' and collect alternatives: the three friends ignore the new boy/one wants to make friends but the other two don't/they all try to make friends but the new kid seems secretive and afraid, etc.
- for each option, draw a branch. Go back to explore each branch by asking further questions and drawing subsidiary branches.

Eventually you will have a tree-like structure that lays out visually all the possibilities you've thought about for the structure of the story. Proceed by following a particular route through the branches, or 'picking the fruit' of especially interesting ideas from many parts of the tree.

Once children are familiar with the story tree concept, use it more flexibly – as a 'Topic tree'. If you are going to teach, say, the topic of animals, create a visual display with branches for various areas of topic. On paper leaves, write intriguing facts, questions and keywords; have children do the same. The power of such a display is that:

- it gives the Big Picture and connects the learning
- it activates pre-processing in the children's minds as they wonder how the tree will be 'filled with leaves'
- it acts as a collaboratively-created preview/review device. Because the children have helped to create the tree, they can more easily feel a sense of ownership, mastery and authority with regard to its contents
- it forms a powerful peripheral learning tool. Even when the children's attention is focused elsewhere during other classroom activities, they will repeatedly and nonconsciously absorb the details of the tree display.

The tree template may also be used in decision-making processes, where the emphasis is on situations and the range of possible options for resolution. By using the tree a number of times for simulated situations – perhaps conflicts encountered in published fiction and/or the children's own stories – it can then be applied more elegantly to real-life situations in the classroom, or in the children's lives more generally.

We are all creatures of habit and pattern. One common and powerful pattern takes a linear approach to dealing with life's circumstances: we do it this way because we've always done it this way. But as the saying goes, 'If you always do what you've done, you'll always get what you've got.'

The branching structure of the options/decision tree template is useful for resolving particular incidents, but also acts as a symbol suggesting that all of life's circumstances may be amenable to change-through-choice.

◆ Looking at the gaps

The spaces between the spokes of a wheel help to define the wheel. Similarly, what happens between scenes in a story has an implicit bearing on the 'manifest structure' of the tale, and is part of its greater context. Obviously, no writer will want to know the minutiae of all of her characters' lives: there is a balance to be struck here; there will be a limit to what the writer wants or needs to find out. Inexperienced writers tend to create stories that are plot driven, fast paced (sometimes unrelentingly so) predictably linear in structure and light on supportive and/or multisensory detail. Such writers have not explored the world of the story sufficiently to draw out enough material to write the best story possible at that time. 'Looking at the gaps' in all its variations helps to redress the balance (Refer also to 'Along the track', p.135 and 'Touching base', p.137).

● look at the time-span of a story and select a character that appears in the tale. Think about the wider context of that character's life; what has happened to account for his/her behaviour? What becomes of that person after the story has ended? As an example take Old Man Jones from 'The Allotment Ghost'.

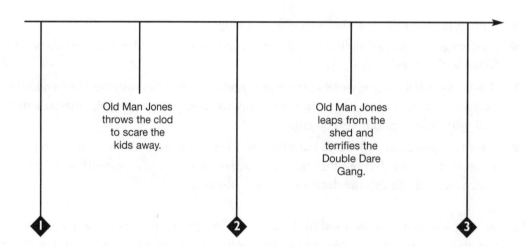

● Even though he's retired from the mines, why does Old Man Jones spend so much time at his allotment?

● How and why has he acquired such a reputation that he terrorises the local children?

● What was Old Man Jones like when he was a kid?

- How does Old Man Jones come to hear of the children's plans to raid his allotment?
- Why is he so possessive of his allotment that he would scare the kids in that way and beat them with a stick?
- What does Old Man Jones do when he's not working in his allotment?

- What contact might the kids in the Double Dare Gang have with Old Man Jones now – what would a sequel to the story be like?
- What do the other allotment owners think of Old Man Jones and his behaviour?
- How might Old Man Jones feel if he became too old to work in his allotment?

- Construct a 'mini time-span' for a character accounting for what (s)he does between appearances in the story.

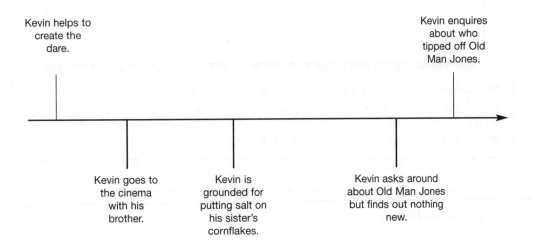

- ## Text gaps

  Cut sections from the text of a story and have children fill in the gaps. To do this effectively they will need to use the skills of attention, observation, deduction and speculation. If the activity is carried out after children have read the entire story, they will also be reviewing and recollecting information. Emphasise that this is not a game of 'guess-the-right-answer'. Any logical outcome is acceptable.

'The raid's off,' I told him, as the faces of the others appeared, all smeared with mud for extra camouflage. ' We can't go and pinch apples from Old Man Jones's allotment.'

'Why not?'

I handed him the page from the paper. The obituaries page.

Nige squinted in the deepening gloom to read what was written in the little black box.

' "Jones, Robert Charles, of Harrod Drive, Kenniston, passed away September twenty-fourth. Beloved husband of the late Martha Ann. Time passes on, but memories never fade..." '

Nige looked up at me and his eyes were big as moons. 'He died. Old Man Jones went and died on us!'

'That's why we can't do the raid, 'I pointed out. 'How could we even think of stealing apples from a dead man?'

The others; Neil, Kevin, Brian, Anthony, looked at one another, than to Nige for guidance.

Nige drew in a deep breath, held it for long moments, then let out a deep sigh.

> **Based on what you know of the story, what do you think Nigel says now?**

Nige beamed perkily. 'That's why we must carry on with the raid!'

He handed out a Tesco's carrier bag to each of us, instructing Neil to go and scrump some apples, Kev to find blackberries, me to find gooseberries, Anthony to go in search of plums, while Nige himself was on rhubarb patrol.

The missing text...

'OK, now let's think about this... Old Man Jones lived by himself, in that big old house at the corner of Harrod Drive and Bowden Road... He didn't have any family left, as far as I know. It'll be weeks, maybe months, before the council gets round to giving his allotment to someone else. By that time, all the fruit and vegetables will have rotted into the ground. The stuff will be wasted. But if we go and take some of that fruit, as we eat it we can think of Old Man Jones and honour his memory...'

● Sub-plots

This activity enriches the context of the story by creating sub-plots to the main narrative. These little 'meanwhile' stories encourage the reader/writer to review what is already known of the tale and create stories that run in parallel. Such sub-plots can interact with the main plot at any point, and may indeed enhance the entire story. Although at the outset 'bolting on' sub-plots can seem artificial, the activity raises children's awareness of the layering of stories to create a richer experience.

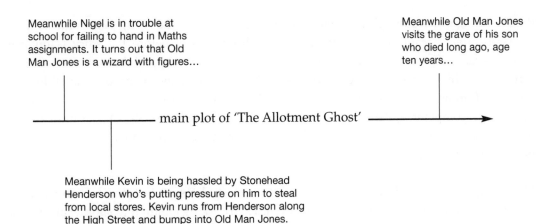

Meanwhile Nigel is in trouble at school for failing to hand in Maths assignments. It turns out that Old Man Jones is a wizard with figures…

Meanwhile Old Man Jones visits the grave of his son who died long ago, age ten years…

main plot of 'The Allotment Ghost'

Meanwhile Kevin is being hassled by Stonehead Henderson who's putting pressure on him to steal from local stores. Kevin runs from Henderson along the High Street and bumps into Old Man Jones.

● What don't I know about this scene?

Take a scene from a story and invite children to speculate around it. This activity encourages recall, discussion, deduction and insight.

> **Example**: The first scene of 'The Allotment Ghost', where the children are spying on Old Man Jones with the intention of raiding his allotment.

- What are the children wearing?
- How big is the entire allotment area? What does it look like? What other gardeners are there?
- What's the weather like in detail? (Note 'the still September air/the afternoon sun'.)
- What is the exact layout of Old Man Jones's allotment?
- What is the route between the allotments and the park where the children go to play football?

This activity only needs to be done occasionally – meanwhile children will automatically tend to fill in extra details in the background of their minds as they read.

◆ Proof-reading

Proof-reading is not exactly the same as editing, though it may form part of the editing process. An effective editor will be supportive and encouraging about the story, wishing as the author does to make the book as good as it can be. The emphasis of the best editorial comment, therefore, is not corrective and critical; rather, it will take the form of a positive critique of the work as it is presented, combined with creative and practical suggestions for refining the idea further. The good editor of children's fiction needs to have an understanding of and empathy with children, children's stories, the writer and the editorial role.

Proof-reading is more straightforwardly corrective. 'Proofs' are the set up pages of a manuscript prepared after the author's redraft has been submitted and before the story is published. Mistakes can creep in at any stage – authorial errors that have slipped through the net, editor's corrections which cause 'knock-on' inconsistencies elsewhere, and mistakes created during the process of transferring the text from the author's manuscript or computer disk into the publisher's computer system (in the old days, the type-setting process.) The most extensive proof-reading will scan for all of these elements, and is usually done by the author or a professional proof-reader.

More simply, proof-reading takes the form of checking for surface technical errors; spelling, punctuation, grammar and obvious inconsistencies. By asking children to spot what's wrong in extant stories, you give them the practice of combing for errors without the pressure of feeling that their own work is under the spotlight. The point is also made implicitly – although you can raise it deliberately – that this kind of 'dotting the i's and crossing the t's' is best done towards the end of the storymaking process. Trying to edit/correct work as you write inhibits the flow of ideas and can make stories stilted and artificial.

Stories on disk or CD allow you to import text straight into templates such as those below. Be aware that you may need to seek permissions to reproduce text in electronic format or copy it for children to use. (The text below can be reproduced for the purpose of the proof-reading activity.)

- The simplest exercise marks out the errors in some way and asks children to suggest suitable corrections.

> We went our **seperate** ways, and after just a few seconds I'd lost **site** of the others in the gloom and was alone with my own thoughts.
>
> What I thought about was Old Man Jones and the years of work he had put into this allotment**,** Although it was a mass of plants, like a jungle in miniature, there was **and** order here, a neatness which meant that **hed** kept everything under control. All of it had been tended and cared-for and nourished. This was his place: his spirit breathed **throw** it, and I was an intruder who had come to do damage and to desecrate.
>
> 'No, no,' I muttered, easing my way past a tangle of blackberry brambles and a clump of blackcurrant bushes. 'It's not like that...We haven't come to hurt your garden...We won't forget you. We respect this place, **mr** Jones... Please believe me...'
>
> Far away, a dog barked in the night; maybe, I thought, the little terrier Jones had chased away. I bet it would never come back!

- Use a side bar to indicate the nature of errors in the text, together with strategies for correction or improvement.

P – paragraph indent **SP** – spelling error **C/H** – confused homophone **Pu** – punctuation error	I walked between two tall rows of bean canes, coming at last to the stand of goosberry bushes near the far side of the allotment. I glanced round to spot the others, but they were invisible in the night. I couldn't even here the sound of apples being picked from the tree or rhubarb stalks being snapped off at ground level... Most gooseberries, when you pick them, are not quite ripe: they're hard and crunchy and very sour, and the stiff hairs prickle inside your mouth? But as my hand ruffled about among the leaves, searching for the fruit, I felt one big goosegog that *was* ripe, just soft enough to give a little between my finger and thumb

◆ Connective prompts revisited

Connective prompts are useful not only for exploring writing blocks (see p.95), but also for plotting. The technique makes use of link words that form a chain of cause-and-effect which can lead to previously unsuspected possibilities. Especially evocative connective prompts are: because, as, since, after, before, meanwhile. Take any situation from a story – Nigel dares the gang to raid the allotment – and 'CP' it.

- Nigel dares the gang to raid the allotment because – he's the boss.
- He's the boss because – he dares to do stuff other kids wouldn't do.
- He dares to do stuff other kids wouldn't do because – he wants to be better than other kids.
- He wants to be better than other kids because – he's scared of being teased or ignored.
- He's scared of being teased and ignored because – he's the smallest and youngest of a large family.

And there we have an insight that even the author had not previously considered! A little practice will train children to know when the reasonable conclusion to a chain of ideas has been reached. The material can then be woven into a story or at least informs the writing even if it is not explicitly mentioned.

Connective prompting can be done as a solitary activity, or as pair-work or in a larger group. Using a spinner to make it a circle-time game keeps children's minds alert and is an effective way of 'having lots of ideas to have good ideas' if you want your group to start their stories from the same point.

Starting premise: Anna Williams decides to join the Double Dare Gang. (See 'Anna and the Rope Swing'.) The chosen prompt word is 'as'.

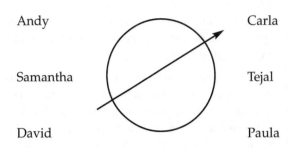

Carla:	Anna Williams decides to join the Double Dare Gang –
David:	As Nigel desperately tries to stop her!
Tejal:	Nigel desperately tries to stop her as Kevin feels quietly jealous of him.
Paula:	Kevin feels quietly jealous of him as Steve thinks Nigel is being unfair.
Andy:	Steve thinks Nigel is being unfair as Anthony worries that Anna's a faster runner.
Samantha:	Anthony worries that Anna is a faster runner as Anna thinks of a great way to complete her dare!

◆ The 'meanwhile' game

This game uses connective prompting to move elegantly from character to character within a story. It can also be used in conjunction with a story map (see p.117) and is a good way of helping children to work flexibly with time manipulation techniques (see p.132). The character focus can be thinking or feeling or doing, or all three. The first example is taken from the Double Dare Gang story 'The Gift'.

David:	Chris shows the adults his amazing powers.
Tejal:	Meanwhile Anna feels terribly sorry for him, because his gifts will not make people happy.
Samantha:	Meanwhile Anthony thinks how great it would be to make things appear like that!
Carla:	Meanwhile Nigel is thinking of a way of rescuing Chris.
Andy:	Meanwhile Mrs Porter-Smith is planning to use Chris to pay off her secret debts.
Paula:	Meanwhile Chris still doesn't understand how greedy people can be.

Example Two is taken from the 6 x 6 story grid on p.114 and uses two connective prompts: 'meanwhile' and 'because'.

Paula:	Three friends go exploring in the northern mountains in search of the Lost Cave.
David:	Meanwhile the evil King Boreas plans to capture the Princess of the Stars because she knows the meaning of Tenumbriel's Dream.
Andy:	Meanwhile the Dragon Helcyrian realises he is about to change with the rising of the Hunter's Moon.

Tejal:	Helcyrian is about to change with the rising of the Hunter's Moon because his destiny is locked within the Crystal of Mondas.
Paula:	Meanwhile the three friends find a wonderful crystal in the Lost Cave, but are trapped there by a lightning storm.
Samantha:	The three friends are trapped by the lightning storm because the Crystal of Mondas is trying to protect itself.
Carla:	Meanwhile the Princess of the Stars has a premonition that the three friends are in danger, because her fate too is linked with the Crystal of Mondas –
David:	Because the Crystal of Mondas contains the whole of Tenumbriel's Dream, preserved forever. It can be used either for great good or terrible evil...

Here the children are working at a high level, generating a great deal of interlinked material as part of their collaborative effort. They are allowing ideas to appear spontaneously, yet are also making intelligent and reasoned links between the story elements in light of what has already been said. Part of the art of using these storymaking activities is in matching one or more of the games to the children's current level of expertise. Most of the games can be used across a wide range of ability, although it is important to ensure that the task set creates a frame in which children can feel confident and safe.

◆ Stepping stars

'Stepping Stars' allow children to step into a story and associate with a character, a setting, a situation, or all three. The activity can be used in several ways.

- Once the basic scenario of a story has been worked out, create a story map. Use a selection of coloured card stars and allocate a star for each character. Ask each child in the group to select a character star. Explain that when they step onto that star they will become that character and can talk about themselves to the rest of the group.

Example: Samantha picks the star that is the Princess of the Stars...

 I am the Princess of the Stars. I am very beautiful, young in looks but ancient in wisdom. I was born in the Primeval Forest, but the memory of my birth and my childhood is being kept from me. Legend says that my parents came from the sky, but no-one knows the truth of that story. Sometimes when I sleep I dream Tenumbriel's Dream. Recently I slept during a huge lightning storm, and the dream told me that Tenumbriel was my father. I woke feeling frightened and confused...

David picks up the star of the Dragon Helcyrian...

 I am the Dragon Helcyrian. I am bound to the Crystal of Mondas in a way that is so ancient all have forgotten, even myself. I have heard through rumour and hearsay that the Princess of the Stars faces great danger – but can rumour be trusted? Besides, I am bound to the ways of the Hunter's Moon. It changes me. Even if I wanted to help the Princess for reasons of good, the light of the moon might cast me in an evil role.

Tejal picks up the star of King Boreas…

 The people of this country are fools! They believe that the Princess of the Stars is innocent and good – just because of her sweet smile. She looks so coy and helpless, and yet night by night she dreams Tenumbriel's Dream and learns its secrets… Secrets of such power that she could hold the world in her hands and crush it like an egg. The Dream soaks her mind with ideas. Slowly she is becoming Tenumbriel, who has been dead for a thousand years. And as the old books will tell you, Tenumbriel was born out of the shadows and the cold.

In this example, the children write creatively to flesh out the characters named on their stars (and there is no better way of doing this than associating with a character and speaking in her voice). A variation of the 'Stepping Stars' game is to link each star with a number of descriptive paragraphs written out on cards. Each card suggests that character's involvement in a story scenario without being too prescriptive. The paragraphs, indeed, might look like the examples above. Once a child has selected her character (at random or by choice), have her talk about the character spontaneously, picking up a prompt card if the flow of ideas starts to falter.

Princess of the Stars

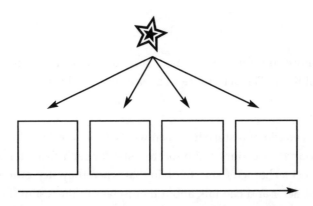

The cards can be written from ideas generated by the group itself, or another writing class, and kept as a permanent resource.

● Use stars to associate in the same way with descriptions of location. Superimpose a grid over a story map so that it is divided into numbered squares, nine in this example. Number nine stars and have children pick them randomly, then 'go to' that place on the map and describe what's there.

1	2	3
4	5	6
7	8	9

So if Carla, for example, picks number 3 she will go to the mountains in the north-east and notice details she may not have imagined before. Extend the activity by allowing the children to use a large open space such as a school hall or part of a playing field. Create markers for the main features of the story map and place them strategically in the space. Once children have selected their area to visit, have them physically visit that place and describe what they imagine. This activity creates a refreshing 'brain break' from paper-based work and also helps to satisfy kinesthetically oriented learners who need hands-on experiences and to move their bodies through space.

● Empathy stars

This variation invites children to 'step into the shoes' of the various story characters and speak from their perspective. It is wisely said that to know a person well, walk a mile in her shoes. Standing on the stepping star of King Boreas and being him and explaining how he feels gives deep insight into that character (and more implicitly, into the mind of the writer!) Record the ideas from all the children who role-play a given character, and work with them to draw out ideas and insights they have in common. These then contribute to the definitive description of that character.

● Spinner links

This activity focuses on the relationships between characters in a story. Let children use a spinner to pair up. Then each pair uses the spinner again to select two stepping-star characters.

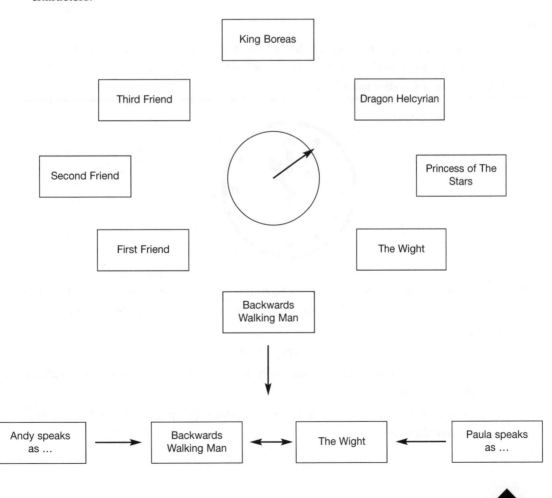

● This activity can be turned into a circle-time game where each child in the group selects a character to represent. The spinner is used to select 'player characters' at random who are invited to talk for a set time (although they can pass if they wish) about themselves, other characters, the unfolding story, etc. A similar structure is a useful way of allowing player-characters to review their roles once the story has been written.

Note: the Stepping Stars idea forms a powerful way of allowing children to discuss real-life issues. See *Self-Intelligence* p.138.

◆ Story circle

You can learn more about a story (at any stage of plotting) by referring to any other part. Professional writers (professional because of their attitude!) pre-process stories for weeks, months or even years before the story becomes consciously realised, coherent and complete. The same 'simmering under the surface' goes on, perhaps to a lesser degree, in writers earlier in their development. In other words, storymakers often know more about their stories than they realise they know.

This phenomenon is exploited in story circle activities, where it is assumed that the complete story already exists at some level inside the writer's mind – as a finished sculpture already exists within the block of stone yet to be carved.

Clock face

Imagine a story divided up into segments like a pie chart, or arranged 'chronologically' around the face of a clock. Twelve o'clock can be taken as the beginning of the story, eleven o'clock as the end (unless the tale comes round full circle).

● Ask writers to indicate in any degree of detail what happens when in their story. If this activity takes place early in the planning process, ideas may be quite vague and generalised:

- between 12 and 1 the Three Friends go exploring in the Lost Cave

- before 3 o'clock the Princess of the Stars dreams Tenumbriel's Dream once again and learns something new about it

- by 6 o'clock the Hunter's Moon has risen and the Dragon Helcyrian has changed into something evil

- In between 7 and 8 the Three Friends are separated by circumstances and get lost inside the Primeval Forest.

● In this example a twelve-hour span is used. You can encourage children to think in smaller-scale detail by splitting each hour into minutes and asking what happens on a minute-by-minute basis:

- at 12.05 the Three Friends come upon the Lost Cave

- between 12.05 and 12.10 they discuss how risky it is to go inside

- at 12.11 they enter the cave and at 12.15 they encounter their first danger.

● For very fine detail, split a 'story minute' into seconds and map out or talk through what occurs during that time:

- at 12.15 and 10 seconds the First Friend sees a strange light up ahead

- at 12.15 and 15 seconds the other Friends have spotted it too and notice an eerie sound in the cave

- at 12.15 and 17 seconds both light and sound come closer

- at 12.15 and 18 seconds the Third Friend starts to panic

- at 12.15 and 20 seconds the Third Friend turns and runs screaming from the scene.

In terms of creating the story, children would now be working at the level of words and sentences. The advantage of using the clock face analogy is that it gives children a familiar template for mapping out their thoughts and offers a natural way of thinking on a variety of scales (hours, minutes, seconds), with a sense of movement and progression built into the model. It also provides the Big Picture – and any number of 'mini Big Pictures' within the overall compass of the story. Children with a more highly developed spatial intelligence are likely to feel comfortable with devices such as the clock face template, story maps, etc., which take the process of story making out into real space and provides a change from the limited linear structure of words following one after another.

● At a later stage of story planning, create a large clock face on sugar paper and ask the writer to note down significant details in their appropriate places on the circle. Use a spinner to pick a particular point in the story and have other children ask the writer questions to find out more about that portion of the tale. If a story is being written collaboratively, co-authors take it in turns to talk about the story segment selected – or may brainstorm ideas if the group is sufficiently comfortable with that technique. (Compare with the connective prompts game on p.41).

Circle story planning

A further variation of this idea requires a large space and plenty of index cards. The writer notes down ideas, motifs (see pp.158–9), snippets of description and dialogue, etc., on the cards. She then stands in the centre of the circle space and lays the cards out in the space by following two rules:

- position the cards 'chronologically', in a clockwise direction, so that they are in sequence

151

- cards that contain enough detail to be used in the story are placed on the circumference. Cards that need more thinking about are placed inside the circle (to be moved to the rim later).

The usefulness of this activity is that it literally gives the writer an overview of her work and allows her in a very real sense to move the story in the right direction.

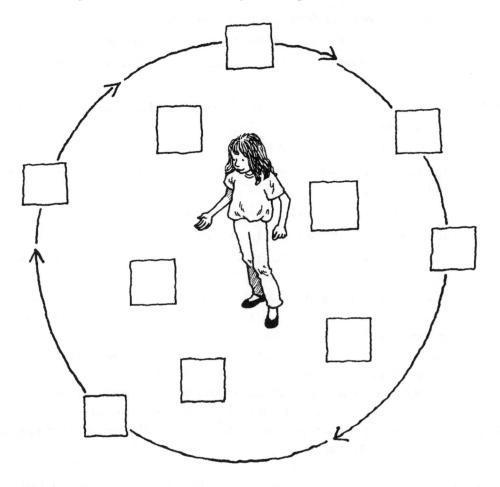

Ups and downs

The story goes that the writer P. G. Wodehouse used to pin the pages of his manuscript around the walls of his study. If a page of text came up to his standards, he would pin it at eye level. If it needed more work, he would pin it below eye level. If it was overwritten, he would pin it above eye level. A similar technique allows young writers to 'come up' to the standards you have set, or that they have set for themselves.

Have children write out their first drafts on file cards. (This can save time, since many children prefer to copy the whole story out again if they make a mistake in their books. This way, they can satisfy that urge by rewriting just the card on which the error occurs.) Encourage the group to arrange the cards in accordance with the following template: children can pin the cards on a board or set them out on a tabletop if preferred.

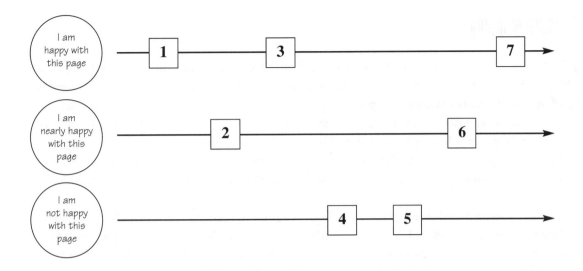

Notes indicating how the story might be 'fixed' can be written on the backs of cards, or on separate cards which can then be clipped together.

The world of the story

Prepare a large circle and scatter pieces of clipart across it. The circle is the world of the story and the clipart images are story ingredients that the writer(s) might choose to use. Organising the images clockwise around the circumference might take place through discussion, starting anywhere. Or the group might be given a theme, proverb or basic storyline as a starting point. The story in-formation might be recorded on tape (audio or video), as notes in a book, or as story segments on file cards.

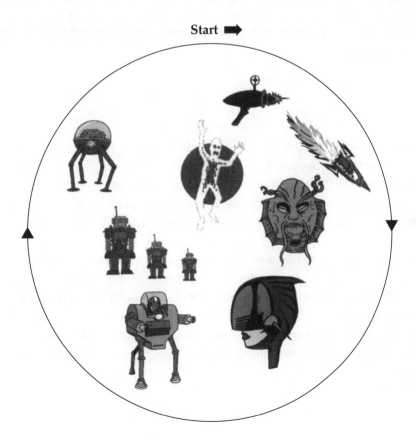

◆ Treasure mapping

Stories are full of treasures. There are characters whose behaviours, attitudes and wisdoms can be modelled; situations whose resolution can have relevance to our own experiences in real life; motifs whose metaphorical power may not be understood until long after it is communicated. The deeper meanings and the core value of stories need not be laboured or taught explicitly as a lesson to younger children – as the saying goes, good teachers aren't frightened of saying something that may not be understood for years. It is enough at this stage to realise that stories, like people, have many layers and that at their heart they have a wonderful potential.

'Treasure mapping' in this sense means that you recognise the potential of stories for developing children's resourcefulness and capability in life. Thus, if story elements are treasures then they can be gathered up and stored and kept safe and be carried through life. One easy way of introducing the concept to children is simply to ask what they would choose if they could go into a story and bring things back. Prime them by suggesting the kinds of treasures they might gather…

- Nigel's daring
- Brian's loyalty
- Anna's common sense
- wide open spaces to play in
- the close friendships of the Double Dare Gang
- Mr Lee's joke shop!

Beyond this, treasure mapping is a growing awareness that when we read stories we can take what they have to offer to heart and make those things our own; and that when we write stories we are always at some level writing about ourselves. (See also Section 5, 'Genre', 'Motifs', p.262, and Section 9, 'Storytelling'.)

◆ Story box

When children play they rehearse the world: its limits, its possibilities, the meanings it holds for them. They are, if you like, learning to organise the mass of information (in-formation) that pours into their heads in an endeavour to form a coherent picture of reality – a map of reality which embodies the world as they perceive it, and which contains the opening chapters (and suggested outcomes) of their own individual life stories.

To deprive children of play is to take away their childhood. When children read and make stories they play vicariously: they create meanings and gather treasures that they apply, more or less deliberately, to their own situations. All good stories contain truth. This may not exactly be the truth that the writer intended her story to contain: as children take stories into themselves, so they draw their own wisdoms from them. That perhaps is one useful measure of a successful tale; that many people can take something different from it and yet leave it complete for those who will follow.

All writers struggle to find their personal voice as they work to articulate their feelings and understandings to a wider audience. We 'write ourselves inside-out' so that we, as much as our readers, can find out what we truly believe. Even the most fantastical fiction contains truth – at least about the inner world of the author, and at best about the wider world at large.

Writing creative fiction, therefore, is educative *per se*, as well as extending and legitimising play as children grow older. An adventure story is 'acceptable play', which is perhaps why so many adult writers remain so young at heart.

'Story Box' brings writing and play together. It is nothing more than the resource of a number of boxes packed with a wide variety of objects which act as stimuli for writing. The contents may be jumbled anyhow, or might be sorted according to genre (a science fiction box, a mystery box, a scary story box), or motifs (natural objects such as stones, shells, bark, etc.; plastic figures of people, toy cars and planes). Items which have contributed to previous stories might be boxed up for other children to use (a Double Dare Gang box, a Princess of the Stars box, and so on). Story boxes can also be made in retrospect. Once a story has been finished, ask children to gather items which represent that tale in some way. Also consider making story boxes from published books the children have read.

Allow children to take items from a box to add another dimension to their story-making. Something as simple as handling, say, a bus ticket can throw up further ideas to be incorporated into a tale. If children use a number of objects, let them sequence the objects in any number of ways. Make use of a story circle, a story map or any other device that helps the organisation of ideas.

Sand tray

Sand play is a standard activity in nursery schools, with the tray marking the boundaries of the imagined world. Sand trays are also used therapeutically: the client is asked to 'pretend' that the tray is his world and that the sand represents the forces running through it. The client is invited to contour the sand in a meaningful way so that it describes the state of his life right now. He then takes objects from a shelf stacked with a miscellany of items and places them in the sand tray to symbolise people, places, situations, hopes, fears, aspirations and strategies for change. He makes a life map and is encouraged to play with the idea of moving things around. And although the map is not the territory, modifying the map rehearses the notion of change and progress in the 'real' world.

On a less formalised but no less important level, allowing children to mould sand and play with story box objects helps them to explore their stories, and by implication themselves. On the surface they are only making a 3D story map, but the matrix of the sand and the nature and configuration of the objects they choose can carry deeper meanings which are appreciated subconsciously before they are consciously recognised.

Metaphorical thinking

If you believe that everything has meaning, then everything has the potential to be of use. This is a key aspect of the StoryMaker attitude. By playing (the word is used deliberately) with the notion that we are defined by our choices, then assuming significance is everywhere leads us to realise the power of choice. We are powerful because we can choose. We are more powerful because we understand the significance of what we choose to leave behind or carry with us.

Metaphorical thinking – allowing ourselves to recognise that everything can have a symbolic quality – puts writers directly in touch with the power at the heart of their stories. Inexperienced writers will often simply reiterate themes, plots, characters and settings taken from books, TV and the movies (and, increasingly, computer games). The main motivation for the writing is excitement – or to complete a school assignment! – and there has been little or no reflection on what the story says about the writer and her life. In that sense the story is junk food – which is not to belittle it, but to suggest that it could be so much more.

Use the items in a story box to introduce the idea of metaphorical thinking. This begins by asking children to consider the qualities of an object. So:

- This shell is both beautiful and practical. It is fragile, and yet within its own world it may last for a long time. Even when it is smashed to fragments, it adds to the seabed on which new life will grow.
- This plastic soldier is tough, but it is inflexible. The soldier stands with his gun aimed and ready, but that's all he can do. To change his stance would be to break him. He is all of one colour. You can paint him to look different, but that would just be on the surface.
- This bus ticket can easily be dropped and lost and forgotten. But it is an important part of the journey. In fact, the journey couldn't happen without it, unless you managed to sneak on board. It tells you where you have come from and where you are going, but it doesn't give you any advice about the best way to get there, or the best things to do on the journey. It might look like a contract, but no-one really minds if you decide to take another route, by another kind of transport.

Tip: Use the 'Off the Top of Your Head' activity on p.70 to get children's ideas flowing spontaneously. Metaphorical thinking is often inhibited by intellectual effort and trying hard to think of an idea.

- Extend the activity by looking more systematically at the elements of a story. Our example is 'The Allotment Ghost'.

    - The fruit is tempting but out of reach. It is at its best right now, and the children realise that very soon it will have dropped from the bushes and rotted away. It has its moment of glory, and afterwards will nourish the ground for the next generation. To get it you need to cross the line into the forbidden place.

    - The children are like different points of view. One is reckless, one is doubtful, one is obedient because he is frightened. In the end they follow the leader's will because that's the way it has always been.

- The dare is exciting and dangerous because it takes you to a place where you shouldn't be. The dare is like a rule that you put on yourself. It becomes more powerful than you are, or so you think. Really, the gang could simply choose not to dare at all. But at the moment they are frightened not to dare because they will be 'yellow-belly chickens' – although they made that rule up too!

- Old Man Jones is the bogey man, the monster in the dark. He is everything the children are not. He is old, fearsome, alone. He owns what the children can't have. His rough hands have cultivated the lovely fruit. There is beauty at the heart of the beast.

- Old Man Jones's big stick is punishment. It has come from the earth, like the fruit. It defends the land. The stick and the fruit, two opposite forces in the lives of the children. Each moves them one way or the other.

- The scar on Steve's leg is the reminder of what he did. It is the mark of the lesson he learnt. When he is grown up he can use it to teach his own children not to go over the line… But maybe they'll decide to go anyway.

Taking this approach with little bits of the story allows children to feel safer and more comfortable than the general challenge of 'What did the story mean to you? ' Even so, asking this is better at the outset than 'What do you think the writer was trying to say?' Fundamentally, it is what a story means to a reader that allows her to see its significance in her own life. In that regard, if children find it hard to switch into metaphorical thinking mode, ask them what they would do if they were in the Double Dare Gang, being dared to go into the allotment. Comprehension of a story (at all levels) improves when the reader can personalise it in some way.

◆ My favourite story

Most people have at least one favourite story from a book, a film, a TV series or whatever. It has importance: it means something to the individual, often many things, even if he hasn't yet fully worked out what they are. Asking children to 'tease out' the elements of why they love a story allows them to recognise its power. Again, chunking the task down into more manageable pieces prevents children from being overwhelmed.

My example

Dr Who and the Daleks
by David Whitaker

(Dr Who was a children's TV science fiction series which ran from 1964 until 1989 on British TV. It has since sold across the world. The Doctor is an adventurer through time and space, travelling in a wonderful craft known as TARDIS – Time And Relative Dimensions In Space).

157

It was the first 'proper' book I ever read. It first came out in 1964 and was based on a Dr Who TV story written by Terry Nation, who is credited with having invented the daleks. At that time I was 11 years old and didn't read books - I only looked at comics and watched TV. My Mum was getting worried about this because she knew how useful the ability to read can be. She also knew that Dr Who was my favourite programme at that time...

The Doctor and his granddaughter Susan, together with two of Susan's schoolteachers, Ian Chesterton and Barbara Wright, travel to the planet Skaro in the Doctor's TARDIS (Time And Relative Dimensions In Space machine). There they find that the evil and monstrous daleks intend to wipe out their ancient enemies, the Thals, by exploding a neutron bomb, the radiation from which will destroy all non-dalek life. The Doctor and his friends rally the Thals and together they storm the dalek city and, after many exciting adventures and cliffhanging moments, destroy the daleks.

Because of this novel, I became more confident as a reader and came to love stories. I think David Whitaker helped inspire me to write stories of my own, so that I can go on fantastic adventures just whenever I choose!

I love this story because of the:

- **themes** – daring to explore and discover/fighting on the side of good/finding your greatest strength in times of adversity

- **genre** – science fiction, which takes ideas and plays with them and is unafraid of the future. The genre by definition embodies curiosity and anticipation, and often comments usefully on the state of the world today

- **motifs** – travelling companions/the quirkiness of the TARDIS – what it can do and the fact that it's 'dimensionally transcendental', bigger inside than out/the fact that the planet's original inhabitants mutated into creatures of beauty, the Thals, and the monstrous daleks. This is a yin-yang, Jekyll and Hyde motif – good and evil stemming from the same source

- **characters** – the Doctor is like the archetypal Wise Old Man, caring, safe, protective, capable, eccentric. Ian is the logically-minded doubting Thomas who is whisked away from the classroom into a thrilling universe of danger, adventure and excitement. (Is there a lesson for us here!) Barbara and Susan prove resourceful in ways no-one had anticipated in the face of danger

- **settings** – in the film the story begins at the Doctor's home, a cosy lounge. His granddaughter is reading a book on Physics while he is enjoying the Eagle! The novel begins 'I stopped the car and the fog closed in around me', which is wonderfully atmospheric. There are also the dramatic settings of the planet Skaro, including a petrified forest where the travellers find a crystallised flower (a powerful symbol), a swamp infested with monsters, a dangerous maze of tunnels through the mountains, and the strangely beautiful but alien dalek city, made entirely of metal.

- other elements –
  - the sense of wonder I felt as a child as the adventure unfolded, and which I still feel now as I think of the story
  - the positive associations of reading/watching the story safe and warm in my home.
  - certain lines from the story which were and are so very striking – *'The whole key to life is discovering things for yourself/To build a planet, now there's a challenge for you/Forget about your planet. We're already in the next universe but one/Learn from this new experience and profit by it.'*
  - opening the TARDIS doors and stepping into another world represents the act of opening a book and going to another time and place, another adventure

The story is me

When we take a story into ourselves in this way, we make it a part of us and its influence can be profound. Recognising this leads us to understand why. Reflecting on a story's significance can provide deep insights into one's own personality. So, as I think about my favourite story…

- **themes** – I realise that I love the idea of exploration, but in reality I'm a stay-at-home type. I prefer exploring ideas to actual places. Maybe like a lot of people I secretly fear adversity and doubt whether I have the strength to cope deep down.

- **genre** – I realise that science fiction satisfies the urge to explore safely. Science fiction is also about pushing out the boundaries of what is known: it deals with challenging believes about what's possible.

- **motifs** – I realise that the idea of companionship is comforting. To go through life alone would be horrible. I love the archetype of the Trickster, and in a sense the TARDIS (which represents the notion that people too are bigger on the inside than the outside) reflects the Doctor's own sense of mischief. I realise that the dark side exists and helps to define the light. In the story the adventurers go into the dark to understand themselves more in the end.

- **characters** – I realise that I need a Wise Old Man to help and guide me. I need somebody to take responsibility for making decisions. I need somebody to lead me. Maybe that Wise Old Man already exists inside!

- **other elements**:
  - *The whole key to life is discovering things for yourself.* I realise that story making is an ongoing process of discovering things for yourself. As the saying goes, 'Somebody showed it to me and I found it by myself.'(Lew Welch)

  - *To build a planet. Now there's a challenge for you.* I realise that the world we make inside defines the world we experience outside. Perception is projection.

  - *Learn from this new experience and profit by it.* I realise that every experience teaches me something. To profit by it I need to work out every time what benefits an experience brings to me, even if the experience is a bad one.

Using stories in this way is a powerful tool in allowing children to understand more about themselves. Naturally enough, as a teacher you need to decide on the appropriateness of such self-exploration and the prominence you give to it in your lessons.

Story diary

One way of drawing out the significance of a story to any child is to suggest that she keep a story diary. The term does not refer to notes the writer makes as she goes through the story-making process. Rather, it requires a child to re-read a story and record reactions to any element she feels the need to comment on. Gently prompt her to explain why she feels as she does.

Set up a template with the story on the right-hand page so that comments can be written on the left. Emphasise that the reader can put whatever he wants, or write nothing at all. This work is not going to be marked or judged in any way, and the reader can keep his notes entirely private if she likes.

The example opposite is taken from the Double Dare Gang story 'The Long School Photograph'.

◆ Story trees revisited

Creating a story is an ongoing process of decision-making. Big decisions are made early on when the writer thinks on the level of themes and genre; smaller decisions (but still important ones) are made on a word-by-word basis at the time of the writing itself. As a child's storymaking skills improve, so will her decision-making abilities. And vice versa.

A story tree is a template that records a number of options at the point when a decision needs to be made. So, for example, let's return to the story of the evil King Boreas and the Princess of the Stars (see p. 113-4). And let's suppose that the story starts with the Three Friends coming upon the entrance to the Lost Cave.

- Option 1 – they all go inside
- Option 2 – two of them go inside while the third keeps guard outside
- Option 3 – they tie one end of a piece of string to a tree outside the cave, so that they can find their way back at any time.

(There are other possible options, but including too many clutters up the tree.)

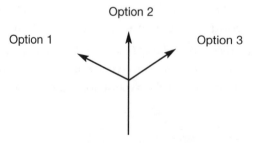

The Three Friends come upon the Lost Cave

There are a couple of teachers I don't like. I'm scared of one of them. The other one doesn't explain things very clearly…

I think 'hate' is too strong a word. I don't hate anyone. Hate makes you lose control of yourself.

Sometimes I shout and stamp because I'm unhappy. Maybe that's Jethro's main problem. I guess he must be a really lonely man.

Yeah, I'm one of those. Sometimes I get picked on too – and a part of me wants to really make mischief and be bad, just to see the worst that could happen! (I don't suppose I'd ever do it though).

I wish I could be like him. He uses his sense of justice to speak out. Lots of times when things aren't fair I just put up with it, and that makes me mad with myself.

I know a couple of kids who have that kind of smile. They're always being told they're insolent. I wonder if that's the real reason… Maybe they don't respect people because those people haven't earned respect. I think treating someone like a human being can earn their respect…

I don't suppose schools have changed much in all that time. Kids were still kids, just like us, and teachers were teachers. Some of them were great fun, some of them you hated. The most hated and feared teacher at the school in the mid-Nineteen-Twenties was Mr Evans – Jethro Evans – who taught Maths.

What nobody could ever understand about Jethro was why he bothered to become a teacher in the first place. He never seemed happy, and he spent most of his time ranting and raving at the kids in his classes. Sometimes, if a class was a bit too noisy coming into the room, he yelled at them and lectured them about good behaviour for the whole lesson. They never learned anything – not even anything about good behaviour.

Being shouted at for fifty minutes was bad enough, but Jethro used to do something even worse. He'd pick on particular children, often the meek and quiet kids who hadn't really done anything wrong, and he'd try to make them cry in front of their friends. That's just about the worst thing you can do to someone – embarrass him in front of his mates. Jethro seemed to do it for pleasure, as a kind of hobby.

Most often, he'd succeed in turning some poor little boy or girl into a sobbing wreck. The other kids in the class would be pale and silent while the torture went on, not daring to say anything in case it happened to them. But there was one boy who did dare to say something: one kid who spoke up more than once when one of his friends was being tormented...

All I know about this boy is that he was quite small, with gingery hair, a cheeky smile, and loads of freckles sprinkled over his nose and cheekbones. It was the freckles that gave him his nickname – Specky. And because Specky spoke his mind and stood up for the weak and the helpless against injustice, Jethro hated him more than any child at Kenniston School – especially because, no matter how much he yelled and screamed at Specky, Specky would never break down and cry. In fact, his cheeky little smile was always there; a smile that earned him plenty of detentions and many hours of standing outside the staffroom with his nose against the wall.

● Work first with Option 1: The Three Friends all go into the cave. What might happen next?

- Option 1/i – they split up to explore further
- Option 1/ii – they are attacked by the Denizens of the Cave
- Option 1/iii – they find a flight of steps going down into the earth.

These further options branch off from what was Option 1.

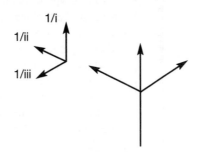

● Now go back to Options 2 and 3 and do the same thing, making a brief reminder note at the appropriate spot. You may find that one scenario catches the interest and imagination of the group more than the others do. Work on that option until ideas begin to run dry, then move on to another. Some options won't lead very far and soon become dead-ends. And so the structure grows until you have a record of many possibilities for the route that the story could take.

'Story Tree' works well as a whole-class activity. All of the children have the opportunity to contribute, and all of their ideas are acknowledged and used. You will need a large space to work with – even a relatively simple tree takes up a lot of room. If you are feeling particularly ambitious, create the tree as a wall display, or use ribbon or string to lay out the tree in an open space such as the school hall. Objects from a story box (see p.154) can be used as visual cues at the option-points. When children are familiar with the activity, let them work in small groups or pairs using sugar paper or flipchart sheets to map out their thinking. Some children subsequently write a story by following a specific route along the tree. Others pluck ideas from different parts of the tree and put them together in a new way.

Extend the activity by having children write-up *all* of the options on the tree to make a 'pick-your-own-adventure' tale…

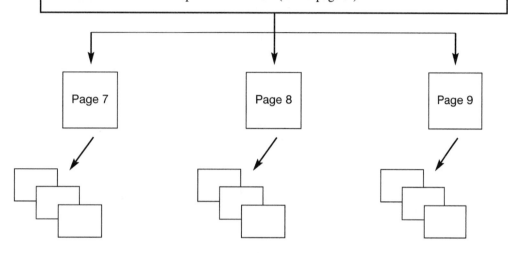

You are walking cautiously through the dank and gloomy passages of the Lost Cave when you come across a flight of stone steps spiralling down into the earth. You suspect this path may lead you closer to your meeting with the mythical mage Tenumbriel. You also realise that following this path may take you into great danger.

What are you going to do?

● We will all go down the spiral steps. (Go to page 7.)

● Two of us will go down the steps and one will keep watch at the top. (Go to page 8.)

● We will avoid the steps and move on. (Go to page 9.)

Page 7

Page 8

Page 9

Tip: The 'Story tree' structure can also be used for mapping topics or programmes of work in other subjects, and as a decision-making device. (See *Imagine That*, p.168, *Self-Intelligence*, p. 189 and *What's The Story?*)

The most valuable insights
come from questioning
the most obvious forms
of common sense.

Alan Watts

Section Four

Character

Life works according to your ability
to process information clearly,
effectively and meaningfully.

Barbara Hoberman Levine, writer and therapist

Section 4 – Character

Page	Topic/activity	Story element covered	Accelerated learning link
169	Getting to know you	*Basic character profiling*	Awareness of mind–body–emotions link/interpersonal skills
171	Classification patterns	*Character description using chosen parameters*	Awareness of classification as an organisational device/awareness of flexible strategies for classification/chunking down
173	Character stew	*Character creation through the use of disparate elements*	Development of observational skills/development of interpersonal skills through the appreciation of uniqueness
174	People are like onions	*In-depth description of character*	Organisation of information / development of interpersonal awareness/neurological levels
176	The world outside	*Development of character within a context*	Observational and interpretative skills/life review skills / application of neurological levels / awareness of subjective-objective balance
178	The world inside	*Development of character within a context*	Self-awareness/interpretative skills/life review skills/point-of-view/application of neurological levels/awareness of subjective-objective balance
181	Mini safari/One unique detail	*Observing characters in life*	Observational skills/development of interpersonal skills through appreciation of uniqueness
181	Character match	*Awareness and refinement of character detail*	Awareness of perceptual filtering
182	Fifty positive adjectives	*Characters and emotions*	Development of self-esteem / positive strokes/affirmation
183	Think bubbles	*Characters and thoughts*	Awareness of facial expression and eye accessing cues / awareness of the dangers of 'mind reading' and projection of one's own impressions
186	Gossip calypso	*Character development through association and first-person thinking*	Accessing subconscious resources/pole-bridging
187	Points of view	*Development of character through multiple viewpoints*	Perceptual positions / development of empathy / development of association-dissociation skills
190	Old Man Envy	*Development of emotion in characters/character types/personification*	Use of metaphor in the development of emotional resourcefulness/chunking down as a problem-solving techniques
192	The mind's ear	*Character and voice*	Development of auditory awareness and submodalities
194	Opinion finder	*Narrative overview / subjectivity within characters*	Awareness of distinctions between observation, deduction, speculation and opinion / addressing generalisation, deletion and distortion as perceptual filters
198	Future diary	*Overview of characters*	Time-line work/success thinking / target setting

199	Belief tree	*Exploration of character through stated beliefs*	Intrapersonal skills/awareness of the subjectivity of belief/belief modification strategies
200	POV grid	*Exploration of character through differences and similarities*	Interpersonal skills/problem solving through sharing strategies
201	But why?	*Character motivation*	Development of speculation and POV skills
203	Eyelines	*Character exploration and description through details of eyes and expression*	Development of interpersonal intelligence
205	Getting into character	*Character development through association and first-person thinking*	Development of empathy
205	Characters as guides	*Character types and the metaphorical dimension*	Use of metaphor for gathering subconscious resources / intrapersonal intelligence

Facts on their own don't
make us wise. Wisdom is
fitting facts together into
a meaningful context.

Joe Griffin / Ivan Tyrrell

Section Four

Character

Characters are of course an essential component of any story. By exploring character, young writers are able to develop their inter- and intrapersonal skills, learning about themselves as they find out more about other people.

◆ Getting to know you

There are many ways of exploring characters in storymaking (see for example *Imagine That*, pp. 117-119 and p.154). A further method uses the template below. Thoughts are related to feelings, which determine behaviours. 'Getting to know you' raises awareness of this principle, so that when children read about characters in other stories or want to create characters of their own, they will understand that people are 'layered', they have depth, and that what happens at one level has consequences at other levels.

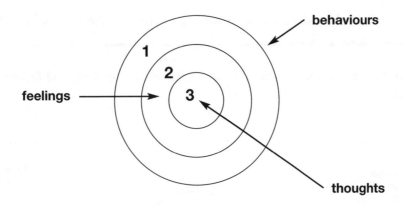

- Develop this idea by encouraging your group to notice people's behaviour. Ask children to speculate about how people might be feeling to account for their behaviour (being at pains to emphasise that these are only guesses).

- Ask children to be aware of their own thoughts and how these create and modify their feelings. Have children put names to their feelings and make distinctions between them. (See *Self-Intelligence* Section 3: 'Enhancing emotional literacy'.) Emphasise the notion that people can change their feelings by changing the way they think about things.

● Encourage the habit of linking thoughts–feelings–actions as children read about characters in stories. Initially you might want to do this as a formal activity (for instance by using the template below, where Paula writes about the character called Neil). Subsequently an awareness of these links will 'run in the background' as part of a child's nonconscious appreciation of a story.

This example is taken from 'The Allotment Ghost'.

Text	Neil's thoughts	Feelings (according to Paula)	Behaviours
'Neil – shut up!' 'It's hurting, Nige... There's a sharp bit digging into my side!' 'It's just a snapped staple. Hang on... Bri, pull the fence up a bit more... That's it. Come on the rest of you, help me get him through...' We lent a hand and dragged Neil through to the Forbidden Zone.	I wish I'd never got mixed up in this! It's OK for Nige – he's the leader of the gang; he's respected. People don't laugh at him... Like they do at me, just because I'm fat. Although they aren't really laughing... Other people laugh, but my mates in the gang understand. I guess they all have something about them people laugh at.	The staple hurts my side... I feel a bit panicky in case someone comes along and catches me... My friends are helping me now. I feel reassured; they won't leave me. They won't run away. We're the Double Dare Gang and I feel proud to be a part of that...	I'm stuck! I'm struggling. Nigel is talking to me... My struggling gets less. I feel calmer now. My breathing is slowing down. I'm sweating even though it's cool tonight... There, I'm getting through the fence now. I'm in the allotment.

In this example Paula has identified with Neil and writes in the first person. Third person annotation is just as acceptable.

A variation of the activity imagines what other characters are thinking and feeling at a selected point in the story.

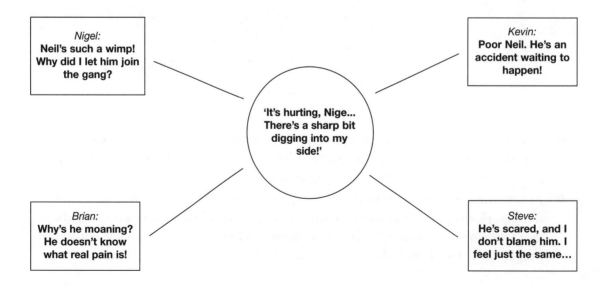

● Use connective prompts (see p.41) to think about the reasoning behind a character's actions. The prompt 'because' works especially well.

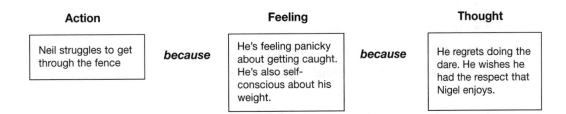

Action		**Feeling**		**Thought**
Neil struggles to get through the fence	*because*	He's feeling panicky about getting caught. He's also self-conscious about his weight.	*because*	He regrets doing the dare. He wishes he had the respect that Nigel enjoys.

◆ Classification patterns

Classifying is an important thinking skill across the subject range (notwithstanding Alfred North Whitehead's assertion that 'Taxonomy is the death of science' and Postman and Weingartner's codicil that 'The memorisation of taxonomies is the death of education') – and it can be used extensively in storymaking.

Hickman and Jacobson in *The Power Process* (see Bibliography) note three rules in the formation of a classification pattern:

● classification must be made on one clear and consistent basis

● if a class is subdivided it must contain at least two subdivisions

● any system of classification must be able to accommodate all the items in a given body of data.

Classifying therefore serves to categorise and often prioritise items according to previously specified parameters. Teaching classification patterns need not be abstract or complicated. Children can grasp the basic concepts by thinking about characters.

● classify characters according to one clear trait, for example:

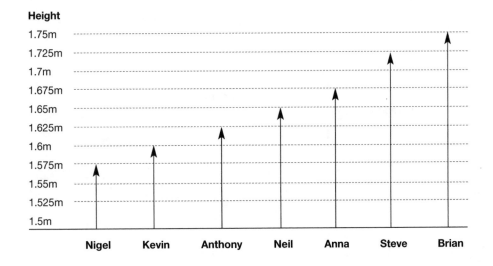

Have children suggest other simple categories for classifying the characters:

● Pick a category and ask children to suggest subdivisions, for example, hair:
  - length (short, medium, long)
  - colour (fair, medium, dark, red)
  - curliness (straight, wavy, loosely curled, tightly curled)
  - smartness (very smart, moderately smart, scruffy)

● Classify characters according to these subdivisions:
  - Nigel – short, medium, straight, scruffy hair
  - Anna – long, dark, straight, smart hair
  - Steve – medium length, fair, loosely curled, moderately smart hair

… and so on. Creating subdivisions in this context means children will need to visualise at the level of submodalities – i.e. subdivisions of the visual sense. Other classification activities, such as subdivisions of the characters' voices, require submodality work within the auditory sense, etc.

● Items can be classified according to two parameters and placed within a frame. The example below deals with emotions the Double Dare Gang might experience on their adventures…(See also *Imagine That* p.132: 'Emotion spectrum' and *Self-Intelligence* p.168: 'Emotions checklist'.)

Frequency of emotion

	common	uncommon	rare

awe

joy

delight

excitement

pride

Intensity of emotion

0

apathy

boredom

envy

regret

fury

horror

This general pattern suggests that the children in the Double Dare Gang experience pleasant emotions more commonly than unpleasant ones – but when you work through the activity with your group the educational value will come in discussing which emotions go where. Extend the work by encouraging discussion on how emotions can be described.

> **Tip**: Make a laminated A3 template and a set of small cards bearing the names of emotions. This creates a tabletop resource that allows children to 'move emotions around' as they work. (This in itself is a powerful metaphor for change!)

◆ Character stew

Sometimes writers base characters wholesale on real people – that is, the character is drawn directly and completely from life. Another strategy is to create characters that combine traits from various people. In this case, part of the challenge and therefore the fun is in discovering which combinations of traits work best, given any character's function within a story.

A 'combination character' is much more than a bolt-on Frankenstein monster, and helps the author avoid drifting into stereotypical thinking. What may happen, however, is that certain character types evolve in the writer's mind over the course of a number of stories. Such character types can preserve their individuality within a story while possessing general qualities the reader can recognise, model and notice in others.

In Steve's writing, two character types have grown which have become very important to him:

- a thin, shy, quiet, deep-thinking boy (often called Tony) whose imagination usually outreaches his nerve. Tony lives largely in his head. He dreams big and lives small.
- a tall, thin, fair-haired girl (usually called Eleanor) who is pretty but who has a low opinion of herself, and frequently puts herself down. She is particularly sensitive to some slight physical imperfection – her nose is too long, her eyes are too far apart, etc. – and lacks confidence as a result. She is very resourceful deep down, however, and exists in stories partly so that she can discover her own courage and resilience.

'Character Stew' is the first step in the multi-stage process of allowing children to learn how to create rounded and believable characters in their stories.

- Ask children to observe ten people carefully (and appropriately, without staring) and to note down a detail about each. You might wish to specify visual details, or auditory traits, or just anything that catches the children's interest. When a classful of children each bring in ten characteristics, you have a lot of material to work with!
- Have groups sift through the observations – some will be duplicated – and put them in order, perhaps making use of one or more classification patterns the children have learned.

173

hair	length	colour	style
eyes	colour	size	expression
nose	shape	length	
head	size	shape	bearing

● Or use an outline and add useful/interesting observations – making a clear distinction between pure observation and an *impression or value judgement*.

striking red hair

beautiful sparkling blue eyes

friendly, open face

tall and *elegant*, upright posture

smart, *fashionable* clothes

sensible brown leather shoes

During this organising process, look at some characters in stories you've read together. Discuss with your group the different functions characters have. What do authors do to make their characters believable?

◆ People are like onions

They can make you cry, and they have many layers. It is all too easy to focus on the external features of a character while paying too little attention to his/her personality and background. A pyramid template like the one below allows children to make notes about aspects of a character other than what's visible on the surface. The sections limit the amount that can be written, and so children need to choose carefully what to write and/or make the language work harder for them.

Use other techniques found in this book (such as dice rolling, picture stimulus, discussion) to generate ideas.

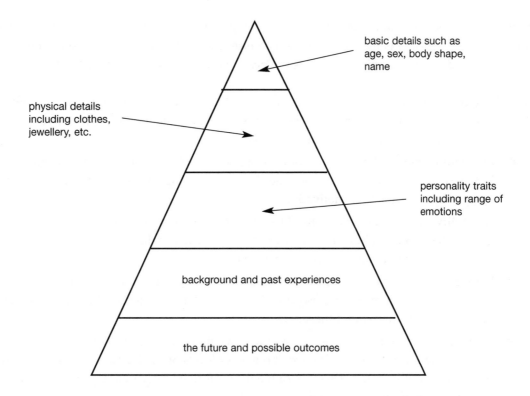

basic details such as age, sex, body shape, name

physical details including clothes, jewellery, etc.

personality traits including range of emotions

background and past experiences

the future and possible outcomes

When children are first planning their characters it is best to draw large pyramids on sugar paper; there may be much crossing out and rearranging of ideas. Finished work can be prepared on A4 sheets and kept as a future resource.

Another, and more advanced, way of using the pyramid is to tie it in with what are called *neurological levels*. This concept was developed by Robert Dilts, a key figure in the field of learning and communication known as Neurolinguistic Programming (NLP). NLP has been called the art and science of personal excellence, and its teachings and techniques have profound implications for effective education. (See Bibliography for further references).

People exist within a layered context that includes the external world and their own personal inner world (which is just as real). Learning and change – and the 'stuckness' that can prevent these from happening – take place on all levels. One way of understanding other people and ourselves better (including the characters we read about and create) is to explore the hierarchy of the neurological levels.

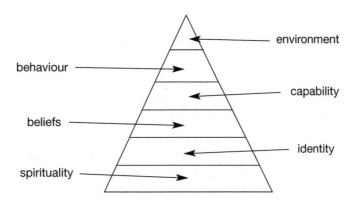

environment

behaviour

capability

beliefs

identity

spirituality

In this version *environment* is like the tip of the iceberg that sticks above the surface – the bit that's seen – while *spirituality* is the base on which all else is built. You may also consider a reversed order pyramid where the spiritual level is the peak of our development as human beings.

- **environment** – means the outer world of people and places; the external factors that we react to. In looking at characters, we can pay particular attention to their environment and how and why it affects them as it does.

- **behaviour** – means the specific actions a character carries out. Those actions will influence and be influenced by the other levels. Exploring such links can provide deep insights into a character's motivations.

- **capability** – means the collections of behaviours, the skills and strategies that we use in life to achieve our goals. Examining how a character does what she does allows us as writers to give her a more believable persona.

- **beliefs** – means the range of ideas we think are true. Beliefs, which determine our actions, can be limiting or empowering. Fleshing out a character's beliefs informs that person's actions throughout the story.

- **identity** – means our basic sense of self; who we think we are. We define ourselves to a greater or lesser degree by reference to the other levels of our being. It is interesting to consider how any character's sense of identity is formed by her environment, behaviour, capabilities, beliefs and spirituality.

- **spirituality** – means how we explore and act upon the great metaphysical puzzles of why we are here and what our purpose might be. The questions we ask in order to explore and explain the universe, the world and our place within it forms the basis on which we build our lives and can lead to the pinnacle of our fulfilment in life.

◆ The world outside

Exploring the world of a character can begin by looking at that character's environment. A simple way to do this is to represent the environment as a circle and include within it icons and images relevant to the character's life. Our example is Steve from the Double Dare Gang.

The items in Steve's world might be literal or representational. This is a good time to introduce the idea of metaphor if you have not done so already. Thus:

 - might mean it's a sunny autumn day, or Steve's generally sunny disposition leads him to perceive the world that way.

 - might mean the tree in Nigel's garden that Steve likes to climb, or it might be the 'Dark Woods' which hide the shadowy and frightening things his life.

 - might mean an advertising poster that Steve has seen in a shop or on TV, or it could refer to the notion that Steve lives for the moment.

Once children come to understand this idea they are on the way to realising that whatever extrinsic meaning the world contains, we fill the world with significance based on our own beliefs and sense of identity.

Perception is projection

We project onto the world our own beliefs and expectations.

We view the world through the filter of our own map of reality.

◆ The world inside

This activity uses the same idea as 'The world outside', although in this case everything in the circle is representational (since we can't help but be subjective in our perceptions). Giving consideration to the way that – in this case – Steve sees the world leads to a much deeper understanding of this character. So:

When you ask your group what the images mean, emphasise that there is not necessarily one right answer. To some extent children's responses will reflect what the icons mean to them, and so a consensus view is no more nor less useful and illuminating than a range of individual opinions.

As a point of information, the author's own interpretation is as follows:

- Steve is reaching the point where he's becoming more aware of girls as girls. Anna Williams is the most prominent female in his life right now. Although she's Nigel's girl, Steve wishes she had eyes for him. The repetition of her eyes and mouth suggests he keeps thinking of her.

- this is Steve's mum and dad. He perceives them as being happy together. They look old fashioned, perhaps because they have old-fashioned attitudes to life.

- this is Steve's perception of himself. He still feels like a little kid in a world that's much bigger than him. Just out of reach is the gift of knowledge and adulthood.

- it's autumn. Fall time. Perhaps deep down Steve feels that his precarious childhood built on a tower of books (other people's words of authority) is about to come tumbling down. Very soon he may need to rely much more on his most powerful resource.

Visual metaphor is the language of the subconscious. We tend to remember the visual aspects of our dreams more readily than auditory or gustatory elements and we frequently recognise our dreams as being highly representational, even surreal, as the logical conscious mind tries to work out what the pictures mean. Daydreams too can have this quality, so that we may not appreciate the nature or detail of our insights. On the other hand, along with a 'flash of illumination' may come the certainty of understanding so that we just *know* something is so. The fleeting subtlety of a daydream or half-awake vision is not to be disdained – as in August Kekule's understanding of the benzene ring and Einstein's daydream of riding on a light beam.

Apart from this, paying attention to the way we represent the world is a step on the path to modifying that representation if it is unhelpful or limiting. The field of NLP relies heavily on conscious intervention to change subconsciously generated imagery that symbolises a limiting belief. The analogy often used is 'replaying the movie'. We may subconsciously make a movie (often a 'tape loop' that repeats without moving on) but by focusing on it consciously we can edit and redirect until it conforms to our conscious aspirations. We only achieve what we can first conceive.

An extension of the 'World Inside' activity is to compare different characters' perceptions of the same thing. Again, this may be done visually, or interpretations can be written down. Artwork software packages allow for quick and easy manipulation of imagery: more simply, children can draw their ideas directly.

In the case of the Double Dare Gang, the kids have differing attitudes towards school…

Nigel's View

Anna's View

Steve's View

Book of Knowledge

Kenniston High

Kenniston High

Anthony's View

Kevin's View

Neil's View

Brian's View

◆ Mini safari

Writers are nosy. They find out by looking within, and by noticing details in the wider world. The idea of a mini safari is to send children searching for some specific impression, detail or piece of information, which may be found outside or inside. Again this will not be the 'right answer' but an observation or idea that proves to be more or less useful in the end.

◆ One unique detail

The poet Gerard Manley Hopkins coined the term *inscape* to refer to the uniqueness of the inner landscape of every created thing. He called the expression of that uniqueness *instress* – the inner tension or force that sustains individuality and lets it shine for others to see. In that sense, every detail of a person contributes to her inscape. But to begin with, it is enough to recognise one thing, one special thing, which makes that person unique.

Begin coaching children in the art of seeing uniqueness by sending them on a mini safari to observe, say, ten people and to notice something individual about each one. This may be a visual detail, the tone of someone's voice, a turn of phrase, the smell of perfume or cologne, or simply a feeling that person evokes in the observer. Emphasise that one-unique-detail should be positive and respectful, and may be recorded literally or representationally in words, pictures, by reference to music, or in whatever way captures the essence of what the children perceive.

Incorporate the idea of one-unique-detail in storymaking. As children plan, write and review, remind them to incorporate 'OUDs' in their descriptions of people, places and events.

◆ Character match

This game highlights the filtering effect of our perceptions – in this case of people.

- You will need a number of pictures of people. These might be children in your class or visuals taken from magazines.
- Distribute the pictures, one picture per group (keep a note of which group gets which picture), and ask each group member to write a description of the person in the picture without revealing any details to anyone. Give each child a number and ask them to write their number on the description they've done.
- Collect up the materials. Redistribute the pictures and circulate the anonymous descriptions around the groups. Have children endeavour to find the descriptions that match their picture.
- Review the work by asking what they did to find the match, and what difficulties they experienced.

◆ Character pyramid match

- Split the class into groups and ask each group to invent a character and type up the information on a computer using a pyramid template (see p.175). Save the work.

- Print off the completed templates and cut up each pyramid into its constituent parts. Shuffle the parts and give out to groups.

- Have the groups working together to attempt to reassemble the pyramids.

- Review the work by asking children what they did to find the matches, and what difficulties they experienced.

◆ Fifty positive adjectives

able	committed	energetic	industrious	persuasive
active	compassionate	enterprising	intelligent	polite
alert	confident	enthusiastic	kind	quick
articulate	conscientious	forgiving	lively	resourceful
artistic	considerate	generous	loving	reflecting
athletic	creative	gentle	mathematical	scientific
bright	determined	gracious	musical	studious
calm	diligent	hard working	original	thoughtful
caring	diplomatic	humorous	outgoing	warm
clever	empathic	imaginative	peaceful	witty

Reproduced from *The ALPS Approach*

Alistair Smith and Nicola Call suggest using these adjectives on desk labels as a quick, fun and effective way of building expectations of success in children. Here are a few more ideas:

- Investigate the etymology of the words and create bits of 'gee whiz' information about the words. 'Compassion', for instance, derives from words meaning to experience, bear or suffer, and is linked with 'pathy' which means 'feeling' in words such as 'sympathy', 'empathy', etc.

- Collect words that are linked etymologically to a chosen adjective – 'lively, live, alive, life, livelihood'.

- Make word clusters that describe the positive qualities of children in the group and characters from stories.

- Make 'yin–yang' clusters in recognition of the fact that people are 'bundles of contradictions'. We all have less attractive characteristics that we can recognise and work on. Steve in the Double Dare Gang for instance can be:

creative	bored
determined	impatient
energetic	lazy
polite	irritable
imaginative	sullen

◆ Think bubbles

Peter Drucker asserts that the most important thing in communication is to hear what isn't being said. Paying attention to facial expressions and postures, and listening carefully to what people are saying (rather than what you choose to hear!) allows us to develop a more powerful rapport with them. We have probably all had a conversation with someone who talks over us to get his point of view across, or whose comments don't seem to connect with the point we've just made. We are most likely guilty of doing this ourselves. Patient observation and active listening helps us to enter and understand more of the subjective world of the people we meet.

One of Steve's trainers had a large notice pinned above his desk: *I am responsible for what I say, but not for what you hear.* Guessing what's in someone's head based on our own reality is a dangerous kind of mind reading that can lead to all sorts of difficulties. On the other hand, playing the game of 'Think bubbles' leads us to realise that (as Anais Nin maintained) the world is not as it is, but as we are.

- Give children a selection of pictures and ask them to fill in the think bubbles based on what they assume is going on…

183

● A variation of the activity uses text with space for think bubbles.

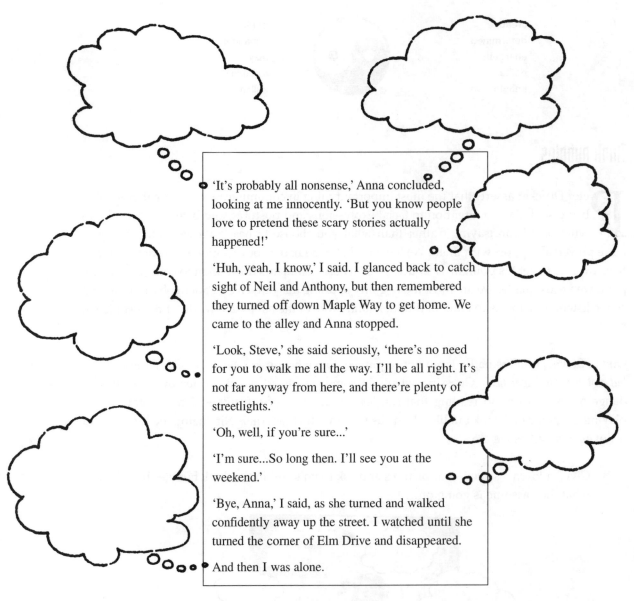

'It's probably all nonsense,' Anna concluded, looking at me innocently. 'But you know people love to pretend these scary stories actually happened!'

'Huh, yeah, I know,' I said. I glanced back to catch sight of Neil and Anthony, but then remembered they turned off down Maple Way to get home. We came to the alley and Anna stopped.

'Look, Steve,' she said seriously, 'there's no need for you to walk me all the way. I'll be all right. It's not far anyway from here, and there're plenty of streetlights.'

'Oh, well, if you're sure...'

'I'm sure...So long then. I'll see you at the weekend.'

'Bye, Anna,' I said, as she turned and walked confidently away up the street. I watched until she turned the corner of Elm Drive and disappeared.

And then I was alone.

From the Double Dare Gang, *The Frankenstein Steps*

● If you want children to generate ideas in a more 'stream of consciousness way', use the following template to have them literally 'write between the lines'...

'It's probably all nonsense,' Anna concluded, looking at me innocently. 'But you

> *I think Anna's scared as well, actually. She's putting on this act of being cool because she doesn't want the boys to think she's a yellow-belly chicken. As the only girl in the Double Dare Gang, she has her reputation to keep up!*

know people love to pretend these scary stories actually happened!'

> *I also think she doesn't really want Steve to walk her home (she'd prefer Nige!).*

'Huh, yeah, I know,' I said. I glanced back to catch sight of Neil and Anthony, but

> *I think Steve fancies Anna a lot. But he's not sure how she feels, and anyway he knows she wants to be Nigel's girl.*

then remembered they turned off down Maple Way to get home. We came to the alley

and Anna stopped.

> *I think this is a difficult time for all the kids in the gang. They've just been children up until now. But suddenly Anna's there and she's a powerful influence. The boys are starting to know what it feels like to grow up.*

'Look, Steve,' she said seriously, 'there's no need for you to walk me all the way.

> *I think Steve's heart sinks to hear this.*

I'll be all right. It's not far anyway from here, and there're plenty of streetlights.'

'Oh, well, if you're sure...'

'I'm sure...So long then. I'll see you at the weekend.'

'Bye, Anna,' I said, as she turned and walked confidently away up the street. I

> *Steve watches her walk up the street and he's thinking it's impossible to get her to like him. Anna's great at pretending to walk confidently!*

watched until she turned the corner of Elm Drive and disappeared.

And then I was alone.

> *You just know that Steve's imagination is going to work overtime now to scare him half to death!*

◆ Gossip calypso

T his is a simple pairwork activity that gives children practice in having stream-of-consciousness ideas. It leads them to realise they know far more than they thought they did about the stories they create. Our pair in this example is Paula and David:

● Ask one of the pair (say, Paula) to create a character or to extend and develop a character taken from another story.

● Meanwhile, ask David to compile a list of questions about the character that Paula has imagined.

● The activity is for David to go through his list of questions with Paula. Explain that there's no such thing as 'I don't know.' Emphasise to Paula that if she hasn't previously thought of the point that David makes in a question, she can make it up as she goes along (writers do this all the time!).

● Explain too that David does not have to stick rigidly to his list. If other questions come to mind, he can go ahead and ask them. Furthermore, he can ask questions which arise spontaneously out of Paula's replies.

The anticipated outcome of 'Gossip Calypso' is that the children will talk easily and naturally about the character as though she was a real person. When the conversation begins to ebb, have the children change roles and use a character that David has imagined. For the purpose of the example we'll pretend that Paula has created the character of Anna Williams from the Double Dare Gang.

David: So what is it about Nigel that Anna finds so attractive?

Paula: Well, he's got a good sense of humour. And I think he's a bit rebellious. You know, he's not a wimp or a coward. He's a bit of a daredevil and I think that appeals to her.

David: But doesn't she find him a bit childish? And anyway, she's so much taller than he is!

Paula: That might be a hangup for you, but not for Anna. OK, so she is more mature than any of the boys in the group, but that doesn't mean she finds them childish. At least it means she can see Nigel's qualities, even if she does sometimes think he messes around too much.

David: Don't you think she was a bit sneaky trying to join the gang just to get closer to Nigel?

Paula: No. I think she knew what she wanted and decided to go for it! She's not old-fashioned, and she's not a wallflower. Why should girls just wait about until boys notice them? Besides, she knew that if she could pass the bravery test Nigel would be really impressed with her. Which he was.

David: OK, I was only asking! What about her family? Does she have brothers and sisters?

Paula: I don't… Um, I mean she has an older brother who works in a store in Kenniston. His name is Greg. He's really easy-going, very laid back. But Anna is much more ambitious. She knows what she wants from life and will go out and get it. She thinks of life as another kind of bravery test, really.

David: Yes. And does Nigel feature in her long-term plans?

Paula: Well, I guess you'll have to ask Anna about that…

Note that the 'Gossip Calypso' technique can be used for any element of a story: plot, settings, motifs.

◆ Points of view

To really get to know someone, walk a mile in his shoes.

Traditional saying

A valuable tool in NLP is the idea of perceptual positions. This means the different viewpoints one can take to understand other people, oneself and the world. There are three perceptual positions: the first, second and third.

The first position is associated. This corresponds to the first person in English – 'I'. Here we experience the world through our own eyes, relating it all to our own framework of reality. It is, if you like, the 'default position' for our perceptions.

The second position requires you to imagine you are experiencing the world through the eyes of someone else. This is still an associated position, except that you are associating with another person – experiencing reality based on their map. Practically speaking, you can never fully and truly live out of someone else's head. But what does happen is that by an act of imagination and will you draw upon your conscious and subconscious knowledge of that person in order to be more in tune with their way of understanding. This act can lead to profound insights into the person that you are associating with, the experiences they are having, and yourself.

The third perceptual position has been called the fly-on-the-wall viewpoint. Here you are dissociated from the experience, perceiving it in a detached and neutral way. If you are remembering an experience in which you were involved, you will imagine yourself from an outside perspective. 'Stepping back' from the field of your perceptions and emotions is in itself a valuable thing to do, insofar as you realise that you have this degree of control and need not be 'trapped' within the frame of your own perspectives.

Assuming the second and third perceptual positions also develops your ability to experience the world through different sensory modalities. If you are, say, primarily visual in the way you represent experience, taking the perceptual position of a tactile person encourages you to 'gather up' what you know about that mode of experiencing. You quickly come to understand that you had this potential all along, and now have another way of developing it. Interestingly, dissociating into the third position requires you to gather up as many details as possible through *all* of the sensory modes.

The three perceptual positions

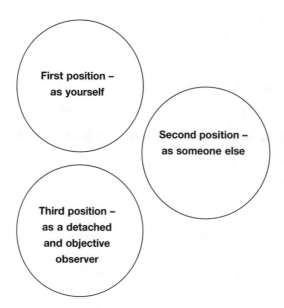

There are several ways of using the notion of perceptual positions:

First	Second	Third
Yourself as writer, creating stories as you normally do.	Yourself as the 'archetypal reader' of your work.	A detached, neutral and expert reviewer of the work.
Yourself as writer at your (perceived) current level of expertise.	Yourself as a much more experienced writer; either a writer you already admire, or your own future self.	A detached observer watching as you write, noting small but important ways for you to become more effective.
Yourself as writer.	Yourself as any/all of the characters in your story.	A 'creator god' who looks upon the world of the story in a detached way and can make any changes (s)he wants.

The tool of perceptual positions can also be combined with time-span work (see p.132), allowing you to adopt a variety of perspectives at any point of the thinking–writing–reviewing line.

● I am an experienced writer. I have completed many pieces of work successfully. I feel confident. I like to encourage writers who are not yet as far as I am along the road. I have some useful advice for young Steve as he struggles to find his own voice...

● I am myself-as-writer. I am my future self. I have just finished my latest story and I feel a glow of achievement. As I look back over the work I can see exactly what needs to be done to make it even better. I also realise some important things about how to plan my next adventure...

● I am Old Man Jones. Steve is writing about me, but he doesn't really understand how I feel. He thinks I hate all kids and would show them violence if they came into my allotment. He thinks I believe that my plants are more important than people. He needs to know that I don't hate kids: I hate disrespect. I hate the way some people come into your life and thoughtlessly trample over what you hold dear. Healthy plants represent the fruit of much care and effort. They are the outcome of hard work and gentleness. Coming in the dark to destroy them means you fail to see what they have to teach. I think I'd better tell Steve about how I feel before he gets it wrong again...

You can also use perceptual positions with the 'Gossip Calypso' technique (see p.186). In this example, Paula is the writer-as-herself (1st perceptual position), Samantha is Anna Williams (2nd position), David is the detached and neutral observer whose function is to sit and record the conversation (3rd position).

We'll assume that Paula has created the character of Anna Williams from the Double Dare Gang. Samantha has read the story and is pretending to be Anna.

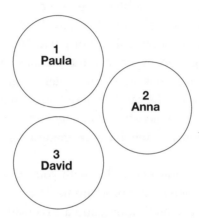

Paula:	So, what did you think of my story The Rope Swing?
Samantha-as-Anna:	Yeah, it was good. I'm not sure I'd be quite so devious about chasing after Nigel. I think I'd take a more straightforwrd approach.
Paula:	Such as?
Anna:	Well, I reckon I'd go right up to him and tell him how I felt. Just because the boys in the gang are pretty immature and unconfident doesn't mean girls have to be.
Paula:	But then there wouldn't be a story –
Anna:	I'm just telling you what I would do.
Paula:	Fair enough. On the other hand, it was *because* you took the bravery test that Nigel came to appreciate you. You proved you were his kind of girl.
Anna:	That's true. And I guess the boys came to regard girls differently too, because of what I did.
Paula:	Yes, that was what I wanted the story to show.
Anna:	Anyway, a lot of the other girls in the class wished they'd thought of it. Stephanie Phillips really likes Kevin Howells, by the way.
Paula:	But I haven't made up a character called Stephanie Phillips!
Anna:	No, but you will…

189

◆ Old Man Envy

A useful way of exploring feelings is to personify them and treat them as characters that you have created. So, for example, we might imagine envy as a skinny old man, bent by the weight of his wanting. He has grown twisted, because for a long time he has twisted what people have said and achieved for themselves. He usually sneers, and when he smiles it is a spiteful, hateful smile because he begrudges the things that he has not got. Old Man Envy will live a long time. His thoughts are small and exist in dark corners. They are not big enough for him to realise that he has been taking happiness away from himself for all these years. Only when *he* changes will life bring him what he wants.

Discussing feelings in this way makes them less abstract and more accessible. Children can hook into the activity by using characters from literature: Scrooge, for instance, typifies miserliness (and happens to be a close cousin of Old Man Envy!). As they practise, however, their personifications will become more individual and original. The activity also allows children to distance themselves from feelings they experience and perhaps haven't yet addressed. They can play the game of pretend. A child who is angry can pretend that the anger is outside of herself, embodied in her character creation. She can talk about anger without reference to herself. She can put her character into situations where that character is 'being herself', being angry. This can lead to insights about the emotion and how it can be modified.

If you have already worked on character creation with your groups, then they are likely to see 'Old Man Envy' as just an extension of that programme. Use any of the StoryMaker techniques to help the children create their personifications, and also consider the following:

● Chunk it down. Using Old Man Envy as an example: ask about his hair (length, colour, style). What about the shape and colour of his eyes? What does his nose look like? Notice his fingernails. What comes to mind?

● Combine chunking with the use of a template and reasoning.

Feature	Details	Reasoning
hair	long, white, dry	Long, because he has stopped caring about himself. All of his attention is focused outside on the things that he wants. White and dry, because the envy has taken away his youth and his energy. He is shrivelled up – he is eaten up with envy!
eyes	green, narrowed, piercing	Green, because green is the colour of envy – but it is not a light grassy green, more of a dark bottle green, the colour of a glass bottle that has been lying on the sea bed forgotten. They are narrow eyes because they don't want to let the light in. They are piercing because Old Man Envy would like to cut you with a glance. He wants to hurt you, because he is hurting
nose	hooked, long, insensitive	Hooked and long because he likes to pry, he likes to stick his nose into other people's affairs. And it is insensitive to fragrance. There is nothing sweet in envy's world.
finger-nails	long, black, broken	Long, because he does not care about his appearance, he cannot be bothered to cut them. Black and broken because envy scrabbles for scraps – he likes to dig the dirt!

● Condense this information down into a brief descriptive paragraph.

> Old Man Envy has shrivelled himself up. He has taken the life out of himself because he always wants to take things away from others. His hair is white and dry and untidily long. His eyes are narrow, like slits, and gleam with a dark green glow. His fingernails are black and broken, as if they have been rooting about in the dirt. They are soiled, like Old Man Envy's thoughts.

● Use the 'Points of View' (perceptual positions) technique (p.187) to allow children to temporarily become the personified character. Have a partner ask Old Man Envy about himself without being judgmental or accusing. Encourage Envy to chat about himself – 'how do I know what I think until I hear what I say'? Note that even if a child is actually envious, he is still dissociated from it because he is being the Old Man Envy character and not herself. The anticipation is that she can learn more about envy without experiencing it now and without giving anything of herself away.

● If you run the 'Old Man Envy' activity with a number of groups, have them compare their ideas and explore similarities and differences in their thinking. Compile a 'character composite' incorporating details from all of the groups.

● Arrange for personified characters to talk to each other. What would Envy have to say to Contentment? What similarities would Envy and Jealousy find between themselves? What kind of place does Envy live in? What changes would he make in his life if other characters could help him?

● Modify characters once they have been created. Give Old Man Envy a haircut. Have him go on a walk in the sunshine and get some clean air in his lungs. Help him decorate his house. Would he like a pet? What sort? Why? Send him an invitation to a party – Contentment will be there. He must of course change before going.

● Use metaphor to compare emotions to objects (which the personification might own).

  - envy is a dark green bottle lying at the bottom of the sea

  - envy is a torch with a dead battery

  - envy is a cracked cup that isn't even half full

  - envy is a withered flower

Note: See *Self-Intelligence* Section 3: 'Enhancing emotional literacy', for more ideas on working with emotions in this way.

◆ The mind's ear

This activity focuses on auditory details. There are a number of variations.

- Ask children to listen to each other's voices and write down what they notice. Extend the activity by having children note details of voices from the TV, the High Street, etc.
- Look at auditory submodalities (applying to all sounds, not just voices):

stereo / mono	distance from listener
volume *(loud – soft)*	duration
tone *(soft – harsh)*	continuous – discontinuous
timbre *(full – thin)*	speed
pitch *(high – low)*	clarity *(clear – muffled)*
Location relative to listener	other characteristics

- Imagine characters' voices using these parameters. (Look back at the 'Think Bubbles' picture on p.183.) Use speech bubbles instead and have children write voice descriptions inside them.

Nigel's voice is moderately loud, fast, thinnish and clear. He likes to be close to you when he speaks. He hates to shout from a distance.

192

● 'Jump into' pictures and encourage children to imagine the sounds they hear there.

I hear the whistle, crack and crackling of the firework.

I hear the rush of traffic beyond the houses.

I hear the gentle rub and clatter of branches knocking in the wind.

I hear the swish of a steady wind through bare branches.

I hear the muffled sound of people's voices in the room.

I hear the squeak and clank of the iron gate swinging open and closed.

I hear the yowl and hiss of the frightened cat.

I hear the plink and tinkle of water trickling into the drain.

I hear the soft rustle of newspaper along the pavement.

I hear the clatter of footsteps hurrying down the street.

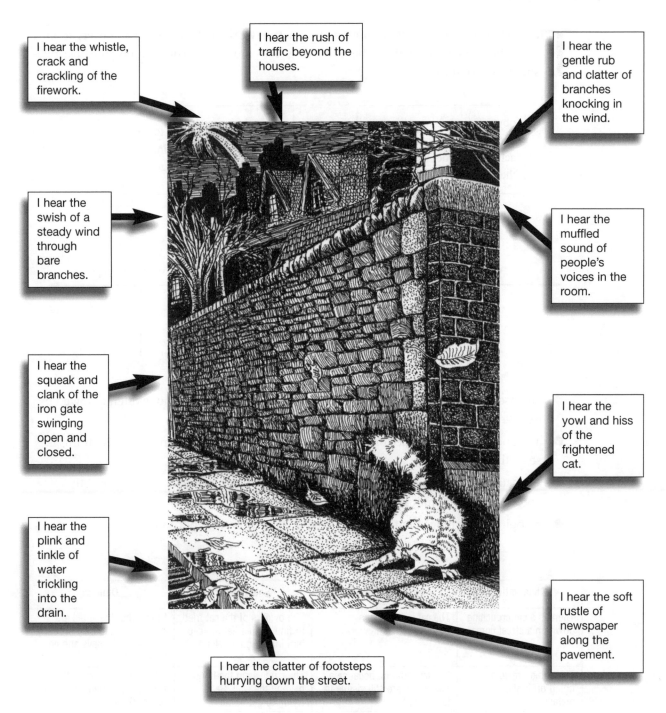

Artwork by Stella Hender, used with artist's permission

● Do an 'auditory audit' of places the children know – the school, the high street, the home. Create sound maps noting details of the sounds to be found there.

● Create a file-card resource of sounds: metal, wood, stone, electrical, animal, etc., for ready reference in future stories.

◆ Opinion finder

The distinction has already been made (in 'Picture work', p.26) between an observation, a deduction and a speculation. These thinking skills move increasingly along the objective-subjective continuum.

objective – dealing with outward things, exhibiting actual facts uncoloured by the percipient's feelings, etc.	subjective – belonging to the consciousness or thinking or perceiving subject or ego.

(Definitions taken from *Concise Oxford Dictionary*)

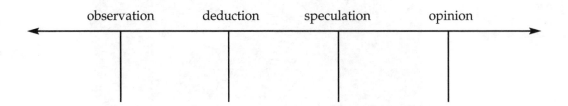

observation   deduction   speculation   opinion

- an observation means noticing something, an object or process, and is often followed by its description uncoloured by the observer's own opinions, beliefs or attitudes.
- a deduction is an inference or logical link based on the observation of details. 'If this is so … then that follows.'
- a speculation is a conjecture, an imagined scenario based upon more or less tightly argued reasoning from an initial premise
- an opinion is a judgement or belief based on 'grounds short of proof'

Observation	Deduction	Speculation	Opinion
There is a cat crouching down on a street corner.	The cat is frightened because of the firework.	The owners of the cat tried to find him earlier to keep him in on Bonfire Night.	I think that fireworks are dangerous and only properly organised displays should be allowed.
There is a firework going off in the distance.	It is late autumn because a few leaves are still visible in the picture.	The cat lives in the house beyond the wall. He is trying to get home.	I think the owners of the cat should have tried harder to find their pet.
There are no leaves on the trees.	It has been raining recently because of the puddle on the pavement.	There is a big bonfire party on the Recreation Ground.	I like Bonfire Night although I think fireworks are much too expensive.
There are houses beyond the walls.	Because of the presence of a few leaves and the firework, the date is on or near 5 November.	The people who own the cat have stayed indoors. They don't like fireworks.	I don't think schools do enough to explain the origins of Bonfire Night.

194

Raise awareness of these distinctions by making use of a picture stimulus (as in the example above). Once children understand these basic distinctions they are in a position to realise more clearly that:

- we all look at life through the filters of our own opinions and beliefs
- although areas of knowledge may progress through the accumulation of data by observation, conclusions, facts and laws can be highly subjective and supported by personal opinion
- some subjects rely more heavily upon speculation and opinion than others. (The relative accuracy or success of a conclusion in mathematics can be measured or judged more objectively than, say, the effectiveness of a piece of prose fiction.)
- opinions count and should be respected, although that 'right of respect' is linked to the idea that opinions should be considered and supported by some justification
- subjectivity – speculation/seeing with new eyes – is as valuable as objective observation. Each is a tool used most effectively in its own particular circumstances.
- knowledge is not static or 'set in stone'. Very often, facts are only facts in light of current understanding. The content of an area of knowledge serves the process of the manipulation of ideas in order to arrive at new understandings.

Opinions may sometimes be held with great conviction, supported by powerful emotions, but with little reflection or attempt at self-justification. Allow children to develop sound platforms for their opinions – or modify their opinions or let go of unhelpful ones – by drawing out their views and exploring them. Working with less controversial ideas to begin with reduces the signal-to-noise ratio: discussion can occur without tempers being lost!

Another technique is to look at other people's opinions initially, so that children are not immediately immersed in their own feelings about any particular issue, or think that their personally-held views are being challenged. So:

Steve: In the story *Anna and the Rope Swing*, the boys don't want Anna to join the Double Dare Gang because she's a girl. Why do you suppose they have that attitude?

Andy: Because girls *are* useless, aren't they!

Carla: Oh yeah, typical stupid boy's comment that is!

Steve: What a minute – stop there. I'm asking you to speculate about what the boys in the Double Dare Gang think. I'm not asking you to give me your own opinions, OK? Do you understand that?

David: OK, well I think that Nigel is the one who really carries that attitude because he feels self-conscious around girls – and especially Anna. He knows she likes him, I reckon. He feels embarrassed about that, maybe because he likes her too, but it's not cool to show his feelings.

Carla: Boys are so immature at that age!

Steve: Let's focus on the story. Carla, are there any boys in the story who are *not* being immature?

195

Carla:	Well…
Samantha:	Steve, the narrator character, realises that Anna is clever as well as brave. That's not being immature – he's not following the crowd.
Tejal:	And Anthony feels frightened for Anna when Nigel challenges her to go on the rope swing. He's frightened to do that dare himself, but he's scared on Anna's behalf too.
Samantha:	And going back to Steve again, he thinks that Nigel's plan to go on the swing to stop Anna is 'stupid and pathetic'.
Tejal:	That's not a mature opinion though.
Samantha:	Well at least Steve realises that Nigel's motives are immature. I think Steve's a pretty understanding character.
Steve:	I agree that my namesake does have many fine qualities.
Carla:	You would say that, sir…

Exploring opinions through stories creates a framework where children are not put on the defensive, and as the example dialogue shows, attention can be focused back into the story when children's own views begin to intrude. Furthermore, the characters and events of a story can offer varying viewpoints that might challenge pupils' opinions in an elegant way: Anna Williams passes the bravery test creatively. She works with resourcefulness in the boys' own world of daring and courage, proving that she has intelligence too. She offers a role model to female readers and gives male readers the opportunity to reconsider their views.

You can capitalise on this element of creative fiction by asking children to step into the shoes of a character…

- The Double Dare Gang stories are written from Steve's viewpoint. Pick a story and rewrite all or part of it from another character's viewpoint.
- Be one of the characters and do some subsidiary writing; write a letter to another character, keep a diary or journal, write a conversation between you-as-a-character and another character in the story.
- Rewrite or retell the story from the viewpoint of a new character who appears in the tale.
- Be yourself in the story: write yourself into the tale and notice your own opinions of the other characters and the things that happen. Think about why you feel as you do.

The thinking tools of observation, deduction, speculation and opinion can be developed through studying text. The concept of 'author intrusion' might be introduced here. It is considered bad practice for an author to impose his or her own opinions on the reader in the body of the text. Opinions – whether the author's or not – should be expressed through the characters.

a)

> Rain had been falling for hours, together with the temperature, promising a typically miserable November night. Despite the dreary weather the Lloyd family decided anyway to go ahead with the bonfire party. The kids had been gathering sticks, old boxes and other burnable rubbish for weeks: it would be a shame to disappoint them now. Fireworks are overpriced and dangerous, so Mr Lloyd himself had chosen the selection and insisted on letting them off. Children usually forget about common sense when they get excited, so Mr Lloyd pushed some bamboo canes into the lawn, strung ribbon between them, and told the kids not to step over the line…

Notice how the author/narrator writes opinions and value-judgements into the text. A subtle shift of emphasis can transfer them to the characters: they are just as valid, and also follow the conventions of good writing practice.

b)

> Rain had been falling for hours, together with the temperature, promising what Mr Lloyd thought would be a typically miserable November night. Despite the weather the Lloyd family decided anyway to go ahead with the bonfire party. The kids had been gathering sticks, old boxes and other burnable rubbish for weeks, Mr Lloyd realised, and it would be a shame to disappoint them now. His own opinion was that fireworks were overpriced and dangerous, so he had chosen the selection and insisted on letting them off. Deciding that children usually forget about common sense when they got excited, Mr Lloyd pushed some bamboo canes into the lawn, strung ribbon between them, and told the kids not to step over the line…

Another way of exploring opinions is to ask precise questions which tease out the roots of the beliefs that support the viewpoint (so-called 'meta model' questions). Such questions may be rhetorical – since Mr Lloyd is a character in a story he could hardly be expected to reply. Alternatively have one or more children get into role and *be* the character and encourage them to answer as, in this case, Mr Lloyd would do.

- Precisely what is it that's miserable about the night we're talking about? [*Mr Lloyd*: Well, I'm miserable, I guess.]

- Exactly how does the weather on that November night make you miserable? [*Mr Lloyd*: I suppose it's the cold and the wet.]

- Have you thought about a selection of November nights in order to decide that cold and rain are typical of them? [*Mr Lloyd*: Well, no. It just seems that way.]

- Could there be November nights that are dry and relatively mild? [*Mr Lloyd*: Um, yes, I guess there could be.]

- What exactly leads you to think that fireworks are overpriced? [*Mr Lloyd*: Their price!]

- With what are you comparing the price of fireworks in order to decide that they are overpriced? [*Mr Lloyd*: Well, with the price they used to be.]

- Do you feel that the price of other items has also risen over time? [*Mr Lloyd*: Yes, that's true enough.]

- Do you feel that the price of fireworks has risen more quickly than the prices of the other things you're thinking about? [*Mr Lloyd*: Um, well, I don't know really.]

And so on. It's important to explain that the use of precise questioning does not seek to undermine opinions; its purpose is to allow an individual to reflect on her views and to become more aware of the part that opinions play in the communication of ideas.

◆ Future diary

Diaries are normally used to record experiences that have already happened. These are usually expressed on a raft of beliefs, which may or may not be helpful in allowing the individual to move on. Story-making is all about 'moving on', in terms both of putting one word in front of another through the story, and of developing one's preferences, style and voice as an author. Writing itself offers a structure one can model in one's own life.

Particular techniques exploit and accelerate the process of moving on...

- 'Future diary': begin by writing diary extracts from the point-of-view of a character. Leap ahead into that character's future and write a diary from that vantage point, describing experiences as though they have already just happened.

- Develop that idea and write a future diary for yourself. Jump along your personal life path and write from the vantage point of your older, wiser self. Look back and examine your past limiting beliefs. Modify them in some way – personify them and talk to them (see 'Old Man Envy', p. 190), shift them outside of yourself (see 'The world inside', p.178), and then explore their origins in the outer world... What exactly is that in the outside world that maintains those beliefs now (see 'The world outside ', p.176)? Are you going to allow those links to continue? What strategies come to mind that allow you to be what you want to be?

- 'Letters to myself': write letters to yourself. If they are letters to your future self, seal them in envelopes and date them to be opened at that time. Put them into your desk diary at the appropriate dates. When you open and read the letters, write a review of their content: How relevant is the information in those letters now? How have you moved on in the meantime? If you haven't moved on, what exactly has stopped you? How many ideas come to mind now which allow you to develop?

◆ Belief Tree

As far as we know, beliefs are a matter of nurture, not nature. We are born with a huge field of potentials (according to Howard Gardner's multiple intelligence theory) which are more or less fulfilled by our upbringing and experiences. We interpret those experiences consciously and subconsciously, and this gives rise to beliefs that filter subsequent events. In other words, we construct the spectacles through which we then look at the world.

Every belief has a story behind it. The device of the 'belief tree' attempts to trace beliefs back to their source. Use it first by speculating on fictional characters. As and when you find it effective, use it for yourself.

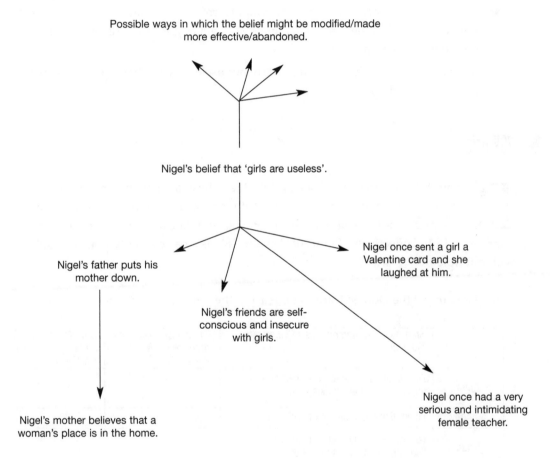

Possible ways in which the belief might be modified/made more effective/abandoned.

Nigel's belief that 'girls are useless'.

Nigel's father puts his mother down.

Nigel's friends are self-conscious and insecure with girls.

Nigel once sent a girl a Valentine card and she laughed at him.

Nigel's mother believes that a woman's place is in the home.

Nigel once had a very serious and intimidating female teacher.

Belief trees for character development show the Big Picture and the logical links between events, beliefs and expectations. The device also acts as a visual metaphor for the notion that beliefs can grow, that they have roots, that they can be changed in a variety of ways.

Techniques such as 'Off the Top of Your Head' (p.70), 'Points of View' (p.187) and 'Gossip Calypso' (p.186) can be used in the construction of belief trees.

◆ Connecting with the here-and-now

Beliefs can be deeply rooted in the past. One way of modifying them is to observe the immediate present and note experiences that do not fit into the framework of the belief. So, using the example above, Nigel could modify his belief that 'girls are useless' by:

- noticing people who are not self-conscious or insecure with girls

- reflecting on why his father puts his mother down. (The pattern of behaviour might have been modelled from Nigel's grandfather's attitude.)

- asking exactly why Nigel's mother thinks a woman's place is in the home

- realising that female teachers can be gentle and caring and understanding (and that Nigel's intimidating teacher might have been like that because of her own baggage)

- daring to send another Valentine card and learning from that experience. Reflecting on the possibility that the girl who laughed at Nigel might have done so because she felt self-conscious and insecure

- noticing instances when girls are clearly not useless. Reflecting on the qualities that allow them to do things effectively.

◆ POV grid

Responsibility means 'response-ability' – the ability to respond in a variety of ways to any situation. This requires a high degree of emotional awareness and flexibility: knowing one's own emotions and those of others, and knowing how one might react most appropriately and effectively. 'Points of View' (p.187) is a basic activity in this area. Follow it up with multiple-POV work.

- How might the Double Dare Gang react in the following situations?

	Stonehead Henderson tries to intimidate the gang.	Another girl becomes interested in Nigel's affections.	Old Man Jones falls ill and can't tend his allotment.
Anna	I'd ask him why he felt the need to be so unpleasant. What's making him so angry?		
Anthony	I'd get Brian to bully him back!		
Brian	I'd make sure my friends didn't get hurt. I'd warn Henderson to back off.		
Kevin	I'd carry a camera and photograph his antics. Then I'd tell him I'd make sure the Headmaster saw them if he didn't leave us alone.		
Neil	I'd stay out of his way.		
Nigel	I'd challenge him to a bravery test. If he chickened out or failed it he'd have to leave us alone. If he passed it we'd pay a forfeit.		
Steve	I'd make sure Henderson knew that the DDG stuck together. If he hassles one of us, he hassles all of us.		

● Another variation is to imagine a conversation between two of the Double Dare Gang characters. Choose two – deliberately or randomly – and role-play their dialogue.

	Anna	Anthony	Brian	Kevin	Neil	Nigel	Steve
Anna							
Anthony							
Brian							
Kevin							
Neil							
Nigel							
Steve							

Suggested topics for discussion:

● One of the DDG sees Nigel's older brother sneaking into a neighbour's garage, clearly looking nervous.

● Nigel confides to one of his friends that he's thinking of issuing a dare that might be dangerous.

● Anna hears from a friend that a particularly unpleasant teacher at school intends to put an end to 'this ridiculous game of daring'.

● Two of the DDG find a wallet filled with money on the linear walkway out towards the Lime Pools.

● Two of the DDG find a dog suffering badly inside a locked car on a hot day.

● The parents of one of the DDG win a large sum of money on the lottery.

● One of the DDG notices another person in the same class cheating in a test. The method of cheating is so clever that there is little likelihood of being caught.

As appropriate, these and other situations can be discussed by children without the device of role-playing another character. (See the Bibliography for *A Book Of Questions* by G. Stock.)

◆ But why?

Things happen for reasons. We have already seen how intention influences effect in writing ('Intention–output–effect', p.20). Characters too are motivated to act as they do within stories. Whatever their behaviour, the author should have considered (or at least know when questioned) the reasons behind his characters' actions.

'But Why?' brings this principle into focus. Begin by reading a story, then use the following template to examine action and reason. Some of the connections will be based on simple observation of what the characters say and do; others will become apparent through deduction;

201

some may be wildly speculative. If you run the activity using an extract from a story that the children have not read, speculative links are likely to predominate.

The example comes from the Double Dare Gang story 'Mollie & The Great Removal Plan'.

Text	Action/Context	Reason(s)
'Now, as I mentioned to you at the start of term, we are having workmen in school for the next couple of weeks. They will be redecorating the staffroom - and about time, no doubt 'Mr Hughes grinned briefly without seeming to enjoy it and looked at the back of the hall where most of the teachers were sitting.	*Mr Hughes the Headmaster is giving out notices at the end of a long assembly. He smiles coldly.*	*Maybe the teachers have been complaining about the state of the staffroom. Perhaps this is one example of a deeper friction between the Head and his staff.*
Mr Hughes half turned and indicated a lady sitting at the end of the row on the stage, next to Mrs Carter the Year Seven Head. She sat like a statue, with her hands in her lap and her eyes staring straight ahead, not even looking at Mr Hughes when he spoke.		*Maybe she (Miss Molloy) is nervous about being in a new school. Perhaps she does not like Mr Hughes. Maybe she has lots of things on her mind.*
'Right!' Her voice cracked like a whiplash. 'You-' She pointed at Wayne Hardy who was sitting by the door. ' Put that chewing gum in the bin! And you - ' Karen Watson flinched as Mollie blazed at her.' 'Stop your chattering now!' Everyone shut up pretty quickly and faced the front.	*Miss Molloy is picking up on the slightest fault or misdemeanour.*	*She wants to impose her authority on the class straight away.*
Mollie's hard glittering eyes moved slowly along the rows, pausing as she caught sight of Ray Vaughn secretly trying to finish off a tangerine. 'You, lad,' she said, not yelling, but her voice dangerously calm. 'What are you doing?'	*She takes advantage of the long silence to further intimidate the children.* *She knows what he's doing. This is a rhetorical question.*	*Maybe she had a teacher like this as a child. Perhaps she's been warned about this class by Mr Hughes.* *She wants to bring Ray Vaughn into the spotlight to make an example of him.*
We had great fun trying on fake noses and moustaches. Neil tried to wear a werewolf mask without us seeing. The he spun round and went RrrrAAArrr! We yawned, but when he took the mask off we all screamed and pretended to dive for cover. And we fell silent with our mouths open when Anna put on a long black lady-vampire wig, stuck her hands on her hips and fluttered her eyelashes at us. We all felt a little bit awkward then, and began busily searching through the racks of tricks and gags, and the novelties stuck to cards on the walls.	*The DDG have decided to play a trick on Miss Molloy. They visit Mr Lee's joke shop for ideas.*	*Neil wants to scare his friends, but they're wise to him. They react in the opposite way to the way he expected, to tease him.* *Perhaps Anna, having proven she's 'one of the boys', wants them to realise she's a girl – after all, she is still fond of Nigel.* *The boys are embarrassed because they have reacted just as Anna wanted them to.*

◆ Eyelines

Very often eyes speak more eloquently than words. Developing the knack of reading a person's expression enhances one's interpersonal skills and provides a useful technique for describing and developing fictional characters.

● Ask children to notice references to eyes and facial expressions in the stories they read. Have them suggest what the references could mean.

Text	Meanings
Nige made a funny expression that had a little bit of disappointment in it, and a little bit of pain. Then a smile came to his face, though his eyes had a gleam in them I didn't entirely trust.	*Nigel's eyes give the lie to his smile. He has something secret planned.*
'Yeah,' Nige nodded with sparkly eyes. 'But even though you were scared, you still had a go'.	*Steve has just passed the bravery test that even Nigel had not dared to do. His eyes suggest a new friendship with Steve and maybe a sense of triumph now that Nigel has done the test also.*
I glanced at Nige and frowned as his expression went all innocent and coy.	*Nigel is about to suggest a scary dare. His expression means he's trying to conceal the truth until the last moment – and perhaps he wants to create the greatest shock impact.*
'What's so special about Old Man Jones?' I asked cheerfully. Anthony's expression was intense. He leaned forward and glared.	*His expression means he's thinking hard and fast at what has just been said about Old Man Jones. He leans forward and glares to make sure that Steve (the narrator) understands the import of Nigel's dare.*

● A visual equivalent of this activity is to present children with pictures of eyes and faces and ask them to describe the expressions and possible reasons for them.

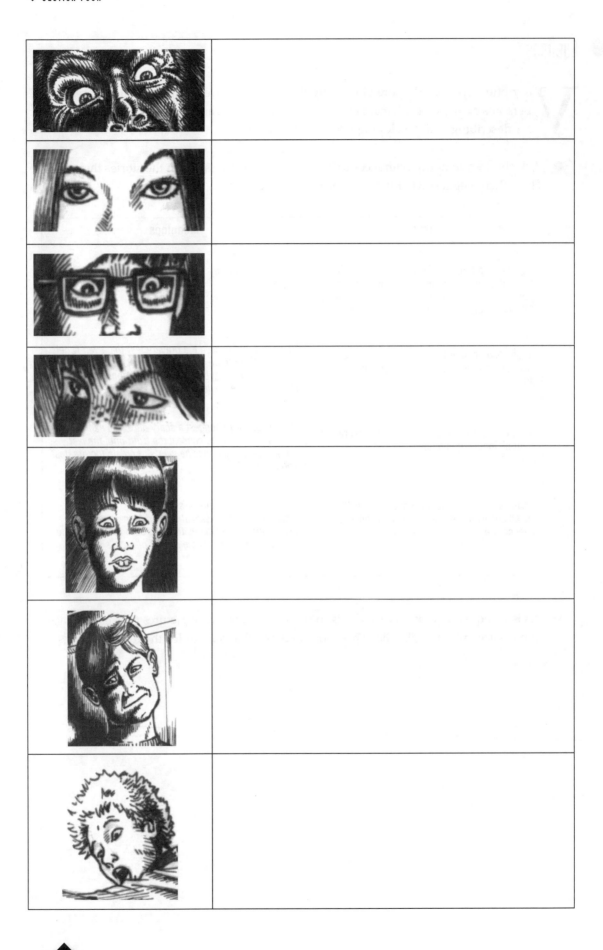

◆ Getting into character

Associating with a character, either 'quietly' through identification and empathy with that character's experiences, or actively through role-play, helps to build self-awareness and the skills of mood and relationship management. These develop 'safely' because you are only pretending to be that person: the character is fictional and anything you say through their mouths need not reflect upon you.

Through the medium of the story, real situations, problems, emotions and resolutions can be framed and rehearsed. Issues can be discussed that in 'real life' would be difficult to talk about. Characters in stories can display the full range of human weaknesses and strengths, make all the mistakes that we would dread to make and allow us to learn from their experiences and the resources they use to survive them. Characters can teach and guide and help us to deal with our own problems. They can remain with us as 'old friends', or we can shut them away in their own world when we fold the book closed, bringing with us only those treasures that we want or need to keep.

By exploring characters we explore ourselves. Encourage children to engage with the characters in stories in the following ways:

- Write letters to characters (and the replies they make!).
- Keep a diary as though you were that character.
- Email characters and construct a reply – or have a partner construct one for you.
- Prepare a list of questions as though you were going to interview a character.
- Be that character and respond to your questions.
- Be a character that you've read about. Write yourself into a prequel or sequel.
- Make notes on a day-in-the-life of a chosen character.
- List similarities and differences between yourself and a character.
- If you could take your pick of these, which would you keep and which would you let go of?
- Talk off the top of your head as though you were a chosen character. Tape your self-talk and comb through it for useful insights.

Characters as guides

Characters can be more to us than fictitious people who move through the events of a story and then are gone. Indeed, for some people fictional characters are alive and rooted in the real world – Sherlock Holmes still gets letters addressed to his rooms at 221b Baker Street, London. When a favourite character triumphs, we too feel the glow of achievement. If he dies, our sadness is real and deeply felt. To some extent characters are the people we would like to be, daring to do the things we wish we had the courage to do ourselves. They can represent our aspirations on all levels, from environment to spirituality (see 'People are like onions', p.174). They can advise and guide us towards our goals; they can console us when things go wrong and when difficulties are encountered; they can walk with us along the way as part of our own life story.

In this sense, characters have a profoundly symbolic quality. They represent aspects of our own lives and personalities. The themes of their adventures connect with the themes that run in our lives. In short, characters and character types carry meanings for us beyond their mere appearance, actions and motivations.

In 'My favourite story' (p.157) we touched upon the deeper significance and linkages of plot, motif, theme and character. 'Characters as guides' draws out one aspect of this principle and develops it so that characters can serve as useful tools in our own self-development.

- Compile a list of characters or character types and work with children to suggest what they could represent. Combing through the literature of mythology and Jungian psychology will supply a wealth of general ideas, but don't let these override the personal meanings that children might attach to particular figures.

The Wise Old Man, the Mage, one who brings wisdom and sound advice.

The Innocent, the child who can always see the wonder and goodness in the world.

The Seeker for Truth, the investigator whose sharpness of mind will not be deceived or outwitted.

The Achiever, one whose dreams have come true, one whose talents are flourishing in the world.

The Traveller, the one who dares to explore and adventure, the one who enjoys the journey without being overwhelmed by the thought of the destination.

Section Five

Genre

You get further if you aim at a star than at the top of the barn.

Unknown

Section Five - Genre

Page	Topic/activity	Story element covered	Accelerated learning link
209	What's in a name?	*Names of characters / manipulation of names for genre use / pseudonyms*	Development of self-esteem / positive strokes/interpersonal skills/ reframing (by renaming!)
212	Title match	*Titles as story-starters / focusing devices*	Reframing/interpretative skills
216	Word maker	*Meanings of words and phrases/etymology / compound words and phrases*	Reframing/understanding the 'Wordscape'/awareness of links between language, thoughts and neurology
218	The scribe's road	*Wordplay/etymology / compound words and phrases*	Reframing/understanding the 'Wordscape'/awareness of links between language, thoughts and neurology
219	Wordbuilder	*Links between fiction and 'real' knowledge / research*	Understanding the interconnectedness of knowledge / transference of skills across subject boundaries
219	The landscape of genre	*Sub-genre/metaphor*	Use of metaphor/chunking down / the Big Picture
222	Genre overlap	*Sub-genre/the links between genres*	Reframing/lateral thinking skills / (nonconscious) understanding of the transference of creative writing techniques to real-life situations
224	Structure & function	*Internal consistency of created worlds*	Awareness of inter-subject links / development of deductive reasoning skills
225	Literal and metaphorical functions	*Internal consistency of created worlds/story motifs as symbolic representations*	Use of metaphor/interpersonal skills
228	Lensing	*Making the most of an idea/inter-genre links*	Perceptual positions/strategic thinking/understanding the flexibility of strategies
229	Themes and motifs	*Understanding the 'layeredness' of stories / generation and development of ideas*	(Nonconscious) understanding of themes and motifs in real life / development of the personal intelligences
230	Practice miscellany	*Consolidation of the above*	Consolidation of the above

Section Five

Genre

This section explains how genre helps children to 'locate' their writing more precisely, and goes on to explore how certain ever-popular genres such as fantasy and science fiction restate the powerful themes and motifs traditionally found in fairytale and myth.

◆ What's in a name?

Choosing names carefully is an important part of the storymaking process. Character names especially can sound artificial and forced if the writer has 'tried hard' to think of them. A number of activities can be linked to the element of names.

● Make dictionaries of first names and surnames available to your groups. Encourage children to check out the origins of their own names and to link them with their own positive personal qualities, attributes and resources.

Anna Williams

Able
Active
Adventurous
Alert
Ambitious
Articulate
Athletic
Anna!

'Anna' - from the Hebrew Hannah meaning grace. The name was very popular in North America. The French form Anne was introduced into England in the 13th Century and has been popular ever since.

Williams is linked to Williamson, 'son of William'. This name is of Old Germanic origin and comes from Willahelm. This is formed from the words wilja meaning will and helm meaning protection. The name was possibly first given as a symbol of hoped-for traits. The name Williams is related to many other surnames and is widely used.

Always cheerful
Never jealous
Now enjoying life
Achieving my dreams!

Symbol

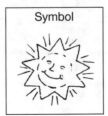

Warm
Witty
Wonderful
Williams!

● Allow access to telephone directories and other name lists. Give children the opportunity to randomly match first names and surnames. They will find that many matches don't fit but that some work wonderfully. This underlines the principle that you need lots of ideas to get some good ideas, and that 'answers' aren't right or wrong, but more or less useful in the end.

● Play name games. A couple are suggested above in the form of a name acrostic and an adjective list of words beginning with (in this case) **A**. Riddles based on names also allow children to imbue their own or characters' names with more meaning:

> I am not in hot but I am in h**at**
>
> I am in **n**ow and also in then
>
> I'm never in where but always in whe**n**
>
> Find me in angel, happy and ch**at**.

- the kenning is an old poetical form built of highly descriptive and active phrases and compound words. It can be combined with a name acrostic to good effect –

> **A**ble adventurer
>
> **N**eat dreamweaver
>
> **N**ifty storymaker
>
> **A**mbitious goal scorer!

- help children to gather up some name-related positive adjectives and put them into a word search on squared paper.
- incorporate names into tongue twisters: **Active Anna added addled adders**.
- work with children to create relationship webs based on their names:

						K				
						E				
		S	T	E		V	E			
		N				I				
		E		A	N	N	A			
B	R	I	A	N			I			
		L		T			G			
				H			E			
				O			L			
				N						
				y						

● Introduce the concept of pseudonyms and point out that a pseudonym can represent a writer's 'alter ego', allowing him to express himself in new ways, or deal with issues that his 'usual self' might find difficult. Emphasise that any writing produced in this way can be completely confidential.* A related activity encourages children to use a pseudonym representing a collection of traits drawn from other people and/or fictional characters.

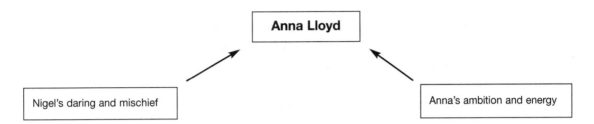

● Playing with names can throw up some good ideas in the field of genre fiction, especially the related areas of fantasy, science fiction and horror. Some techniques to bear in mind are:

  - alternative spellings of ordinary names to produce futuristic or 'otherwordly' names: Bryan, Steeve, Aana, Chrys.

  - transposing and/or dropping letters: Brin, Niel, Kven, Thony, Thon.

● Create a 'multi-person pseudonym', an author whose work is composed of the writing of a number of students. Some children's series of books are created this way, often when the initial author of the work has become highly popular. Beyond a certain point his/her name is used more as a marketing device, and ghostwriters pen most of the stories. The educational value of such a scheme in schools is that children must to some extent work collaboratively and to a previously agreed 'formula', template or brief.

● A similar idea is embodied in the creation of a fictitious place or setting where a number of stories can occur. In *The Double Dare Gang*, Kenniston is a made-up town composed of bits and pieces from many other locations. Manipulating geography in this way is not only good fun, but gives children the opportunity to plan settings carefully and, if working as a group, negotiate the placement of the location's constituent features.

* Steve wrote some adult Horror novels under the randomly – and serendipitously – chosen pseudonym of Ben Leech. Ben allowed Steve to express anger he was feeling at the time. Subsequently Steve used 'Len Beech' as another pseudonym in a collaboration he felt was not working. A further incarnation has been Philippa Stephens, for a teenage romance novel; while 'Stephanie Phillips' has appeared as a character in a few of Steve's other stories.

◆ Title match

Some writers insist on having a title to work to before they write; others are happy to let a title come to them during the writing. Having the title of story beforehand helps to keep the writer focused and to the point. Playing with titles is also a useful way of exploring genre.

● The titles below are taken from the linked genres of science fiction, fantasy and horror. Have children separate the titles into these three genres. Ask them to articulate the reasoning behind their choices.

House on Haunted Hill	Saturn Three
The City and The Stars	The Green Man
The Day the Earth Stood Still	The October Country
The Lord of The Rings	I am Legend
The Thing from Another World	Heart of Darkness
The Weirdstone of Brisingamen	Darkfall
Journey to the Centre of the Earth	Out of the Silent Planet
Close Encounters of the Third Kind	Quatermass and the Pit
The Fury	Creature from the Black Lagoon
Fantastic Voyage	The Illustrated Man
Forbidden Planet	An American Werewolf in London
From Beyond the Grave	The Changeling
Destination Moon	Planet of the Vampires
Stargate	Silent Running
The Time Machine	Dragonheart
It's Alive!	Don't Look Now
A Nest of Nightmares	I Walked with a Zombie
Somewhere in Time	

Note: If a title doesn't seem to fit clearly into any particular category, look at the activity called 'Lensing' on p.228.

● The same titles are reproduced below. Have the children cut them up and mix-and-match them to produce new titles (a few ideas follow). Collect titles relating to other genres to give the activity an extra dimension.

Example combinations:

An American Prophecy

Silent Changeling

Silent Invasion

Out of the Legend

The Illustrated Country

The Lord of the Haunted Hill

Time Encounters

The Thing from the Centre of the Earth ...

Tip: Use other StoryMaker techniques to develop the stories suggested by these recombined titles.

Destination Moon	Somewhere in Time
Stargate	The Green Man
The Time Machine	The October Country
It's Alive	I am Legend
A Nest of Nightmares	Heart of Darkness
Saturn Three	Darkfall

House on Haunted Hill	Journey to the Centre of the Earth
The City and the Stars	Close Encounters of the Third Kind
The Day the Earth Stood Still	The Fury
The Lord of the Rings	Fantastic Voyage
The Thing from Another World	Forbidden Planet
The Weirdstone of Brisingamen	From Beyond the Grave

Out of the Silent Planet	Planet of the Vampires
Quatermass and the Pit	Silent Running
Creature from the Black Lagoon	Dragonheart
The Illustrated Man	Don't Look Now
An American Werewolf in London	I Walked with a Zombie
The Changeling	

◆ Word maker

Exploring genre leads naturally into other areas of study:

- science fiction tempts one to learn more about science and technology
- fantasy encourages the reader into realms of mythology and legend
- horror too draws upon folklore and myth and shines a light into the darker corners of the human psyche.

Keeping these ideas in mind allows young readers and writers to understand the concept of genre more thoroughly, and helps to avoid the gratuitous use of motifs, characters and events.

While writing should always be fun, stories can have a depth that takes them beyond mere entertainment. Horror stories, for instance, have long been popular with children. While it is easy to disapprove of the – admittedly frequent – use of gratuitous violence and other generic effects, perhaps a more helpful strategy would be to guide children into using the motifs of the genre more meaningfully.

Steve has found that boys particularly love the gruesome and the grotesque in horror. If a group wants to make a story filled with zombies, for example, Steve explains that he's read dozens of zombie stories and he's bored with them now – so how will this one be original and interesting? Similarly, if the plot of a child's story is a direct copy of a film he's seen or a book he's read, Steve asks the writer to think of six changes or differences to make his story more individual. Combined with techniques such as 'Intention – output – effect' (p.20), these challenges often result in children looking at their stories more carefully and with a greater sense of purpose.

Exploring any genre necessitates looking at the vocabulary of that genre. Consider the following activities:

- **historical stories**: look at 'the words of the period'. Investigate how they were used and how they have changed over time (or why they have disappeared from the language).
- **romance stories**: look at the 'language of romance' and discuss the meanings of the words. Explore the emotions of romance and their nuances. (What are the differences between 'love' and 'infatuation', for example?). Investigate cliché and stereotype, and why the genre is so popular among certain sections of the population.
- **horror/mystery/thriller stories**: these genres often rely heavily on mood and atmosphere. Scan stories for 'mood-making' words and phrases. Look at scary, menacing and sinister scenes (from book or film) and discuss how the writer/director has achieved that effect.
- **science fiction**: examine the language of technology in SF stories. How do writers manipulate the language to create a sense of the future? Gather relevant prefixes and suffixes and recombine them to create new ideas for machines, etc. (See below.)

- **fantasy**: some fantasy tales are rich in the vocabulary of the genre: Tolkien virtually invented a new language for *The Lord of the Rings*. Trawl through fantasy stories to gather up the names of people, places and creatures. Investigate their etymology. Use them as inspiration for creating new words of your own.

Prefix-suffix mix

Have children add to the following lists, then mix-and-match (using root words as necessary) to invent new SF ideas and bits of technology. Allow alternative spellings and other manipulations so that the words look and 'feel' right as far as the children are concerned.

Prefix	Suffix	Root
ante- (before)	-able, -ible (capable of being)	aqua (water)
bi-, bis- (two, twice)	-ain, -an (one connected)	audio (I hear)
circum- (round)	-ance, -ence (state of)	centum (a hundred)
com- (together)	-ant (one who)	creo (create)
contra- (against)	-el, -et, -ette (little)	fortis (strong)
cyber- (steer)	-er, -eer, -ier (one who)	manus (hand)
ex- (out of)	-ess (female)	octo- (eight)
fore- (before)	-fy (to make)	porto (I carry)
hyper- (over, above, exceeding)	-icle, - sel (little)	primus (first)
inter- (between)	-less (without)	scribo (I write)
post- (after)	-ling (little)	unus (one)
pre- (before)	-ment (state of being)	vanus (empty)
re- (back)	-oon, -on (large)	video (I see)
sub- (under)	-ory (a place for)	voco (I call)
trans- (across)	-ous (full of)	volvo (I roll)

Even from this small selection a little wordplay will give us:

aquarette   *a little water capsule*

scribatory   *a place where writing experiments are carried out*

cyberling   *a little steersperson*

octofy   *(verb) to turn into eight of something as in 'Steve, will you octofy that cake for me now please?'*

interport   *a half-way house where you can stop on a journey*

audioon   *a large sound. This may be like a cannon shot, loud and brief, or like distant thunder – softer, but creating an impression of huge size*

◆ The scribe's road

Wordplay can also be used to look at objects anew. 'What's in a name? If a rose were called a sausage it would not be regarded the same!' Anglo-Saxon stories and poems are a rich source of descriptive phrases that give a new freshness and elegance to the things we see around us. Examples include:

war hedge   *the men in the second rank who held their shields over their heads as a protection*

giant works   *impressive architecture (left by the Romans)*

swan's way   *the sky*

rooftrees   *the supporting beams of a dwelling*

throng-noise   *the roaring of a crowd*

The strong and vibrant language of the Anglo Saxons is powerfully evoked in *Wordhoard* by Kevin Crossley-Holland and Jill Paton-Walsh, and *The Earliest English Poems*, translated by Michael Alexander (see Bibliography).

The act of reframing the language in this way helps children to see with new eyes. The activity also develops confidence in the use of words, encourages creative connections and offers insights into word origins. Have children make up new terms, like the examples below. Challenge another group to suggest what the terms refer to.

meltstone   **wordhoard**   **sky arrow**

              firestick   **datacoin**

       imagebox   **hourcircle**   **imageportal**

◆ Worldbuilder

The children's SF and fantasy writer Douglas Hill loves to set his adventures on fresh and original worlds that he has created from scratch. An important motivation must be the creative challenge of doing so, but Doug has also admitted that if anyone picks him up on some aspect of his setting he can reply with mischievous glee, 'Yes, I know the river is flowing vertically upwards, but it's *my* world and I can do what I like in it!' It goes without saying that the river is flowing upwards for good reasons, and those reasons will relate to the internal consistency of the story in terms of technology or the, perhaps altered, laws of physics. Thus like all good writers, Douglas Hill makes the world of the story believable, however fantastical it may be in terms of our reality.

Challenging children to make a world creates an opportunity to draw in knowledge from other subject areas. If a child wants a river to flow uphill in a story, then as part of her thinking time she must consider the dramatic reasons for the effect, as well as investigating ideas of gravity and/or the technological means to accomplish her vision. Beyond a certain point, what isn't acceptable is the assertion that the river flows upwards 'because I wanted it to'. If it flows by magic, then there should be at least some underlying rationale behind the magic. (Refer to Philip Pullman's *Dark Materials* trilogy to see how this is done superbly well.)

'Worldbuilder' requires careful thought and a certain amount of research. Numerous examples from science fiction and fantasy testify to the thorough planning writers put into the worlds they create: when we are there, we don't see how it could be any other way! When working with children who are just starting out on the scribes road, begin with little brainstorm games such as, 'What if gravity switched off unexpectedly every day for five minutes? What would the world be like? What problems would we have? And how might we solve those problems?' Questions like these allow children to have ideas and fun.

◆ The landscape of genre

An effective way of understanding genre is to use the metaphor of a landscape. Considering a genre in these concrete and visual terms allows children to see the Big Picture and chunk down this large idea into the smaller and more manageable concepts of sub-genre and motifs. As a child's wealth of reading experience grows, she will also be able to 'locate' the books she's read on the genre map in her mind (and wall display if you make it an ongoing class project!).

Studying a range of genre-based stories will provide the basis for mapping out the context of the tales. So:

- This story is spooky and mysterious and there's a ghost near the end!
- This story is about how a person thinks she's being haunted. But is she really? Maybe it's all in her mind?
- This story is about vampires and it's set in Transylvania in the 19th century…
- This story is set in the modern day and it's about giant monster mice that attack a town!

In creating the map you might use the actual titles of books, or just the main motifs to be found there. The result might look like an annotated story map (see p. xxx) or a tree (see p. xxx). Or perhaps you and your children will devise something refreshingly different.

The notion of sub-genre might be introduced at this point. A sub-genre is like a side branch off the main trunk, or a particular location on the map. There are generally recognised sub-genres, but there's nothing stopping you from thinking of your own. So, looking again at horror:

- Gothic horror involving tractless forests, gloomy castles, lightning storms, vampires
- modern urban horror featuring the city and a threat in the form of a human, non-human or animal
- atmospheric horror depending heavily on setting and creating a sense of menace; often includes ghosts and hauntings
- psychological horror - closely related to atmospheric horror, but with the element of ambiguity that the haunting (or whatever) is occurring within the mind of a character
- so-called 'body horror', which concerns itself with physical transformation
- supernatural horror which deals with occult matter such as witchcraft, etc.

As a teacher, reflecting on these sub-categories allows you to explore the issue of what you consider suitable material for children to read and write about. Horror has been used as an example because its content can be controversial – and because it is so popular among young readers. (Steve has written horror stories for both children and adults. Practically speaking, if children enjoy horror then by the time they enter secondary education most of them will be reading adult material. It is Steve's contention that stories written for children (whether they are horror stories or not) should take account of the age of the audience. That said, issues should not be avoided, nor material censored or 'sanitised'. Training children to be creative, flexible, independent thinkers with high emotional resourcefulness is the best way of allowing them to decide for themselves what they read, and to deal with the issues they encounter.)

Once children become familiar with the idea of genre, they are ready to start using their understanding through activities such as 'Genre overlap' and 'Lensing' (see below).

◆ Horror genre map

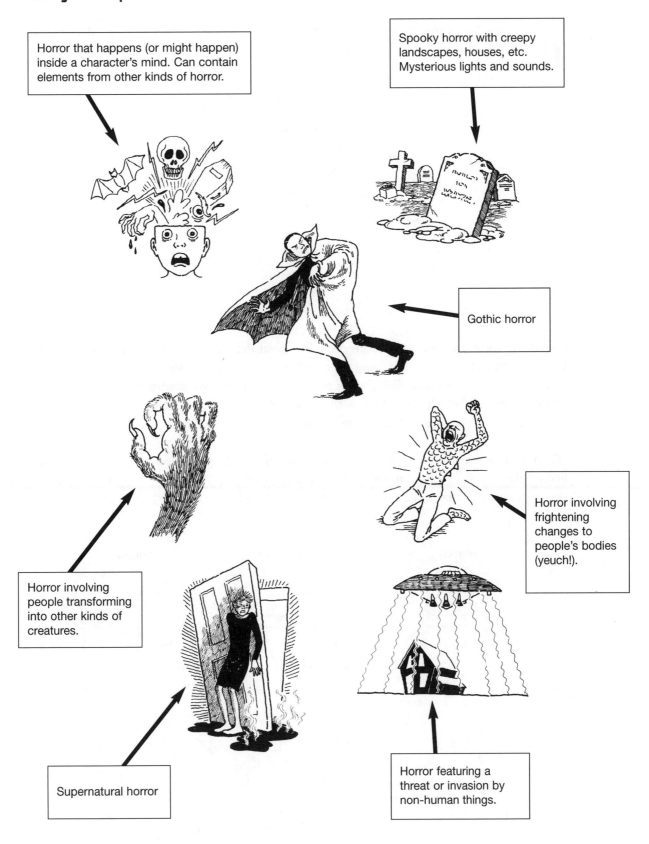

Horror that happens (or might happen) inside a character's mind. Can contain elements from other kinds of horror.

Spooky horror with creepy landscapes, houses, etc. Mysterious lights and sounds.

Gothic horror

Horror involving frightening changes to people's bodies (yeuch!).

Horror involving people transforming into other kinds of creatures.

Supernatural horror

Horror featuring a threat or invasion by non-human things.

◆ Genre overlap

If we consider genres as landscapes, then they are not separate unconnected territories. Rather, genres can overlap in all kinds of interesting ways.

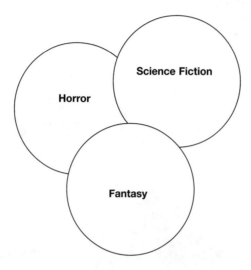

Looking at these areas of overlap can provide a great deal of useful material for storymaking. What would a story be like that contained elements of science fiction and fantasy? Or fantasy and horror? Or horror and SF? These genres in particular have traditionally been linked in literature, film and television – they are the Three Sisters in the world of fiction. But the possible combinations are far more extensive (see below).

When using genre overlap techniques, gather ideas for settings, characters and motifs through books, film, etc. Give children plenty of material to work on. You might also consider creating sets of genre cards that could be shuffled and recombined in an endless number of ways.

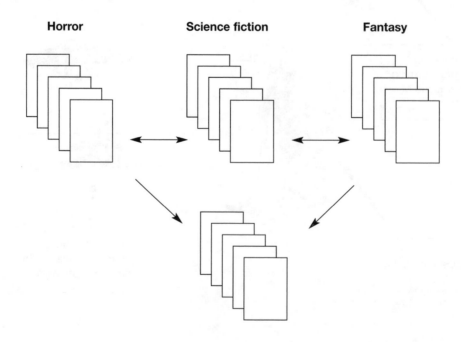

- Create sets of cards for a number of genres. Make each card specific, so that it includes ideas for a setting, character or motif.
- Shuffle the cards together to create a 'multi-genre' pack.
- Deal out the cards and brainstorm ideas as 'raw material' for storymaking.
- Use other StoryMaker activities to refine and develop the ideas.

Discard what doesn't work – write what does!

◆ Genre mix and match

	SF	Fantasy	Horror	Romance	Crime	Mystery	Western	Historical	War
SF									
Fantasy									
Horror									
Romance									
Crime									
Mystery									
Western									
Historical									
War									

Mix and match any two genres and explore what a story would look like containing elements from both of them. You might choose simply to brainstorm ideas or look in books and at films, etc, to choose specific elements for use in your 'genre story combo'.

◆ Genre coins

A more sophisticated technique is to prepare a number of cardboard discs. Write the name of a genre on each disc. Toss the discs and brainstorm a story combo based on the discs that overlap – *and in proportion to the degree of overlap:*

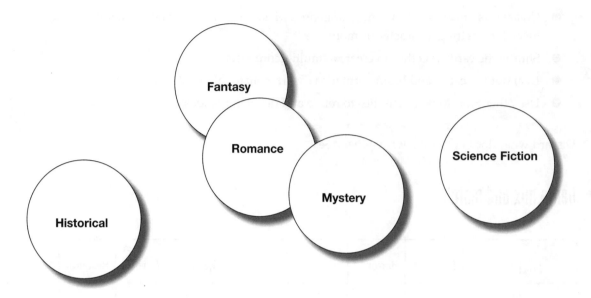

In this case the story would be a fantasy-romance with some elements of mystery.

Tip: Use similar cardboard coins as a random selection device for *any* story elements – characters, motifs, settings

◆ Structure and function

Structure and function is an important principle in science. The form of an animal, for example, fits with its environment and way of life. A giraffe has a long neck to reach leaves high up. New World monkeys have prehensile tails to help them swing through the trees, and so on. Similarly the design of machines is closely related to the job they have to perform.

Children's awareness of the principle of structure and function can be raised through the process of storymaking, and is linked with the idea that elements of a story are included for a reason that the author has considered. (See 'With good reason', p.128; 'But why?', p.201; and 'World-builder', p.219.) This notion can be expressed with particular clarity in genre writing, especially science fiction, where the 'internal logic' of the story has to be consistent, however closely it is related to the technology and physics of the real world.

Begin working with children in this area by looking at a small-scale and easily understood idea related to structure and function; for example, the colour and patterning of animals.

Animal	Colour/pattern	Reason
lion	tan colours, yellowish brown	to blend in with the grassy plains where they live, so that their prey won't spot them so easily
stick-insects	green/brown	to look like sticks or leaves as camouflage
humming-birds	various very bright colours	for display in mating and to distinguish between species

Look in the same simple way at other aspects of animal design.

Animal	Structure	Reason(s)
humming-birds	long, thin beak	to reach deep within the petals of a flower to draw nectar
iguana	eyes that can move independently in any direction	to spot prey and predators as early as possible
scorpion	powerful pincers/stinging tail	pincers to grapple with rivals and hold prey fast/stinging tail can arch over the scorpion's back – this makes it look more menacing, and the scorpion can also deliver its venom while holding its prey

Elaborate on the idea by examining the advantages and disadvantages of design features in a given example – in this case, us!

Feature	Design	Advantages	Disadvantages
eyes	two at front of head	high up on body for distance vision/two eyes allow for stereoscopic vision	relatively poor night vision / limited angle of vision
mouth/throat	connected to digestive system and lungs	muscles around mouth, the tongue, the larynx and connection to lungs makes speech possible	eating-digestive and speaking-breathing functions make choking a possibility
two legs/bipedal	upright posture supported by the spine	creates height for distance seeing/frees hands	posture puts pressure on spine leading to structural weaknesses

Subject specialists will be able to supply further examples and give insights into the structure/function relationship. Follow this up by gathering artwork and descriptions of creatures, aliens, environments and technology from the literature of science fiction. Encourage children to explore the examples further by using templates such as those suggested. Ask them to reflect on how likely/believable/improbable they find the aliens, planets and spaceships. Link this with the writer's intention. This leads to understandings that certain elements are included simply for dramatic effect.

◆ Literal and metaphorical functions

A further dimension to the structure/function relationship is that of metaphor. A story element that may not be literally accurate or true or very believable could nevertheless contain profound symbolic meanings. Many myths, legends and folk tales operate on this level as do motifs to be found in the 'Three Sisters' – the genres of fantasy, SF and horror.

Story element	Source/origin	Metaphorical function
Giant insects invading the Earth	1950's American SF movies. The 1954 movie *Them* is one of the best examples.	Insects represent the 'invading hordes'. The US was / is protective of its boundaries. In the 1950s the Soviet threat was very real. Insects also represent what is alien, mindless, relentless. Their giant nature represents the size or imminence of the menace. Gigantic insects or monsters were often created by atomic radiation, and so their use in stories symbolised a fear of the unpredictable, unknown and menacing changes it was felt that radiation could cause.
Dracula/vampires	Traditional element of folklore. Popularised in 1897 in Bram Stoker's *Dracula*, and throughout the 20th century in film and latterly on TV. Examples include Bela Lugosi's portrayal in the 1930s-1940s and Christopher Lee's interpretation in the Hammer films of the 1960s-1970's. Recently 20th Century Fox's series *Buffy The Vampire Slayer* has appealed to a massive worldwide audience, especially the teen market.	The vampire as an icon has altered over time, reflecting both its multi-faceted nature and the public's changing interpretation (influenced at least in part by the media). Originally vampires were parasites, to be feared because human beings were their prey and because they represented what was evil, unknown and tainted. More recently portrayals have imbued the vampire character with a certain pathos, coupled with a sense of suaveness and mystery, and even a sexual attraction. Recent interpretations have cast vampires as 'anti-heroes', misunderstood and feared but fighting on the side of good.
Dragons	Mythology, legend and folklore throughout history and across the world	Dragons have a huge and complicated mythology. They have been seen as both evil and good, benign and malicious. The ancient Chinese believed that solar eclipses were caused by a huge dragon trying to swallow the sun. They beat gongs and made a racket to scare it away. Christian tradition portrays the slaying of the dragon by St George as the triumph of good over evil, although modern readings of the pagan origins of the story assert that the dragon and dragon-slayer are locked in eternal battle, one never winning over the other. This represents the essential tension and balance of the cosmos embodied in the symbol of Yin-Yang. Recent filmic portrayals of dragons cast them as benign helpers of humanity, or even comic/cartoon characters.

Dreams also have a deeply metaphorical/symbolic structure. The literal aspect of any dream element is often a minor surface feature. Dreams have been called 'the language of the subconscious'. There is a large and growing body of literature linking myths and dreams – for example Roselle Angwin's *Riding the Dragon: Myth and the Inner Journey* – see Bibliography.

◆ Yin-yang thinking

One aspect of stereotypes and stereotypical thinking is the tendency to see things in black-and-white. Characters are either good or bad. Help children to give depth to their understanding of characters and genre by pointing out that we all have the capability to be both.

Use the following template to examine aspects of a character or character type. Invite children to place character elements on the side of good or bad – then help them examine how a 'bad' aspect could be used beneficially and how a 'good' aspect might be used for ill. Point out also that what is seen as good or bad depends partly on the context or circumstances and the interpretation we place on events based on our systems of belief.

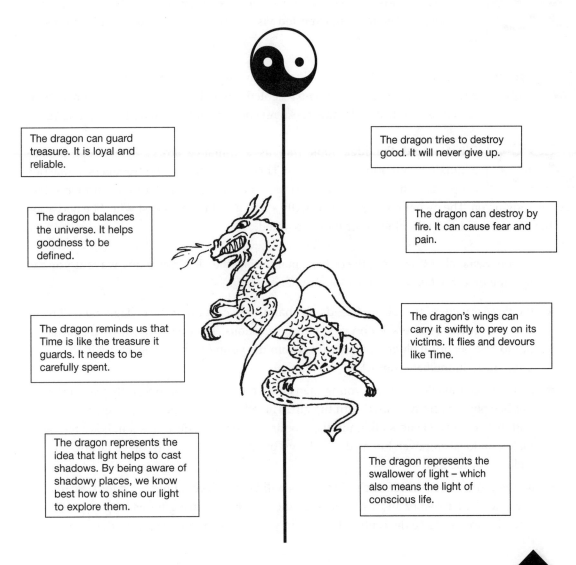

The dragon can guard treasure. It is loyal and reliable.

The dragon tries to destroy good. It will never give up.

The dragon balances the universe. It helps goodness to be defined.

The dragon can destroy by fire. It can cause fear and pain.

The dragon reminds us that Time is like the treasure it guards. It needs to be carefully spent.

The dragon's wings can carry it swiftly to prey on its victims. It flies and devours like Time.

The dragon represents the idea that light helps to cast shadows. By being aware of shadowy places, we know best how to shine our light to explore them.

The dragon represents the swallower of light – which also means the light of conscious life.

◆ Lensing

One idea does not necessarily make only one story. The principle of 'squeezing the orange' - getting the last drop of potential out of an idea – is a useful one for the working writer. One aspect of this process is *lensing*, which is looking at an idea in a number of ways, in this case through the spectacles of the different genres.

Take in initial premise –

> *Three people, a man and two women, are travelling along a forest road when their car breaks down. They leave the vehicle to find help and soon become lost. Presently they come upon a rather large and ramshackle old house in the middle of nowhere.*

 **What would this look like as a fantasy story?** Maybe the group finds that the house is enchanted and is the doorway to a wonderful magical realm.

 **What would the idea look like as a science fiction story?** Perhaps a brilliant but eccentric scientist owns the house and is engaged in dangerous genetic experiments. The three unexpected visitors provide ideal guinea pigs in his (or her) work.

 **What would the idea look like as a horror story?** The house is (of course) haunted by an angry spirit who resented the highway being driven through his land after his death. He now seeks revenge on all those who travel along it.

 **What would the idea look like as a romance story?** The house is well maintained but apparently empty. There is no phone. The travellers, a married couple and the wife's sister, decide to stay a short while to refresh themselves before moving on. The owner returns unexpectedly – and it is the man's first wife. She had a son by him, but gave birth to the child after they separated.

… And so on. Remember to squeeze the orange: manipulate the idea in as many ways as you can think of at the time. So, taking our idea for a romance story:

- the three travellers are college friends; the handsome captain of the college football team and two female admirers, both vying for his affections. The owner of the house turns out to be a beautiful older woman with whom the young man falls instantly in love. This causes immediate conflict.

- *or*: the three travellers are two young men and a girl. They are supposedly just friends, but one boy is secretly in love with the girl. The other boy has persuaded them to come with him for a weekend's hiking in the woods. The empty house (it's a holiday retreat) makes an ideal stopover, but as the hours go by the second boy discovers he also has feelings for the girl.

- *or*: the girl cannot decide which of the boys will be the object of her affections. Really, she enjoys their rivalry and wants to keep them both on a string for as long as possible. The plan for her to be the centre of attention works fine for a while, until the owner of the holiday cottage turns up – she's young, stunningly beautiful, and becomes immediately interested in both of the boys.

● *or:* the girl and one of the boys collude to make a plan to compromise the second boy, who comes from a rich and respectable family. However, he is no fool and sees through their scheme of blackmail. He pretends to play along, while secretly planning his revenge.

When you run this activity you are likely to find that ideas flow easily for a while but then begin to dry up. Once this happens, take a brain break and then switch to a different genre before proceeding. Out of the wealth of ideas you'll find some good ideas that you can begin to develop. 'Squeezing the orange' works especially well in conjunction with a Story Tree (see p.139).

◆ Themes and motifs

The mind makes meaning by association. The richer the map of reality and the more one practises the technique of making connections – and anticipates success – then the more easily and prolifically ideas will flow.

Accelerate the process by cross-connecting themes (which form the supporting framework of a story) with motifs that help to define its texture and style. Match a theme to one or more motifs and write down the ideas you have.

Themes	Motifs			
	Character	*Text*	*Place/Object*	*Situation*
Stepping over the line into forbidden territory.		They shook hands on the deal, although only Baxter was smiling.		Two characters, both desperate to outrun the past.
You get nothing for nothing. There is always a price to be paid.		'It doesn't matter what was said. The show must go on.'		If she can play her part well enough, the game will be won.
Change and transformation.		After what had happened life would never be the same again.		Two friends have one chance to mend the past and save the future.
Huge endings come from small beginnings.		'Don't worry. I'm sure you'll be able to get through this!'		Such a simple thing heralded the calm before the storm.

◆ Practice miscellany

H ere is a selection of simple activities you can use with children to improve their genre-based writing skills:

- **Saga retellings**: have children retell their own or someone else's story in a given number of words. Suggested lengths are –

    - mini-sagas – 50 words exactly plus a title of up to 10 words (or get as close to 50 words as you can)
    - midi-sagas – 100 words
    - maxi-sagas – 250 words
    - (for a real challenge) microsagas – 25 words

- **Acrostic list**: use a genre-based word as an acrostic to gather related ideas.

    A - attack, awesome, artificial, angry

    L - lizard, lifeform, lost, legendary

    I - interplanetary, invading, insidious, invisible

    E - Earth, energy, enter, engineer, egg

    N - night, nest, nervous, nemesis

- **'How would I do it?'** Notice how another writer has achieved a particular effect; a character description, setting a scene, evoking an emotion. Reflect on how you could/would do it differently. Or, deliberately emulate another author's technique in a different story or context. (This is not plagiarism!).

- **Guided fantasy**: work in pairs or small groups. All read the same story. Extract a number of key words that capture the essence of the tale, or at least evoke it in some way. One member of the group reads the words out, one at a time, with long pauses in between. The rest of the group, in a relaxed but alert state, allow the words to recreate the memories and experience of the story. (See Section 8, 'Visualisation'.)

- **'Just for starters'**: collect memorable opening sentences from stories children have not read. Discuss possible storylines from them.

- **'Twist in the tale'**: Cover up the final paragraph or page of a short story. Invite children to finish off the tale. Compare versions.

- **'From screen to page'**: watch a scene from a movie and write it out as a piece of narrative.

- **'Movie-maker'**: obtain a film script (You can often find extracts on the Internet and in some DVD packages). Study a scene and discuss how you would film it – What would the set look like? What camera angles would you use? What directions would you give to the cast?

- **Seed words**: Take a word and write a scene that exemplifies it – for instance, 'bizarre'.

- **'In new clothes'**: read classic genre tales or watch old genre movies. Rewrite them in up-to-date language in a modern setting.

- **'Blue pencil'**: have children edit each other's work. This does not mean mark or correct it. Ask children to pretend they are editors of a genre magazine. Help them define the aims, policies and standards of the publication. Decide on criteria for judging submissions. Help editors/editorial panels to apply and be true to those criteria as they consider work for publication. (Time permitting, why not publish the magazine afterwards?)

It is always possible to
use language in new
ways.

David Bohm

Section 6

Flexible text formats

Thoughts are things and the mind is the builder.

Edgar Cayce, healer

Section 6 — Flexible text formats

Page	Topic/activity	Story element covered	Accelerated learning link
234	Flexible text formats	*Layout/dialogue/visual (film) format/redrafting*	Strategies for skills development / visualisation/preview-review process/ preprocessing
240	The story so far	*Story summary*	Pre-processing/peripheral–subliminal learning techniques
241	Font styles & point sizes	*Layout/on-screen composition/font styles and 'mood'*	Pre-processing/peripheral–subliminal learning techniques
243	Elaborating text	*Appreciation of a story / review*	Pre-processing/ nonconscious learning and development of understanding
243	Subliminals, peripherals and nonconscious learning	*Insights into the creative process*	Subliminals, peripherals and nonconscious learning

Flexible text formats

◆ Flexible text formats

Text is most usually presented to children in large blocks (pages) which are split into smaller blocks (paragraphs) containing linear sequences of information (sentences) composed of individual units (words) joined in an infinite range of combinations. Although some account is taken of point size, with larger print being used for younger children or supposedly poorer readers, text size and style (font) remains constant throughout the writing. However, applying creative thinking skills to the formatting of text and the layout of pages allows children to access information in a variety of ways and therefore caters to a greater range of learning needs. Similar flexibility can be employed by young writers to plan, compose and review their own written work.

A selection of ideas is offered below. Feel free to adapt and add to these techniques.

Standard text

'Right, off you go. You have *all* of this lesson to work on your drafts, and *because* you'll be concentrating hard, I will expect absolutely *no* noise or talking *at all!*'

I got down to it after chewing my pencil for a few minutes...

'We were just ordinary kids from an ordinary town. There was no reason at all why it should have happened to us in particular...'

Actually, I ended up quite enjoying myself, and thought it wouldn't be a bad life to be a writer. I was almost disappointed when Kev put up his hand and waited for Mollie to notice him.

'Yes, Kevin?' she said heavily, pausing in her marking.

'Please Miss, my rough book's full. Can I have a new one?'

'You know it's your form tutor's job to give you a new book –'

'I'll carry on in my English book then, shall I Miss?'

'No, that's for your *best* work. This is only a *draft* of the story, remember...

Consider emphasising dialogue in a different way:

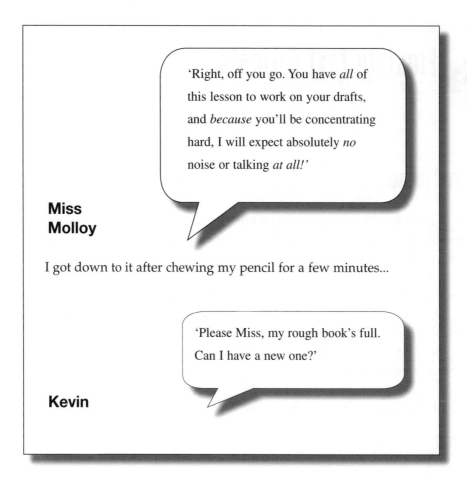

Miss Molloy: 'Right, off you go. You have *all* of this lesson to work on your drafts, and *because* you'll be concentrating hard, I will expect absolutely *no* noise or talking *at all!*'

I got down to it after chewing my pencil for a few minutes...

Kevin: 'Please Miss, my rough book's full. Can I have a new one?'

Prepare formatted pages that guide children in the balanced use of dialogue and narrative. This is of course a highly artificial approach, but you can wean young writers away from it when they begin to use dialogue more elegantly –

- to develop character
- to move the story on.

A suggested format is given in the following template. There are two characters. The unbroken rectangles indicate narrative overview.

Whole stories can be 'templated' in this way to give children definite but not restrictive support and direction in writing. Variations include:

● Have children pretend that they are film directors. The director has the use of up to three cameras. He or she can make notes in the side boxes about how the cameras capture the action as a scene unfolds.

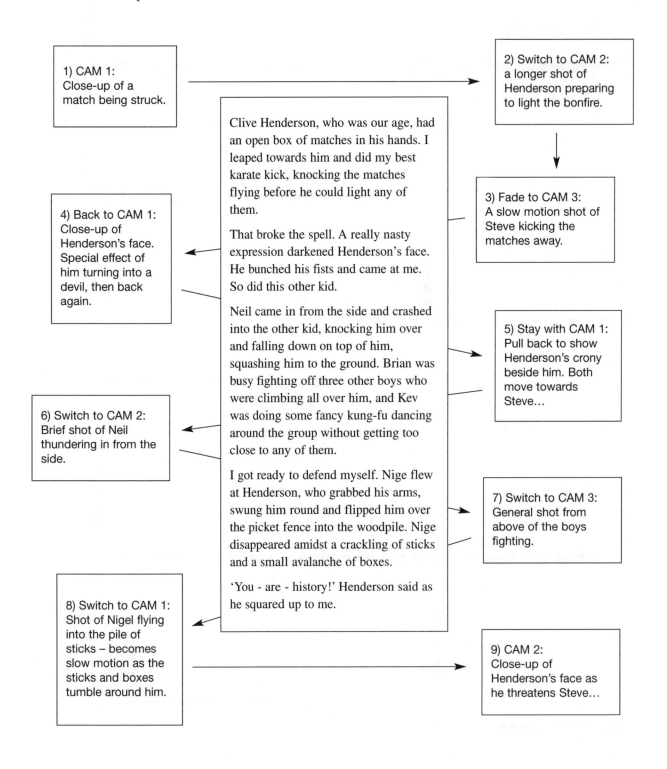

1) CAM 1:
Close-up of a match being struck.

2) Switch to CAM 2:
a longer shot of Henderson preparing to light the bonfire.

3) Fade to CAM 3:
A slow motion shot of Steve kicking the matches away.

4) Back to CAM 1:
Close-up of Henderson's face. Special effect of him turning into a devil, then back again.

5) Stay with CAM 1:
Pull back to show Henderson's crony beside him. Both move towards Steve...

6) Switch to CAM 2:
Brief shot of Neil thundering in from the side.

7) Switch to CAM 3:
General shot from above of the boys fighting.

8) Switch to CAM 1:
Shot of Nigel flying into the pile of sticks – becomes slow motion as the sticks and boxes tumble around him.

9) CAM 2:
Close-up of Henderson's face as he threatens Steve...

Clive Henderson, who was our age, had an open box of matches in his hands. I leaped towards him and did my best karate kick, knocking the matches flying before he could light any of them.

That broke the spell. A really nasty expression darkened Henderson's face. He bunched his fists and came at me. So did this other kid.

Neil came in from the side and crashed into the other kid, knocking him over and falling down on top of him, squashing him to the ground. Brian was busy fighting off three other boys who were climbing all over him, and Kev was doing some fancy kung-fu dancing around the group without getting too close to any of them.

I got ready to defend myself. Nige flew at Henderson, who grabbed his arms, swung him round and flipped him over the picket fence into the woodpile. Nige disappeared amidst a crackling of sticks and a small avalanche of boxes.

'You - are - history!' Henderson said as he squared up to me.

● Two text boxes side-by-side allow for easier redrafting. Alterations to the original text can be written into the right-hand box.

Original draft

Clive Henderson, who was our age, had an open box of matches in his hands. I leaped towards him and did my best karate kick, knocking the matches flying before he could light any of them.

That broke the spell. A really nasty expression darkened Henderson's face. He bunched his fists and came at me. So did this other kid.

Neil came in from the side and crashed into the other kid, knocking him over and falling down on top of him, squashing him to the ground.

Redraft ideas

Clive Henderson was our age, but much bigger than any of us except Brian. He was holding an open box of matches in his hand. I knew at once what he was going to do –

I leaped towards him…

… His expression darkened.

… this other kid, who was shorter and skinnier but looked just as mean.

Suddenly Neil …

Clearly this technique, along with other formatting devices, works well on-screen. If the activity is to be paper based, use loose-leaf sheets rather than notebooks and/or file cards, which can be physically moved around and, as necessary, dis-carded.

● *Side bars* accompany a writing space. They can be used for any purpose, but generally serve to carry reminders before and during composition, and for review notes afterwards. A sheet can easily be formatted to include them.

Preview	Do	Review
Remember apostrophes! Begin with Steve and Henderson. Then general action. Should Henderson already have lit the fire? – dramatic backdrop of flames. Lots of strong verbs. Plenty of action, not too much violence.	Clive Henderson, who was our age, had an open box of matches in his hands. I leaped towards him and did my best karate kick, knocking the matches flying before he could light any of them. That broke the spell. A really nasty expression darkened Henderson's face. He bunched his fists and came at me. So did this other kid. Neil came in from the side and crashed into the other kid, knocking him over and falling down on top of him, squashing him to the ground	'held', not 'had' I like the slightly comic touches. This isn't a hard or bleak story of the streets. It's kids up to mischief – a bit escapist maybe. Neil appeared suddenly from nowhere and crashed…

Use side bars for visual reminders. Ideas and prompts can be elegantly consolidated in children's minds as they prepare to write and then compose their first draft. (See also 'Grading and assessment' (p.93) and 'Subliminals peripherals and nonconscious learning' (p.243).)

Prompts	Main text
splat! " "	

◆ The story so far

Side bars can be used for brief summaries of the story up to that point, allowing readers to pick up the plot threads quickly and sail on with the action while nonconsciously also absorbing the concept and structure of such summaries and how these precede further story development.

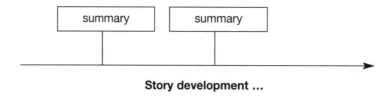

Story development ...

Use the same device for key words and key concepts paragraph by paragraph. Although children may not deliberately and thoroughly read this information, they will see it peripherally and assimilate it on a subconscious level.

The story so far:		It was hard work, because there were two of them on the Rope Swing: Nige keeping his face screwed up and turned aside, and Anna, who was looking at me seriously. I knew what her eyes were saying - that I was the only one stopping her from joining the Double Dare Gang. I was the only one left to tig.
Anna Williams wants to join the Double Dare Gang (really because she likes Nigel). Nigel, embarrassed by this, sets her a bravery test that Steve feels is both unfair and dangerous – going on the rope swing without help.	determination	
However, Anna's cleverness is revealed when she reaches the swing while Nigel is on it by climbing out of the oak tree. She has almost completed her challenge…	fairness	And I thought then, that Anna had been braver and sharper than any of us. She'd been given the challenge, and had planned it all carefully, even daring to go on the Rope Swing (though it hadn't been swinging at the time). And she'd done it all because she fancied Nige. I was almost jealous. As I hauled the swing in closer, Anna let go with one hand, and held her hand out for me to help her on to firm ground. I saw Kev's expression of shock as he realised what was happening.

◆ Font styles and point sizes

Increasingly children are and will be composing stories on a computer. One day (and sooner rather than later no doubt) pocket PCs will be commonplace that act as e-readers for downloadable books, databases with Internet access and fully functional word processors. Handwriting style has always been important, and these days an awareness of on-screen page design has to be too.

- Have children look at different fonts and discuss the mood they evoke and the kind of story they might be suited to. Here are some examples:

  - A quick brown fox jumps over a lazy dog   (Comic Sans SF)

  - A quick brown fox jumps over a lazy dog   (Garamond)

  - A quick brown fox jumps over a lazy dog   (Marker Felt Thin)

  - A quick brown fox jumps over a lazy dog   (Impact)

  - A quick brown fox jumps over a lazy dog   (Blippo)

  - A quick brown fox jumps over a lazy dog   (Times New Roman)

- Traditionally larger print has been used for stories for younger children. If composing on screen, consider using different point sizes (and perhaps font styles) – not just for ease of reading generally, but for different reasons within the same story: larger text could indicate faster pace, or something even more exciting or scary about to happen. Such emphases act as visual cues which reinforce the story content and help prepare children for what is about to happen.

From: The Double Dare Gang: 'The Frankenstein Steps'

I walked through the alley between the houses, and the wind caught me as I reached the top of the steps; which wound down the hill like a broad ribbon to the distant lights of the railway station below. Beyond the station was the river, and past the river was the park, and across the park was the main road and my house.

It seemed like a million miles away.

The chilly gust had made my eyes water. I rubbed at them, then scanned the steps carefully for any sign of someone – of something – lurking there. Of course, there was nobody; though it would have been nice if a train had just stopped at the station, and a load of people coming home from work had been making their way up towards me.

I had never counted the steps, but I reckoned there were about a hundred and fifty of them. There was a streetlight at the top (I was standing right under it), one in the middle, and one at the bottom...

With great stretches of darkness in between.

Even though I kept telling myself that Anna had just been trying to scare me, I felt all fluttery inside. And I didn't want to begin the journey down, because I thought that if I began to panic, I'd just run faster and faster – until I couldn't stop – and the wind would whirl me up – right into the arms of the man who'd been hanged on the Bowden Hill gallows – and then we'd both haunt the Frankenstein Steps forever!

In the town, I heard the church clock striking the hour. Six o'clock. I knew that Mum would be worrying – So I took a deep breath and started on my way.

As the brightness of the streetlight faded and the shadows gathered round, thoughts of ghosts and monsters and things that lived in darkness began growing in my head. I began counting the steps out loud, to calm myself down.

'One... two... three... four...' Then I counted seconds to keep myself busier. 'Five-one-forty... Six-one-forty... Seven-one-forty...'

After a couple of minutes I reached the safety of the middle streetlight; a pool of comfort where I could rest for a moment or two.

The night was huge on either side of me. I looked down to the bottom of the steps. They were deserted. I looked back up to the top –

And a figure was running down after me, his arms held out in front...

◆ Elaborating text

This term embodies the idea of creating or working out further detail within the world of the story, based on the material you are presented with. In other words, any device that prompts you to explore the story beyond what is actually given encourages you to elaborate the text.

Side bars are handy for asking questions to facilitate this process: again, you may direct children's attention towards specific questions, or make no mention of them and allow the ideas to be processed subconsciously.

I wonder what you would do if you were Steve? What other qualities does Anna have? I wonder how Nigel will feel about Anna now? Why do you suppose Steve is 'almost' jealous? Why 'almost'? What does Kev's expression indicate?	It was hard work, because there were two of them on the Rope Swing: Nige keeping his face screwed up and turned aside, and Anna, who was looking at me seriously. I knew what her eyes were saying - that I was the only one stopping her from joining the Double Dare Gang. I was the only one left to tig. And I thought then, that Anna had been braver and sharper than any of us. She'd been given the challenge, and had planned it all carefully, even daring to go on the Rope Swing (though it hadn't been swinging at the time). And she'd done it all because she fancied Nige. I was almost jealous. As I hauled the swing in closer, Anna let go with one hand, and held her hand out for me to help her on to firm ground. I saw Kev's expression of shock as he realised what was happening.

Discuss with your groups further ways of using side bars and other flexible formatting techniques. Be inventive!

Subliminals, peripherals and nonconscious learning

We learn with our whole brains and through all of our senses. Absorbing information, assimilating and 'incubating' it to come up with meanings and understandings is as natural a human activity as breathing or digestion. While we live, we learn anyway.

Traditionally formal academic learning has been highly selective in both its content and methodology. Recent and ongoing discoveries in neuroscience are verifying old wisdoms and giving new insights into how more effective, 'whole brain' learning can be achieved. One important finding is that although we do not pay conscious attention to all of the data that pours in through our senses, it is processed at a subconscious level and may with training be

243

consciously accessed more systematically – in other words, brought into the spotlight of consciousness to be developed further through our range of conscious (intellectual and logical) thinking tools.

Storymaking offers a wonderful example of how this entire process can work. 'The muse' has long been the friend of the writer. She has been mysterious, capricious, mischievous, elusive – a force to be cultivated and wooed. Accelerated learning concepts and techniques lead us to realise, however, that she can be called upon at any time and made to work to our will.

In the same way that vast quantities of information are woven to make meanings subconsciously, and then brought into consciousness to be exploited, so ideas can be introduced without conscious awareness and effort. So-called subliminal learning is coming to be seen as an important tool in the educational workshop.

Some terms:

- **subliminal** – 'below the line' or threshold of conscious awareness. Any information that enters the brain without being consciously noticed or processed is subliminal. Perhaps not surprisingly, *most* of our understanding of the world is built upon subliminal data. For instance, it has been calculated that ten million pieces of kinaesthetic data reach the brain every second. And yet, until it is brought to your notice, you have probably not been aware of your blinking, breathing, the position of your hands, the gentle feel of your clothing on your skin…

- **peripheral** – 'around the edge' of our conscious awareness. Peripheral information can be external or internal. External peripheral information might be something seen out of the corner of your eye, or a gentle sound you barely hear, or an aroma that evokes thoughts and memories that linger even though you have not consciously registered the smell. Internal peripheral information would include a tune that repeats itself in your mind, but which you only notice occasionally; or an idea that rests 'on the tip of your tongue'; or something that you know you have to do but you can't quite remember what it was… Internal peripheral information is more easily accessed without 'trying hard'. Achieving a state of relaxed alertness where you are receptive to the subtle presence of insights, intuitions, hunches and gut feelings brings subconscious material to the surface.

- **nonconscious** – that which is not conscious at the time; that which is working at a subconscious level. Our nonconscious field of mentality represents a massive resource. The therapist David Lesser once demonstrated this to a group of students in a large lecture hall: 'Hold up a fist,' David said. 'That represents the conscious part of your mind. Your subconscious is represented by the rest of this room.' Being aware of these ideas allows us to exploit subliminal learning techniques that enhance the work we do within the conscious arena.

Some suggestions for using subliminals, peripherals and nonconscious learning

- **Massage the senses**:
  - consider using music to create a range of moods within the classroom. Gentle ambient music is a relaxant. Baroque music resonates with the alpha rhythms of the brain to enhance that powerful learning state. Specific musical extracts can also be used in storymaking (see pp.286–7).
  - Create a colourful and visually rich environment. Incorporate peripheral learning devices into your displays (see below).
  - Use subtle fragrances to establish an association with positive expectation and the excitement and anticipation of learning. Practise VAK in the real world as well as in the world of the story!

- **Use spatial anchoring to accelerate learning**:
  - choose discrete areas in your classroom to associate with specific learning outcomes. You might, for instance, designate a spot where you deliver praise, another where you impart information for the first time, another where information is elaborated and developed, another where discipline and related classroom management tasks are dealt with, etc.
  - you can choose to tell your groups about these spaces or you may decide not to. The point is that they work subliminally: children will come to link the spaces subconsciously with their chosen purposes.
  - after a time you can use the spaces elegantly by moving between them as you deliver your lessons. As ideas are developed, go to the 'give praise' spot and the children will 'know inside' that you appreciate their efforts. If the class is too buoyant or inattentive for your liking, drift towards the 'give discipline' area and it's increasingly likely that they class will quieten as you pass through the discipline space to the 'give praise' area once again. Inventive assignment and use of spatial anchors will act as a subtle and powerful background feature of the learning environment you engineer.

- **Create display cards featuring key words, concepts, visuals, affirmations**: arrange them around the walls of your room above eye level. Children will look at these deliberately for a time perhaps, but then cease to pay them conscious attention. However, each time they glance upwards – which many people do as they remember or imagine something – they will be reminded of the content of the cards. Such nonconscious reinforcement coupled with skills to access subconscious information will boost children's learning ability.

- **Vary the font and/or point size** of text on your worksheets. This will subliminally reinforce key words and instructions.

- **Consider using coloured paper** for worksheets and for children to compose their stories. Anchor that colour with feelings of positive anticipation, enjoyment, achievement and success.

- **Make a text board** to allow children to understand sentence structure and punctuation. A text board takes the form of a large, laminated sheet featuring a story extract with the punctuation omitted. Provide card cut-outs of punctuation marks (or simple objects like counters, beads, shells, etc to represent punctuation) and allow children to move these items across the board into their correct positions. Their bodies will remember this learning experience.

- **Make bookmarks upon which you write** (or have children write) key words, spelling and grammar rules, useful concepts, affirmations, etc. Create a 'bookmark store' where readers can go to select a bookmark for their own use. They may study it briefly, and thereafter its content will be reinforced subliminally.

- **Have children write affirmations, key ideas, etc., on post-it notes** which can be stuck inside lockers, on books, on walls – no damage, temporary untidiness, permanent learnings.

Whether the techniques in *ALPS StoryMaker* apply directly to the conscious part of the mind, or whether they bypass conscious awareness to feed the creative subconscious, their aim is to use the external environment of the classroom to structure, modify and optimise children's inner environment – for it is there that stories are created as part of their greater understanding of the world.

Section Seven

 # The inner world of the writer

Always bear in mind that your
resolution to success is more
important than any other thing.

Abraham Lincoln

Section 7 — The inner world of the writer

Page	Title of unit	Story element covered	Accelerated learning link
249	Writing rituals	*Preparing to write/a resourceful state of mind*	Positive anchoring techniques/VAK
250	Six Big Important Questions	*Self-evaluation/a sense of purpose/greater control over the writing environment*	Independence of judgement/review skills/development of self-awareness / feedback
251	The confidence to write	*Self-evaluation/engineering a positive approach to writing / greater control over the writing environment*	Independence of judgement/review skills/development of self-awareness / feedback/neurological levels / emotional intelligence/anchoring techniques
254	Power reverie	*Visualisation skills/the active use of imagination*	Meta-thinking — awareness of and control over the conscious point-of-attention
255	Spiderweb daydreaming	*Visualisation skills/the active use of imagination/planning strategies*	Meta-thinking — awareness of and control over the conscious point-of-attention/target- and goal-setting strategy
255	Writing the wrong	*Writing blocks and strategies for overcoming them*	Strategic thinking skills/'meta writing' — writing about the writing process/use of metaphor and allegory to explore issues
257	Spin-a-yarn	*Planning and preparation using a web template*	Strategic thinking skills/goal-setting
258	Be an expert	*Detailed exploration of areas of a story*	Development of interpersonal skills / strategies to develop knowhow, authority and mastery within a context
260	Icon annotations	*Evaluation and analysis of text / distinction between fact and opinion*	VAK/developing an awareness of thinking skills/developing an awareness of subjective - objective statements
261	High on a hill	*Use of landscape metaphor for influencing attitude / development of confidence*	Use of landscape metaphor for influencing attitude/development of confidence
262	Motifs and meanings	*Awareness of the multilayered meanings of stories/metaphor / allegory/personalising story content*	'Meaning-making'/metaphor/allegory / personalising story content
264	Story symbol	*Consolidation of personal meanings in stories*	Anchoring/metaphor/allegory / personalising story content
265	How am I?	*The therapeutic value of writing*	Development of self-awareness / decision making and problem solving skills/chunking/feedback/strategies for working in a group
266	Uniquely me	*Awareness of connections between roles, relationships and attributes in characters*	Development of self-esteem and interpersonal skills/awareness of connections between roles, relationships and attributes in characters
267	Today's dare	*Development of self-confidence and resourcefulness in writing*	Framing techniques for resourceful states
269	The write attitude	*Consolidation of above*	Consolidation of above

Section Seven

The inner world of the writer

◆ Writing rituals

One of the hardest things for most writers to do is just sit down and start to write; surely this must be true for all deliberately creative people? Some kind of preparation is needed before the doorway to the subconscious can be opened, the conscious mind is receptive, and the world of the story is entered.

Such preparations may indeed be entirely subconscious. In this case, we simply 'feel in the mood' to write, or ideas begin to flow of their own accord. The writer Douglas Hill anticipates the enjoyment of the next day's writing before he goes to sleep – and wakes up eager to sit at his computer and carry on with the story (see 'Sleep on it', p.25). Steve has identified three distinct means of getting ready to write:

- sitting at the computer is a spatial/kinaesthetic anchor linked with the easy flow of ideas – just being there ready kickstarts the process
- re-reading the previous day's work mobilises the subconscious to 'pick up the threads' and continue weaving them
- using a 'worry chain' gives Steve something to do while his mind switches to relaxed alertness mode as he reviews the last sentence, paragraph or page and prepares to write the next. On no account does he try hard to think of what to say next!

Some writers have developed their 'preparation ceremonies' almost to the level of rituals. One novelist likes the have the house clean and tidy before he can settle to his work. It was said that Ernest Hemingway sharpened pencils to get him in the right (write) frame of mind. Marcel Proust supposedly kept overripe apples in his desk drawer and used the smell of them to set the creative saliva flowing (an olfactory anchor).

Although anything can potentially be used as a 'writing ritual', the device you use for yourself and your groups needs to be practical. Actually the entire classroom environment that you engineer might serve to create a sense of delight and anticipation at the thought of writing soon. The very act of looking forward to their writing time with you can be enough to prep-up children's minds to achieve. (Think of how story time is often arranged in primary school: there is a specific space set aside for the activity, which (preferably) is colourful, comfortable and relaxing. Going to the story corner and sitting down to listen is the little ritual children use to prepare to be enchanted.) More specifically, any specific sensory anchor can create the same effect:

- a particular sound, musical extract or style of music. (The storyteller Pomme Clayton sets out a square of colourful cloth before her sessions. She lays musical instruments out on the cloth, little bells and chimes and whistles, and uses them just before telling her story – 'to attune the listening ear'.)

- an aroma you use every time you want creative writing to occur. (You can even use different aromas to access the different intelligences children possess. Thus, you can have a numerical intelligence perfume, a linguistic intelligence fragrance, a personal intelligence scent, etc.)

- an 'ideas lamp' – an ordinary table lamp which you can switch on when you want the children to switch on to writing. The lamp represents the illuminations you know will occur as they create.

- a notebook specifically used for having ideas, and/or a general writing book where, for example, left-hand pages are used for scribbling ideas and overall preparation, and right hand pages are used for composition. (See 'Annotated notebooks' in Steve's *What's The Story?*)

- writing paper of a certain colour

- a particular pen each child uses for creative writing. (One of Steve's old jokes is 'What does the writer do when his pen runs out? He runs after it!')

- a mental device/visualisation that children can access. Here they will find all the resources they need to write successfully (See 'Safe havens' in the Visualisation section, p.279.)

Taking the time and trouble to allow children to prepare themselves effectively for writing will save more time and trouble in the long run.

◆ Six Big Important Questions

Although *ALPS StoryMaker* addresses the issue of creative writing in a classroom context, it also aims to act as a vehicle for resources that can be used throughout life. Writing can easily evolve from a pastime to a passion, from a hobby to a way of life. Whatever the scale of one's writing aspirations, it is important to ask the six Big Important Questions as a way of reviewing the preparations and learnings already made, and previewing one's ongoing intentions.

- When do you want to write?
- Where do you want to write?
- What do you want to write?
- Who do you want to write about?
- How do you want to write?
- Why do you want to write?

As a teacher you can ask these questions of yourself, and reframe them for your children to consider – When do I want my class to write? etc. There may be some discrepancy between the needs of the curriculum and the developing agenda of young writers (although it's always likely there will be plenty of overlap), so provision should as far as possible be made for those children whose imaginations have been fired by the idea of storymaking. A writing club during school hours or as part of an extracurricular programme is ideal.

In asking the six Big Important Questions, be sensitive to feedback and what that indicates. Children's responses to the questions will tie in with Dilts' model of neurological levels (see p.14) and provide a direct line to children's beliefs about what they can do. Most significantly, when children ask the Big Six for themselves, they will be well on the way to becoming independent creative thinkers – which is the ultimate aim of this book.

◆ The confidence to write

Creative writing, like every aspect of education, is a process that occurs on all levels – mental, emotional, physical. The 'storm of thoughts' that swarms through the mind as one learns, or is inhibited from learning, is reflected in a constant stream of emotional and physiological responses. Learning to notice these within oneself and others boosts one's personal intelligences. Follow this process:

- think about the next thing you want to/are required to write, and pay attention to your own reactions… What images and other thoughts passed through your mind? What feelings were you aware of? What other physiological responses came to your notice?

- go ahead and write for a short while. Once you have stopped, review the Six Big Important Questions and how what you did or were required to do fitted with what you wanted or needed to do. All the material you gather during this activity is significant. Move through the neurological levels and check back with yourself for positive or negative responses.

	Positive anchors	Negative blocks
Environment		
Behaviour		
Capability		
Belief		
Identity		
Spiritual		

- **environment** includes where and when we do things. What aspects of this support and boost your writing? What aspects inhibit the flow of ideas?

- **behaviour** means the details of what we actually do when we write. How do you sit to write? What implements/instruments/materials do you use? How do you use them? How do you manage the peaks and troughs of your concentration during writing? And so on.

- **capabilities** means how well we think we do things. As you write, what is going on in your mind of a self-evaluative nature? Do these thoughts serve to elevate or deflate your feelings of yourself as a writer? Let these feelings take you to a memory. Our responses are supported by a 'history of incidents'. What has happened to cause your current response?

- **beliefs** means why we think we do things. Take a little time to reflect on the purposes behind your writing. For every negative reason that occurs to you (if any do!) create a positive one. Reluctant writers may find the construction of a negative list an easy thing to do: offer them the challenge of matching that with a positive list. They may not believe those positive purposes, but at least their presence helps to cancel out the drip-feed of negative beliefs to the subconscious.

- **identity** means who we think we are, and how (in this case) writing contributes to it. Since we are largely defined by our choices, the ability to choose is a powerful force in life. Storymaking is all about making choices: it is a process that models what we do as we create our own life-story. Writing can also be a very therapeutic, a very liberating experience. It clarifies our ideas and feelings; it builds a framework within which we can dare to dream (within a time-scale!). For many writers, the act of writing makes them what they are. *

- **spiritual** means an awareness and understanding of the deepest purposes of our existence, a connection between the individual and the cosmos. In this regard 'spiritual' need not mean 'religious'. Spiritual aspects of life are to do with the capacity to wonder and the ability to realise occasionally that simply being here now is in itself a wonderful thing. ** Spiritual awareness, like having ideas and watching them unfold on the page, is an *allowance of something happening*; it is not forced, nor largely the product of intellectual effort. To give permission to yourself for compassion and awe and reverence in the face of all created things is, if you like, returning to a natural state of being. To *be the process* of living in this state literally embodies and expresses spirituality. This level of ourselves is both the platform of life and its peak of experience. ***

* The writer Douglas Hill was once taking questions from a young audience. One little boy said, 'Doug, do you love to write?' To which he replied, 'Son, do you love to breathe?'

** Zen koan are elegant little puzzle-stories that can lead to illuminations. One of the most well known and delightful concerns the learner who said to his teacher, 'Master, I have been here for a long time now and I still don't think I understand the highest purpose of life.' The master replied, 'Have you finished your rice? Yes? Then wash your bowl.' That was the essence of his lesson.

*** The notion of 'Spiritual Intelligence' builds on Howard Gardner's idea of multiple intelligences. Our capacity to be spiritually oriented beings is a potential we all possess. Like Maths, language, music or any other ability, 'SI' needs to be developed and explored through systematic programmes of training and learning – like creativity, it is not mysterious and elusive, but a vital energy we can come to understand and exploit.

- Take a feeling (such as a lack of confidence when writing). Give it the following: a name (any name), a colour, shape, size, texture, weight, temperature, a sound when you tap it with a pencil, a location inside your body (notice where you feel it within). Now – change each parameter one by one but quickly, without giving yourself time to 'try and think of answers'. When you have shifted the re-formed feeling somewhere else inside, do something outrageous with it: give it wings and let it fly away, dissolve it in water and pour the water down the drain, scrunch it up like paper and toss it into the waste bin. Give your imagination free rein (free reign?). Now how do you feel? (For an explanation of this technique, see *Self-Intelligence* p.103: 'Dealing with feelings'.)

- Write about a feeling that you want to change. Describe it, personify it (see 'Old Man Envy', p.190), explore it. Put the notes into an envelope and write a date on it – the date by which you will have changed that feeling. Each day between now and then, write down at least one thing you can do to change the target feeling. A week after you have started your 'list of changes', begin to implement them one at a time. Take positive direct action on a regular basis. When you arrive at your target date, open the envelope and immediately write down how the feeling has changed – plus any insights for transforming it completely. Act on those insights in the same systematic way.

- 'Consolidation anchors': 'Writing rituals' focused on creating positive associations as you prepare to write. 'Consolidation anchors' uses writing itself as a resource, plus any other activity that fills you with pleasure, pride and a sense of achievement. This is how to do it:

  - Select an anchor. This is something you think, say, do – or all of these – to which you can attach your bundle of positive feelings. (You need to decide to 'fire the anchor' consciously. One of Steve's anchors is to rub together the thumb and little finger of his left hand - this is an action that you are not likely to do unintentionally.)

  - Each time you do something which gives you pleasure, confidence, etc., notice how you feel and fire your anchor. You will soon come to associate those positive feelings with the anchor. Whenever you encounter limiting circumstances or feelings, fire the anchor and notice the wash of positive feelings you get.

  - As it becomes appropriate to do so, link your anchor to the writing process. As you write, and enjoy it – fire your anchor. As you read through your day's output and feel that sense of achievement – fire your anchor. Make it part of the total experience of gaining satisfaction and personal power from your storymaking.

You can create a menu of anchors for different purposes, allowing you to deal more effectively with different situations and blocks. As these become more powerful and effective in yourself, consolidate them by linking them to a symbol of your choice. This might be a physical object, but also an image in your mind. Whenever you touch or think of your consolidation anchor, you are tapping into the resourcefulness you've created for yourself.

Steve's consolidation anchor is a spider-web. All routes lead to the centre, and from the centre expansion can occur in any or all directions.

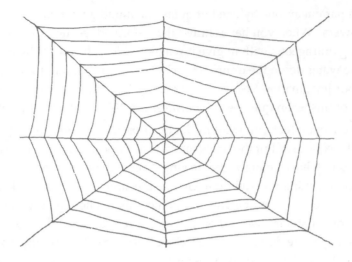

◆ Power reverie

Daydreaming has acquired the reputation of being a pointless waste of time, whereas in fact that state of mind – where the conscious attention is relaxed and uncritical and where the door is open to the creative subconscious – can be used for a variety of purposes. Indeed, writers may very accurately be described as professional daydreamers!

Common-or-garden daydreaming is usually unintentional. We 'lapse' into a daydream and let our attention idle. Images come and go, drifting across our mind's eye. Sometimes a short run of thoughts link together and make sense – a 'train of thought' – but then we settle back into the peace of passively listening to the subconscious mind's endless, busy chatter.

It need not be so. Reverie can be induced at will and for a purpose. It is important to have a purpose that is clearly imagined, simple, straightforward and precise. If the issue is a lack of confidence in writing, affirm to yourself that you will have an insight as to the cause of that behaviour – just one memory that makes sense to you. Stare at a blank space (this is often better than closing your eyes, which has associations of sleep) and let your thoughts drift. Make no conscious effort to remember: let the imagery come to you.

Like any skill, 'Power reverie' needs to be practised. Be patient with yourself, yet be quietly determined that you will succeed. Once the reverie is over, ending spontaneously or through choice, jot down any ideas that have occurred to you. It doesn't matter if these don't make sense, or don't seem significant. They soon will.

Steve once showed a writer friend how to use 'Power reverie'. Chrisy's particular problem was that, once she had planned her story, she found it very difficult to make progress with the actual writing and felt constantly frustrated by her efforts. Allowing herself to relax, Chrisy decided she would soon understand the reasons for the problem. Within minutes, two clear images came to mind… The first was of herself typing at the computer *with the monitor switched off*. This was both an insight and a resolution: Chrisy knew she had been trying to edit as she composed – two conflicting actions.

The second image showed two acquaintances who also had aspirations to write and who often advised Chrisy on her own work. They were crossed out like incorrect maths problems. Chrisy knew that their advice was not needed, and may anyway not have been well-intentioned.

◆ Spider-web daydreaming

This is another way of using reverie – relaxed alertness with the attention internalised – more systematically. Imagine a spider-web, or work from a picture. Imagine that the problem lies at the centre of the web and that a range of possible solutions lies at the margins. Imagine that your daydream will take you there in a series of clear steps…

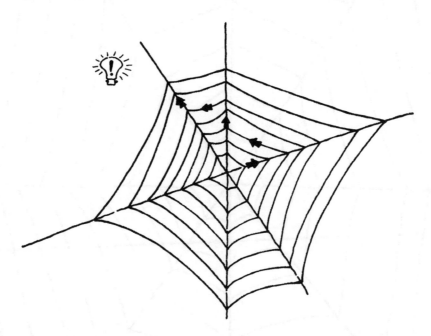

This activity works well with a partner, who can ask you simply to describe your impressions as they come to you (pole-bridging), and focus your attention with a few well-placed and elegantly-framed questions. Tape-recording the session allows you to create and 'edit ' your output separately!

◆ Writing the wrong

Sometimes when writers are faced with problems in their work, they give up through a failure of nerve or a failure of imagination and the story is left abandoned as a potent symbol of that-which-was-not-achieved.

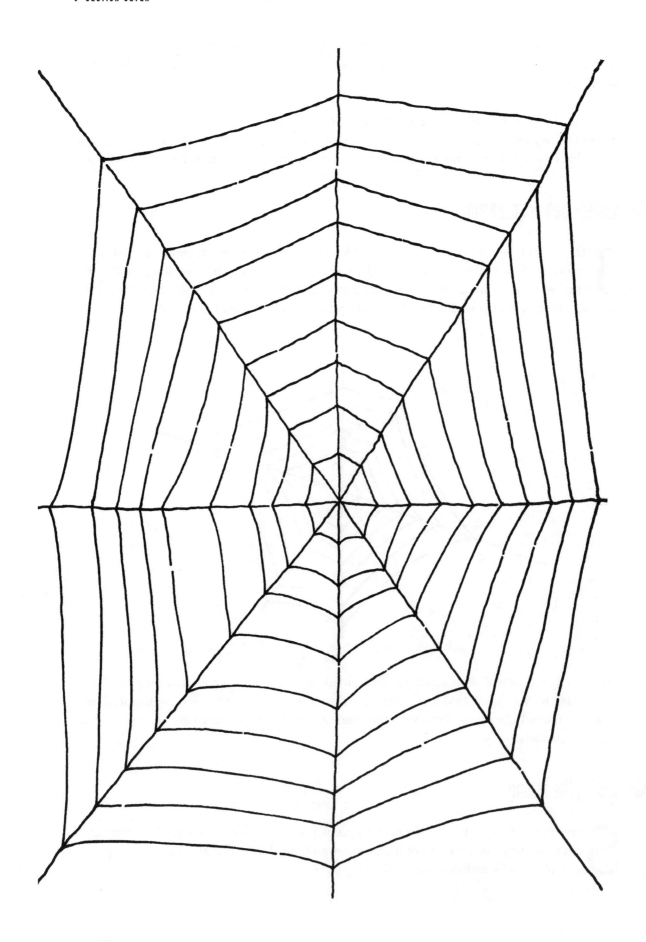

One strategy for resolving (re-solving) the situation is to write your way out of trouble – keep writing until the block has cleared and you know you are sailing in open waters again. You can go about this in a number of ways:

- Have two projects running concurrently, a major piece of work and a minor enterprise. If you experience a difficulty or block with the main endeavour, set it aside and move to the minor work. When you have finished it (remember to fire your consolidated anchors!) return to the big project. You are likely to find you can continue unhindered.

- Most writers have several projects 'incubating' at different stages of formation. If you have problems with the work you are actually writing, direct your attention to a story you are still just thinking about. Make some notes, develop it a little, get excited about it. You can return to your big project energised and refreshed.

- Do 'meta writing' – write about your writing and the difficulties you've encountered. Apply storymaking techniques to the problem itself. Write about a writer having the problem you had. How did he/she overcome it? Learn from your character.

- Turn your problem into a character and chat with him/her. Use perceptual positions (see p.188) to gain different perspectives. Be the problem and explain yourself (away).

- Use metaphor: create a parable – make it up as you go along – which indicates at least one way out of the difficulty. (See *Imagine That* pp. 126-130: 'Day-to-day parables'.)

◆ Spin-a-yarn

Link this activity to 'Spiderweb daydreaming'. The initial premise for the story (an idea for a character, a picture stimulus, a context sentence, whatever) is placed at the centre of the web template. Developments of that idea can proceed in any direction. Children can work by themselves, in pairs or small groups. The template can then be used in several ways.

Imagine that each point on the circumference of the web is a story ending/resolution. What might they be? The activity then involves working out what can happen, in various storylines, to link the centre to each outer point.

Use a dice to move freely about the web, though with the intention of reaching the outside from the centre: 1 = up, 2 = down, 3 = left, 4 = right. A decision relating to the progress of the story lies at each junction. At that point, roll the dice to see where it takes you. If you go back, review the story up to that point, take out any elements that don't work and add any that work better. If you go left or right, switch to another character or scene happening concurrently with the point you've just left. If you go up, your new scenario must move the action or character on in some way towards the resolution of the story's original conflict.

Imagine that the centre of the web is the story's initial premise/problem. The points on the circumference represent a range of viewpoints or perspectives in dealing with the issue. These may be embodied by children in a group and/or characters from this or another story. Each step taken towards the centre represents a decision made or an insight gained. Cross-links represent opportunities for children/characters to talk together and swap ideas. A step towards the centre is taken only when a child is confident of the effectiveness of her decision or idea in moving the story forwards.

The centre of the web represents where a character or author-narrator is standing in the landscape of the story. The concentric rings of the web represent an increasingly expanding viewpoint as the character/author learns more about the story and has insights as to how it might resolve. The points on the circumference represent the range of resolutions possible through reflection, insight and decision-making. This technique is a bit like standing in a story map to explore the geographical setting and, simultaneously, the structural context of the narrative.

There is a clear analogy between the web and the process of goal-setting. Either the centre or any of the outer points represents a fixed goal. The strands of the web represent chains-of-decision towards that goal. The nodes represent targets on the way to achievement. The crosslinks represent the idea that strategies are not fixed as the goal is fixed, but that any number of routes towards that goal are possible. Furthermore, backtracking to an earlier node is not an admission of failure or defeat, but a shrewd move involving re-evaluation of information and the opportunity to take a more useful or effective way forwards.

The 'Spin-a-yarn' template can be used as a straightforward plotting device. It is included in this section because once children are familiar with the concept they can use it as a tool in the broader context of their lives to define, explore and resolve issues.

◆ Be an expert

If the process of creative writing is conducted in a supportive environment where curiosity, independence of judgement and willingness to explore are celebrated, then children can very easily feel a sense of ownership and authority with regard to their creative fiction. This is a very different scenario to that of young writers offering up some fragile personal creation solely for comparative assessment and critical evaluation. These are necessary, perhaps, given the current educational ethos, but should be introduced when children's emotional strength and resiliency allows them to have a healthy perspective on an adult's subjective opinion of standards.

'Be an expert' can be used effectively with other storymaking techniques. Individuals or groups are directed to explore a certain area of the story; to find out more through discussion, questioning, research, dice rolls, etc, and then to report back their findings to the whole group. It is explicitly understood that they will be the voice of authority for that part of the story. So:

Story map

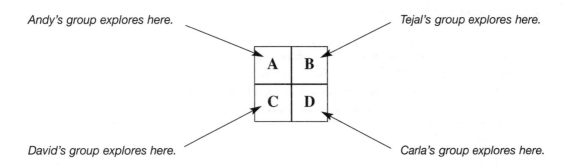

Andy's group explores here.

Tejal's group explores here.

David's group explores here.

Carla's group explores here.

The different areas of the map may contain elements previously created by the whole class: A might feature mountains, B a town, C an abandoned building, D a forest, etc. Groups can also be put in charge of different characters in the story, fleshing out basic details agreed earlier.

Story tree

Andy's group explores here.

Tejal's group explores here.

David's group explores here.

Carla's group explores here.

Story path

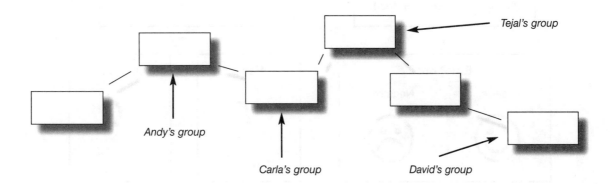

Tejal's group

Andy's group

Carla's group

David's group

In the case of the Double Dare Gang, groups could be asked to find out more about the characters' families and backgrounds, do research on the setting for the stories, draw a more detailed map of the allotments and who tends them, etc. The opportunities to allow children to feel a sense of ownership and authority for their work are numerous.

> 'The process of being consulted, having one's opinions seriously considered, feeling that one's contributions are valued and that they may well result in change for the better are all powerful builders of morale, confidence and commitment' (with reference to the BASIS model: HMI 1989, *Effective Primary Schools*, quoted in *Accelerated Learning in Practice* p. 102).

◆ Icon annotations

The distinction between observation, deduction, speculation and opinion has already been made. Children can practise these thinking skills by inventing icons to represent them and then using side bars to annotate text. If working on-screen the icons can be cut-and-pasted pieces of clipart: if the work is paper based, simply drawn shapes or coloured sticks may be used.

Work with the children to devise an appropriate menu of icons. Some suggestions are:

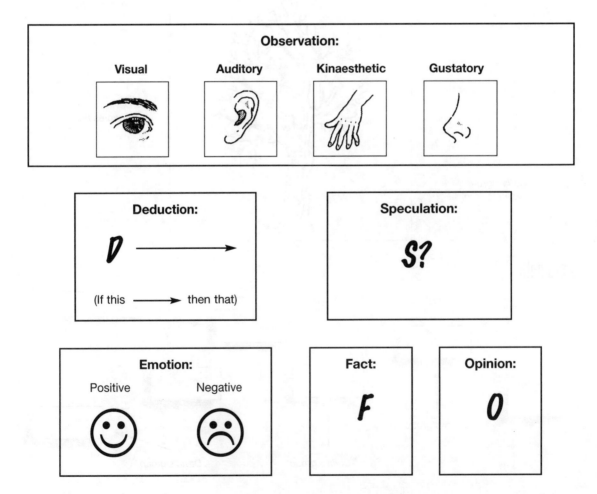

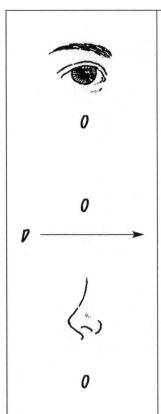

We reached the shop in plenty of time before it closed. The town centre was busy, with queues of rush-hour traffic waiting at the lights, their exhaust smoke blooming in the air. People were hurrying home wrapped up in hats and coats and scarves, and the coffee shop on The Square was busy behind its steamed-up windows.

Mr Lee's was a tiny, **tatty-looking** shop down a side street just off the main thoroughfare. It was squashed between a newly-opened Balti house and a mobile phone showroom. The smartly dressed young man in the phone shop glared at us when we pressed our faces against the window, and mouthed something that made Nige laugh. When he got up from his desk and headed for the door, we legged it and piled into Mr Lee's...

Mr Lee had been around forever. My Dad said he used to come into the Joke Shop when he was a kid, like centuries ago. **And Mr Lee seemed the same then as he did now**, Dad said. He was a long, thin man with a slight stoop - probably caused by his years of bending to avoid hitting the rubber bats and horror masks and vampire wigs that hung from the ceiling.

The shop had an odd smell; not nice but not nasty - both at the same time. A nostalgic smell. Sometimes when I went in there to buy or browse, I thought I could smell the sulphur stink of fart powder; sometimes the air was peppery; and sometimes quiet with the scent of make-up and cardboard boxes and plastic.

Not that it mattered; **I just enjoyed going in there**.

Mr Lee smiled at us vaguely as we entered…

Once children become familiar with using these and similar icons, they can be applied in other contexts, such as the children's own diaries and journals, and pieces of non-fiction. Although the language of the sciences aspires to be detached and objective, closer inspection often reveals opinions mixed with facts, and speculations and value judgements which may well amount to the opinion of the writer and/or a particular section of the scientific community.

When children realise they have expressed an opinion or value judgement, they can be encouraged to look at the information and ideas on which these are based. Opinions are fine, but are acknowledged and respected more when they are soundly based and well considered.

◆ High on a hill

The outer environment helps to define the writer's inner world, while his 'map of reality' shapes his view of the world outside. Perception is projection. The notion of landscape can be used in a metaphorical way to help an individual to explore issues, gather resources, develop self-awareness and modify behaviours.

Work with children to develop a list of features from the landscape. Consider any negative connotations as well as positive ones, so that a deliberate choice can be made to go with the positive: this may also lead to insights related to negative thinking and blocks in an individual's development.

Here are some suggestions:

Feature	Negative aspect	Positive aspect
River	Follows the same course. Can get blocked. Never direct.	Goes with the flow and can move over and around obstacles if necessary. Constantly changing in its nature depending on outside circumstances – but always essentially itself. Without the river, the surrounding landscape would suffer.
Mountains	Hard to climb. Cold. Exposed to the elements.	A challenge to climb. Once at the peak, they offer a wonderful vantage point. Strong and upright. They help to define the character of the land around.
Forest	Dark and impenetrable. Unknown.	Can be explored, given curiosity, care and a strong light. Forest tracks can usually be found. The forest is a haven for a rich diversity of life. Only unknown until it has been investigated.
Desert	Hostile. Hard to live there. Shifting sands.	The desert is shaped by its circumstances, but is fully itself. Only hostile until you understand its ways. Learning to live there requires awareness, ingenuity, resourcefulness. The sands shift to accommodate the winds, but the wind does not destroy the character of the desert.

Once these connections have been made, a story map (see, for example, p.117) takes on a deeper significance, and insights into allegory and parables can occur more readily.

◆ Motifs and meanings

Although every element in a story should serve a purpose as far as the writer is concerned, it isn't necessary of course that stories be multilayered, deep and meaningful, or offer an elegant commentary on the human condition. However, as 'My favourite story' (see p.157) asserts, readers will often draw personal meanings out of a story that the author did not intend in any general sense to include. Stories form the interface between writer and reader; they are complex and elegant structures that evoke meaning making at all stages of their existence. Stories hold lessons for us at many levels, whether or not they set out explicitly to teach. That is the power of the tale, which people can take into themselves and use within the greater context of their lives.

The link between motifs (the constituent features of a story) and meanings has been made throughout this book. A variation of this process encourages children to apply what they learn from stories in their own lives. This is not to say that they 'have to obey' the lesson of the story: a story is not – or should not be – a commandment to be slavishly followed. (Steve's Double Dare Gang stories were originally declined by more than one publisher who thought they were 'subversive'. One editor felt she couldn't possibly accept stories that depicted children stealing and playing practical jokes on teachers. Steve's response that the stories raised issues in order to suggest resolutions went unanswered…) Rather, it is what the writer Barbara Hoberman Levine calls a 'seedthought', or rather a bed of seedthoughts, which grow in their own time into understandings offering choice.

Techniques such as 'Questioneering', 'Unfolding' and others found in *ALPS StoryMaker* serve to encourage the process, but do not aim to boost children to a certain level of comprehension by the time they have reached a particular age. The mind is not a vessel to be filled, but a fire to be kindled. Stories 'prime the potential' and strike a few sparks.

The following template is offered to clarify the idea of motifs and meanings. It is not suggested that children should fill in dozens of examples. Once the idea has been understood, links will be made nonconsciously. Note the relationship between what certain motifs might mean and the intended themes of the story (and possibly themes that run through the lives of some readers).

Example story: 'The Allotment Ghost'

Motif	General significance	Have you experienced anything similar? What happened?	What does the experience mean to you?
The allotment	It's someone's territory. There are boundaries around it. What's in it is precious and has been cultivated with care.		
Sneaking into the allotment	This is about risk-taking. It's also about the pressure to do what your friends are doing. The 'dare' is like a chain that links you all together.		
Old Man Jones	He is like the ogre or the fierce dragon guarding the treasure. He is 'the enemy' to be feared but challenged.		
The gooseberry	This is the forbidden fruit. It is not eaten, so remains untasted. It also represents everything that has been grown in the allotment.		
The big stick	This is punishment, the rule by fear and pain.		
The broken glass	This is nemesis; a punishment inevitably attached to the act. In this case it comes by some unexpected means. The lesson to be learned is cut into the boy's flesh. He carries the scar to remind him that memories are stored in the body as well.		

263

◆ Story symbol

In a way, a story can be a 'bagful of symbols': for the reader, everything can be meaningful. An extension of this idea is to consolidate those meanings by asking the question, 'If you could choose anything to represent this story, what would it be – and why?' An answer to this amounts to a metaphorical representation of the story content and suggests what meanings and significance the reader has drawn from the tale. Such a story symbol might be something taken from the story itself, though it need not be. Some examples below illustrate the point.

Story	Symbol	Significance
The Allotment Ghost	The ripe gooseberry	It is something ephemeral in itself, and yet it's linked to a lesson that is remembered forever.
The Frankenstein Steps	A spark	The moment when your imagination can overwhelm you with something frightening is like a spark in your chest.
Mollie and The Great Removal Plan	A 'laugh-in-a-bag'	It is the capacity to laugh even at an unpleasant experience.* This shows you have learned something from it and grown. It is also the laughter of the Trickster, who makes mischief in the universe.
The Gift	The snow	The snow is a gift and a true treasure. Like the people of the Earth, each one is different. Like a life, each flake is fleeting and unique.

* An ancient Arabian proverb says 'The situation is impossible, but not serious'.)

Note that the examples and rationales given above are my own. Children may be less sophisticated in explaining why a symbol is significant – indeed, they may not be able to explain it at all. That's fine. As the wisdom has it, you don't need to understand something completely to use it effectively. A symbol can hold great significance even if the understanding and justification come later.

Consolidation symbols

Look back to the idea of 'Consolidation anchors' on p.253, and see *Self-Intelligence* p.138: 'Stepping stars'.

In the same way that we can summarise and symbolise the complex of meanings enfolded into a story, so can we represent a network of skills, resources and achievements in our own lives through the use of a symbol. This may be a visual image, a real or imagined sound, an aroma, some physical object. Once we have decided upon such a symbol, we invest it with more meaning whenever we bring it to mind and link it with some positive aspect of our lives. Increasingly, an image (or sound, etc) of the symbol will 'come into our heads' spontaneously as a subconscious acknowledgement of the positive power of the representation.

Steve's consolidation symbol is a little caricature of a wizard, complete with pointed hat, long dark robes decorated with stars and a black wand crackling with energy. When the wizard holds out the wand Steve imagines grasping the other end in his left hand and not letting go. The wand is the magical link between the creative subconscious and the rational, ego-centred, conscious 'I'.

◆ How am I?

Writing can be deeply therapeutic: many people keep diaries, for instance, that are of great benefit when it comes to expressing feelings, exploring issues and admitting things to oneself which could not be admitted in any other context. Poetry too serves to sum up an experience elegantly and succinctly. The act of putting things down on paper has a symbolic value; it helps us to 'get things out of our system'. And because the words on the page are now separate from us, we have in a sense stepped back from the issue or problem or feeling and can look back on it in a more detached and rational way.

As children become more familiar and comfortable with the notion of manipulating ideas and words through various written forms, the concept of writing as a 'dealing and healing' strategy can be emphasised. Here are some ways in which the therapeutic power of words might be used.

- Write letters to your past and future self. Ask questions, give advice, offer reassurance.
- Keep a 'side-by-side' diary of events in your life (a) as they happened and as you reacted to them; (b) as you would like to have reacted. Explore why you did not react in that way. Devise strategies for gathering the resources that will allow you to react as you want to in the future.
- Put yourself in a story where you react in a situation as you would ideally like to do.
- Write letters to the characters in your stories. Be those people and, in character, write back to yourself.
- Personify emotions (See 'Old Man Envy', p.190) and explore that character using StoryMaker techniques.

- Work with a group to create storylines that explore issues which concern you. Swap strategies with your co-writers about how they might resolve those issues. Use what works well for you.

- Reflect on the qualities you notice in fictional characters. Chunk down those qualities to see how they work. Build those elements into your behaviours.

- Ask 'How am I?' Notice yourself. Use your thoughts and feelings flexibly.

◆ Uniquely me

Negative thinking in both children and adults often focuses on one's sense of self-identity, although it may start at the level of environment, appearance, capability or behaviour. (Cf. Robert Dilts' 'neurological levels', p.14). Such thinking is selective and generalised, and may easily become habitual - 'Oh, I'm no good at anything. I'm useless', or 'Nobody likes me, and I don't blame them.'

'Uniquely me' emphasises the positive and particular in people, in terms of roles, relationships and attributes. Stage one of the activity draws out these ideas by working on characters from fiction.

	Roles	Relationships	Attributes
Nigel	Leader of the Double Dare Gang.	Respects his friends, helps Mum at home, (secretly) likes Anna Williams.	Mischievous and sometimes a little reckless, untidy but organised.
Brian	Bodyguard and protector of the Double Dare Gang.	Commands respect from others. He has a natural ease and warmth people respond to.	Placid and fair, friendly and loyal.

This process allows children to select out what's positive in these characters who, despite their faults (which are in no way denied) have some worthy attributes that make them unique individuals.

Stage two of the activity invites children to select out each other's positive qualities, and finally for children to reflect upon themselves in this way.

> 'The quality of life (depends) on how we feel about ourselves and not what happens to us.'
> (Mihaly Csikszentmilhalyi, quoted by Alistair Smith in *Accelerated Learning in Practice*)

◆ Today's dare

To dare is to push the limits a little, and in pushing those personal limits we enlarge our world. Doing it once sets the precedent; from then on to dare to make progress becomes less frightening and more exciting and challenging. We dare by recognising what has limited us previously and then by making a conscious decision that we will act to overcome that which has constrained us in the past. As the saying goes, 'If you always do what you've always done, you'll always get what you've always got.' To dare to move beyond that is a liberating experience. People get the taste for it – daring becomes a self-reinforcing behaviour!

To dare is not to be reckless. Recklessness is acting without consideration or a regard for consequences and responsibilities. Daring successfully implies that we have thought about the context within which we will act, have some sense of what has limited us in the past, and have considered the consequences/benefits of our decisions. To dare is to use resources that have lain latent inside us, waiting to be used but for the will to use them.

The storymaking process models life in this regard. We can dare to jump in to that blank page and fill it with meanings. We can dare to show our work to someone else. We can dare to contemplate writing 'the book inside' - taking that magical step from short story to novel. We can dare to master the act of writing stories and so prove to ourselves that we are capable of mastery.

We can dare to use our new resource in the wider arena of life…

- Today I dare to ask questions.
- Today I dare to think of three possible ways of feeling a sense of achievement.
- Today I dare to give sincere praise.
- Today I dare to respect myself.
- Today I dare to understand how someone else feels.
- Today I dare to think about what I'll dare to do in the future.

The Double Dare Gang

Code of Honour

- LIVE TO DARE - DARE TO LIVE!

- HONOUR THE DOUBLE DARE GANG!

- HONOUR YOUR FELLOW DOUBLE-DARERS.

- SHOW RESPECT - HURT NO-ONE.

- THE WORLD IS THE QUESTION - YOUR LIFE IS THE ANSWER.

- THE GREAT ADVENTURE HAS BEGUN.

We are defined by our choices
DDG Forever!!

◆ The write attitude

As a teacher —

- Use non-threatening, non-judgmental activities to cultivate an ethos of confidence and enthusiasm for language.
- Encourage open questioning.
- Link the development of social skills with literacy.
- Make fun-with-words a multi-sensory experience.
- Encourage individual 'meaning-making' and the personalisation of knowledge.
- Allow children to see beyond the immediate context of the work – outline the 'Big Picture'.
- Invite children to take an active role in generating ideas through language.
- Create cohesion in learning by offering children structures that provide them with the means to achieve the tasks you set for them.
- Create the opportunity for frequent feedback so that children can express their individual learnings.

As a writer —

- Everything that happens to you is useful material for writing.
- Experts can only tell you how they do it.
- Use what works for you and discard what doesn't.
- Write for several good reasons. Take strength in a sense of purpose.
- Realise that nothing's perfect. Looking back on a story and knowing you could do it better now means you have moved on.
- When you are pleased with your achievement, thank yourself. Enjoy your sense of pleasure at the successful completion of a project.
- When you create a story (or whatever) do it uncritically. Write for the joy of seeing the language unfold at your fingertips. Put the editorial hat on later, and polish your work firmly, fairly, creatively.
- Never throw any writing away! (See 'Everything is useful'.)
- Write your way out of any difficulty to do with your writing.
- Consider applying whatever you learn from storymaking in the wider arena of your life.
- Realise that in making marks on paper you are developing your own talents to make your mark on the world.

We struggle, not to win
or lose, but to keep
something alive.

T. S. Eliot

Section Eight

Visualisation

In the space age the most important
space is between your ears.

Thomas J. Barlow

Section 8 – Visualisation

Page	Topic/activity	Story element covered	Accelerated learning link
273	Teaching Alpha	*All elements*	Awareness of brain waves and corresponding mental-emotional states/accessing the Alpha state of relaxed alertness
279	Safe havens	*All elements*	Accessing the Alpha state / positive anchoring within a visualisation
282	Walk with me along the path	*All elements*	Awareness of prompted, guided and scripted visualisation/using a 'seedthought' stimulus for visualisation
283	Gathering treasures	*All elements*	Using visualisation to develop 'The new 3Rs'
284	A trip around town	*Settings*	Training for concentration and the direction of the conscious point-of-attention/VAK and submodalities
286	The music man	*All elements*	VAK/using auditory input to enrich visualisations/using the Alpha state for free writing

Section Eight

Visualisation

◆ Teaching 'Alpha'

Common sense tells us that we are not constantly aware of all of the information that exists in our minds. Most of what we know remains out of our conscious awareness until we think about it, either by choice or because we are 're-minded' of it in some way. For convenience (because the philosophical debate about this is profound, tortuous and ongoing) we can say that our consciousness includes a point-of-attention, a spotlight of awareness that shines on past experiences, our present environment, and future possibilities. It also includes the ability to manipulate information intelligently in order to come to new understandings.

Largely outside our conscious awareness lies the subconscious realm (again a label of convenience). This forms the bulk of the 'mindscape' or 'map of reality' by which we live our lives. Popular belief in the past would have it that the subconscious was like a vast basement store room where piles of mental junk, along with some gems of wisdom perhaps, lay about gathering dust as it were. This idea is deeply erroneous. The subconscious is not the passive recipient of 'facts' – it is not a vessel to be filled; it is not a *tabula rasa* to be written on – but an actively thinking part of the whole being whose construction of a working model of the world never ceases. We are 'meaning-making' beings throughout every second of our lives, so that even when the conscious mind is 'switched off' in sleep, the subconscious endeavours to dream its way towards a greater truth. And 'truth', by the way, tends on an individual level to mean what conforms to the framework of our pre-existing beliefs. We look at the world through subjective eyes: we think about the world according to what has already happened to us in our lives.

There is a constant communication between the conscious and subconscious levels of the mind, and between the mind and the external world. The process of creative thinking can be seen as a feedback loop between the inner and outer worlds of our experience through the interface of the conscious awareness.

Although this process happens anyway (it is a natural and inevitable consequence of being human), we can develop and accelerate our capacity to think creatively in a number of ways, one such way being to use our conscious point-of-attention more deliberately.

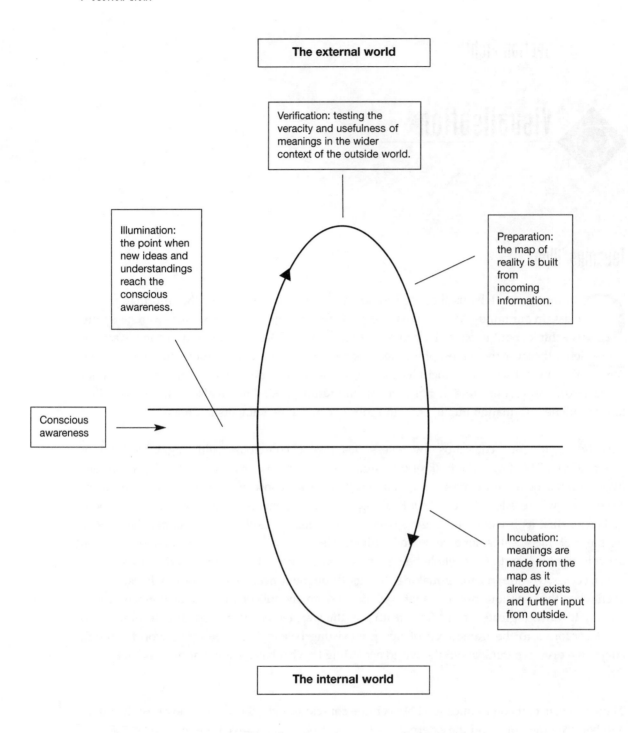

The external world

Verification: testing the veracity and usefulness of meanings in the wider context of the outside world.

Illumination: the point when new ideas and understandings reach the conscious awareness.

Preparation: the map of reality is built from incoming information.

Conscious awareness

Incubation: meanings are made from the map as it already exists and further input from outside.

The internal world

Think of that point-of-attention as a compass needle swinging freely on its pivot. When we are asked to 'pay attention' our awareness is externalised and focused for a certain time (depending on a number of factors, including how interesting the stimulus happens to be!). If we are distracted, then our attention is split between the original focus and the new stimulus. We can refocus our attention by an act of will.

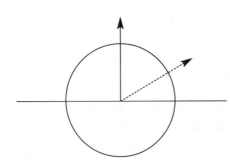

When we daydream, our conscious point-of-attention tends to internalise and we become more aware of the drift of thoughts through the mind. Those thoughts may seem disconnected and meaningless, or they could amount to a deep understanding of something new which, at that point, we can explain logically to ourselves and to others. This is a moment of illumination, a 'Eureka moment' that moves us forward in our thinking.

Trying hard to have eureka moments is fruitless. It's like struggling to remember a name that's 'on the tip of your tongue'. The more you try, the more elusive the information becomes. What is possible, however, is to access the state where the conscious point-of-attention is internalised and where you remain aware that you are aware – that is, you do not lose yourself in daydreams which slip away and are forgotten when you return to the here and now.

The state of mind (and body) where 'systematic daydreaming' happens may be called relaxed alertness or quiet consciousness. You are simply sitting peacefully, taking note of the ideas that flow through your mind – without bothering about whether they are consciously constructed or subconsciously generated.

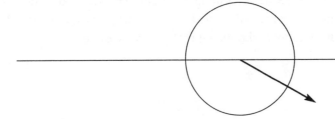

Sitting quietly, doing nothing, just noticing the drift of your thoughts…

The first step in practising this technique, therefore, is just to lapse into tranquillity and remain self-aware:

- arrange for a quiet environment free from distractions
- make sure you are physically comfortable
- focus your eyes on a blank space – a wall, a sheet of paper
- focus your attention on an idea, a mental image, a memory, etc.
- allow the image to shift of its own accord to other thoughts, ideas, insights and understandings
- without effort follow the train of thought, realising that you are doing so.

In a classroom context the technique can be practised with a group by taking note of the following points:

- use temporal anchors – run the activity at the same time each day/every other day, or whatever schedule you choose
- use spatial anchors – talk about 'daydream practice' in the part of the room you have chosen to create positive anticipation of success (having first explained it in the space where you deliver new concepts and information)
- use visual anchors – nominate a blank wall area as the 'staring area', or if you wish children to gaze at blank sheets of paper, use the same subtle pastel colour of paper each time
- use auditory anchors – frame the session with suitable music before and after. You might use the same music playing unobtrusively in the background when the children are writing creatively.
- maintain a safe learning environment. Explain the educational value of what you are asking your group to do, but emphasise that the children are not in competition with anyone, there's no single right way of daydreaming, and the experience can vary from person to person. Outcomes are individual.
- emphasise also that each child is in full control of the experience. You can come out of a daydream whenever you want. Sometimes a bad memory can arise spontaneously. Even before this develops, you can choose to come back to the here and now.*
- make it clear that all creative people daydream. (The writer David Gerrold maintains that a truly creative person is a 'perpetual notion machine'.) It simply means paying quiet attention to the ideas that are always forming deep in the mind. If education is about acquiring new information (commonly called the syllabus), it is also about what you do mentally with that formation, and noticing that you have done it.

* Unpleasant memories that seemingly arise spontaneously often represent a deliberate, subconscious attempt to alert the reflective/decisive, conscious part of the mind that here is some 'unfinished business' that needs attending to. Some techniques for dealing with this can be found in *Self-Intelligence*.

The stimulus for daydreaming has been termed a 'seedthought' - a picture, key word, aroma, musical extract, object – which for our purposes is deliberately planted in the fertile soil of the imagination and then allowed to grow. Part of the fun of creative thinking comes in anticipating the unexpected connections made by the daydreaming mind. And much of the satisfaction of this process comes in the elegant interplay between our purposeful intention to create and ideas that are simply allowed to drift to the surface and come under the scrutiny of the conscious attention.

The power of seedthoughts can be appreciated by developing the analogy of growth and the endlessly branching structure of a tree. It is a well-known fact that in some species the root network is as extensive as the spread of branches above ground. And so it is in our minds: a single thought might radiate outwards into an array of ideas and possibilities, and at the same time form a rich complexity of links with information already present in the subconscious map of reality.

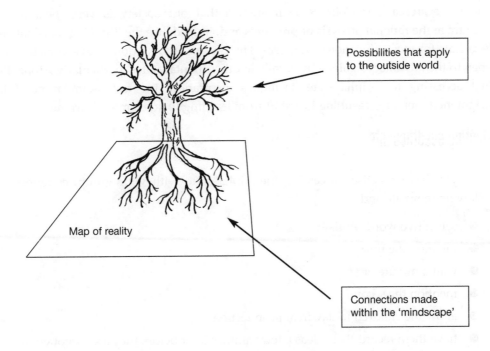

Possibilities that apply to the outside world

Map of reality

Connections made within the 'mindscape'

Creating a daydream state and practising accessing that state regularly allows us the best of both the conscious and subconscious aspects of the mind.

The brain continually generates minute electrical impulses which are part of the physical expression of the mind's ceaseless activity. Researchers in the field recognise four main frequency ranges corresponding to four distinct mental states:

- **beta** – 13–25 cycles per second [cps] – which characterises conscious logical thought and analysis
- **alpha** – 8–12 cps – which characterises 'relaxed alertness' in all its forms; daydream, reverie, meditation. An alpha state allows the conscious point-of-attention to move easily between the external and internal worlds

- **theta** – 4–7 cps – which characterises deep meditation and daydreaming involving greater levels of self-absorption
- **delta** – 0.5–3 cps – which characterises dreamless sleep where consciousness is absent.

This (highly simplified) continuum suggests that in the beta state the conscious mind is 'turned up to full volume' and the attention is externalised. Alpha maintains conscious attention but conscious processing of information is quiescent and the attention drifts between the external world and information rising from the subconscious. The theta state sees the further 'dimming' of conscious attention and awareness. In this condition the individual becomes more suggestible; information arises readily from the subconscious, but may not be consciously noticed or even processed to any great extent. (Hypnotherapists elicit this state in their clients as part of the therapeutic work they do.) Delta sees consciousness 'switched off' so that all mental activity occurs at the subconscious level.

The writer/researcher Colin Rose maintains that our society is very 'beta oriented'. We encourage the rational analysis of problems and, indeed, use the 'thinking tools' inherent in the Beta state for most educational purposes. Thus, he asserts, we don't leave ourselves sufficiently open to the advantages gained by accessing other mental states, particularly Alpha. Rose states that accessing the Alpha state 'facilitates inspiration, the fast assimilation of facts, and heightened memory,' resulting in a shift from learning to accelerated learning.

Planting seedthoughts

Once you have practised accessing the Alpha state with your group, combine it with the following template and:

- select two words initially
- mention the first
- wait a minute or so
- mention the second
- allow the children to daydream connections
- have them record their ideas a few minutes later before they are forgotten.

	1	2	3	4	5	6
1	glue	pen	weight	chain	paper	stone
2	link	file	clear	container	stretch	glass
3	stand	write	warm	store	record	pin
4	tidy	watch	time	flower	cap	display
5	shelf	backup	memory	key	frame	cover
6	bag	box	corner	space	card	stack

In this case the task is very open-ended. The children's thinking has been framed only by the time-span of the activity and the two words; some of these are concrete, some abstract, and they are vaguely suggestive of an office or study. Extend the activity subsequently by increasing the time-span/the number of words/the proportion of concrete words/the degree of direction you give to the task. To say, 'We are going to think of a new way of filing information and here are six words to help us do it' the first time you run the activity invites rational analysis and conscious effort – the children will be trying hard to comply; they will be 'beta dominant'. When they are more familiar with the alpha state, ideas will tend to flow more easily and creatively. And out of that mass of ideas some good ones are likely to emerge.

Although the emphasis of this book is on storymaking, the mental processes required to do this can and should be applied to all other areas of the curriculum. The seedthought template can be subject-specific or, even more interestingly, contain words from two or more subject areas. The cross-links that the children make will give them insights into the subjects themselves, and will help to counterbalance the limiting compartmentalisation of subjects which is such a powerfully ingrained feature of our current educational system.

◆ Safe havens

'Visualisation' is a catch-all term referring to our capacity to move mentally beyond the here-and-now. In other words, we can access information that we have already experienced through recalling our memories; and we can construct new scenarios and experiences through the power of the imagination. The word itself is obviously a visual reference, although in fact we remember and imagine through all of the sensory modalities: we see through the mind's eye, hear through the mind's ear, touch through the mind's fingers, and so on. Furthermore, visualisation is not just a mental activity; it is also an emotional/physiological process. Think back to some pleasant experience and you are likely to notice a shift in your feelings. There will be corresponding physical changes such as facial expression and perhaps body posture, together with a range of internal physiological effects you may not detect at all. Recollection or imagination of negative or unpleasant experiences is similarly reflected in how we react on a physical level. Stress is as much to do with so-called 'catastrophic thinking' as it is with ongoing external circumstances.

We visualise anyway. It is a natural feature of being alive and conscious. Education would be a meaningless concept without our ability to recall or imagine (indeed, concepts themselves could not exist!). The term 'visualisation' is usually taken to mean the deliberate and systematic direction of the conscious point-of-attention upon some mental scenario, recalled or imagined, or both. So we all visualise but we are not all effective visualisers. Learning the skill aids storymaking and vice versa, but there are a number of specific activities which can accelerate the process.

A 'safe haven' is an imagined pleasant place you can go to as a preliminary to further visualisation work. It is a halfway house which you develop over time. This makes it a powerful positive anchor and an effective component of any writing ritual (see p.249).

The 'Safe haven' visualisation might be done from a script – see example 1 – or as pair work – example 2 – where the visualiser and 'visualisee' construct the scenario together. The advantage in the first case is that the safe haven remains entirely private, although pair work is more interactive and the visualisee can react to any aspects of the visualisation which are creating difficulties or concerns for her partner.

● Begin the visualisation by creating quiet time in the classroom.

● Ask the children involved to gaze at a blank space on the wall or at a blank sheet of paper.

● Explain that the purpose of the activity is for them to imagine a pleasant place full of good things. This will give them good feelings inside. The children can feel entirely comfortable and safe in the place where they imagine themselves to be.

● Then begin the work. If you use the following script, read it out slowly with a pause between each sentence: give the children's imaginations time to fill in the details. And notice how, to aid this, the language is 'artfully vague', referring to colours and sounds without any specific references.

Example 1: Visualisation script

And now I'd like you now to gather your thoughts together to think about a place – a place that's pleasant, comfortable and enjoyable for you. And to make sure that place is vivid and powerful in your mind, take all the time you need to notice the colours you find there – picking out all of those clear and separate colours, in this place where you imagine yourself to be...

... And you can notice the sounds you find there – becoming more aware now of all of those individual and very distinctive sounds, in this place where you imagine yourself to be...

... And at some point, pay attention to the textures you find there – and if you want to, in your mind you can reach out and feel the surfaces and textures of things, and find yourself delighted by the great variety of textures in this place where you imagine yourself to be – this place which is so pleasant, so comfortable, and so enjoyable for you...

... And however these thoughts come into your mind, you can make your safe place even more enjoyable by noticing lots and lots of interesting details. So continue to do this until you are ready to come back to the here-and-now, feeling pleased with what you've done.

Example 2: Pair work

Steve: OK Phillipa, gaze at the blank sheet of paper and begin to imagine a pleasant place for yourself. You can make it up from places where you've been, or where you'd like to go, or a mixture. Just tell me as much as you want to about the place in your mind...

Phillipa: Well, I'm inside quite a large, round, one-roomed hut. It's made of wicker work or palm leaves. It's very light and airy. I imagine that I'm sitting cross-legged on a colourfully-patterned rug. There is an earth floor. The soil is dry and compacted down.

Steve: OK. Can you see outside?

Phillipa: Yes. There's a doorway right ahead of me, about ten feet away. The hut is on top of a grassy hill. Beyond I see a forest panorama. It's a lovely sunny day. The sun is high above in a blue sky, and there are some dazzling white clouds drifting by.

Steve: Notice some sounds now. What do you hear?

Phillipa: Well, mainly it's quiet inside the hut. But the wind is kind of lifting the fronds of the roof and hissing between the fibres – and farther off the wind is roaring through the trees. It's a lovely big strong sound, but gentle too.

Steve: What aromas do you smell?

Phillipa: Oh, well now you mention it I can smell the sweet grassy-straw smell of the hut itself. And the earth smells fresh and clean...And there's a faint smell of perfume, a very natural smell – flowers maybe.

Steve: All right. And now you can notice details, things nearby –

Phillipa: Yes –

Steve: Can you pick something up now and tell me what it feels like, how heavy it is, what it's made from?

Phillipa: Well, I've picked something up. It's a treasure. I can feel it in my hands. But it's something private, so I won't tell you any more.

Steve: OK, you go on enjoying your safe place for as long as you like.

◆ Walk with me along the path

All visualisation work of this kind needs to be done respectfully. There should never be any pressure on a visualiser to reveal information if he does not want to. Helping someone to visualise means supporting him through the process, walking with him along the path.

That said, visualisations can be highly structured and filled with fine detail, or remain wonderfully nebulous and vague. For convenience, we might make the following distinctions:

- **prompted visualisation**. This consists of a number of disconnected words introduced separately, like a few of the dots in a join-the-dots picture

- **guided visualisation**. This is more structured but 'artfully vague' (See Example 1 above), like a join-the-dots picture suggesting a general outline

- **scripted visualisation**. This is a highly structured 'tour' through a scenario previously imagined. The script draws the visualiser's attention to a range of specific details. A story might be thought of as a highly organised scripted visualisation.

A prompted visualisation might make use of a word grid similar to that used in 'Planting seedthoughts' (see p.278), where connections (some of them new) between the items are more important than the items themselves. A variation of the activity is to lift 'prompt words' from a story that's already been written, but not read by the visualiser. As a starting point, you can mention that the aim of the visualisation is to begin to enter the world of a story: you might have specified a theme/genre/conflict beforehand. So:

Stage 1: Comb through text for suitable prompt words. In the following example, prompt words are highlighted in bold type.

Extract from 'The Frankenstein Steps'

I had never counted the **steps**, but I reckoned there were about a hundred and fifty of them. There was a **streetlight** at the top (I was standing right under it), one in the middle, and one at the bottom...

With great stretches of darkness in between.

Even though I kept telling myself that Anna had just been trying to **scare** me, I felt all fluttery inside. And I didn't want to begin the journey down, because I thought that if I began to panic, I'd just run faster and **faster** - until I couldn't stop - and the wind would whirl me up - right into the arms of the man who'd been hanged on the Bowden Hill gallows - and then we'd both **haunt** the Frankenstein Steps forever!

In the town, I heard the church clock striking the hour. Six o'clock. I knew that Mum would be worrying - So I took a deep breath and started on my way.

As the brightness of the streetlight **faded** and the shadows gathered round, thoughts of ghosts and monsters and things that lived in darkness began growing in my head. I imagined the girl who had no heart, that poor **lost** little soul; and the Halloween Man with a pumpkin for a head; and the railway phantom...I even pictured my plesiosaur rising up from the green depths of the Lime Pools, breaking surface and letting out a **mournful**, bellowing howl...

I began counting the steps out loud, to calm myself down.

Stage 2: Reiterate any decisions already made about theme/genre/conflict. 'This will be a ghost story based on the theme of *stepping over the line*. It will feature two major characters who have been lifelong rivals.'

Stage 3: Run the visualisation. You can either speak the words individually with a space between each (15–30 seconds should do), or as pair work where the visualiser's response is requested after each word.

Steve: Steps…

Phillipa: OK. I see some stairs leading upwards to a dark landing. I'm in a big house – it's occupied, but I don't know if anyone's here at the moment.

Steve: Are you one of the characters in the story?

Phillipa: No – OK, that means I can go to any part of the house or the story… I know there's a woman on the landing. She's waiting for someone to arrive. Her rival maybe.

Steve: Streetlight…

Phillipa: Ah, there is someone coming towards the house. It's a man. He walks up to the door. The woman on the landing can see his silhouette through the glass panels of the door. There's a streetlight behind him.

Steve: How is that important?

Phillipa: I don't know –

Steve: Pretend you do. Make something up.

Phillipa: He was expecting to surprise her – Yes, that's it. He is in love with her, but she doesn't love him. He has a rival, someone else that the woman's in love with.

Steve: Faster…

Phillipa: His heart is beating faster because he's thinking about seeing her…

Steve: And her heart?

Phillipa: Her heart… No, her heart isn't beating at all. *She's the ghost in the story!*

◆ Gathering treasures

Visualisation work lies at the heart of all storymaking. It can also be used to develop greater resourcefulness with regard to one's attitude as a writer. Once children are familiar with 'systematic daydreaming' in this way, explain that the next visualisation is to be a treasure hunt. As they imagine their way through the adventure, they will notice a number of things which will be significant and useful. The children may not know how or why these treasures are important, but at some time in the days or weeks to come their relevance will become clear.

◆ **283**

'Gathering treasures' can be incorporated into the reading or telling of a story (a scripted visualisation). Prime the group by suggesting that each child can 'bring back' up to six treasures once the story is finished. Point out that these things might not even be mentioned in the story – but children can notice them anyway. Have the children make a note of their treasures and ask them to scribble down any other linked ideas in the days that follow.

◆ A trip around town

Ask children to work in pairs. Supply a map of their home town. Pick two spots: A and B. Explain that one child is to visualise and describe a journey between the two points, prompted and guided by her partner.

Follow up the activity with a similar visualisation of the setting for a story. Some authors include maps of the locality in their books, but if not basic maps can be constructed by reading the story through. This is an act of visualisation in itself, of course: 'A trip around town' adds many interesting details.

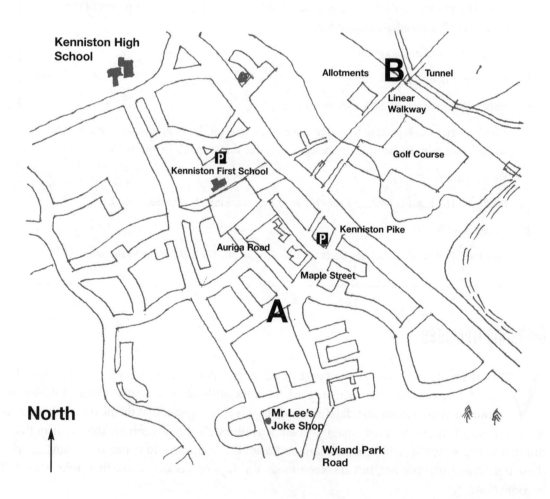

Steve: OK, we're starting at point A. Imagine standing right there. What do you notice?

Phillipa: It's a fine sunny day, a bit cold – it's September time. I'm facing northeast. Just across the road I can see Maple Street stretching away towards the Kenniston Pike.

Steve: What time is it?

Phillipa: It's fairly early in the morning, say nine-thirty. The busy traffic rush has finished, but the Pike is still busy. But if you turn left at the end of Maple Street there's a set of traffic lights and I can cross there.

Steve: OK, go down Maple Street…

Phillipa: There was a rain shower earlier. I see some puddles on the pavement, and people's gardens smell wet as I pass – quite a strong smell of leaves, flowers, damp soil. Cars go past and I can smell their exhaust fumes. I can see them too, billowing out of the tailpipe because the air is cool.

Steve: OK. Are there people about?

Phillipa: Not many. There's a man walking his dog on the other side of the road. I'm moving away from the main shopping area so I wouldn't expect to see many folks… I'm at the Kenniston Pike junction now. There are the traffic lights, a hundred yards to my left. I see the row of poplar trees across the Pike. They conceal the golf course beyond. Over the road and to my left, past the traffic lights, I see the little lane that leads to the linear walkway, which I'll follow up to the allotments…

◆ I spy

Working with a partner allows the visualiser to construct a more elaborate scenario. In the example, Steve can suggest changes in perspective, place emphasis on different sensory modalities, explore submodalities, introduce story elements and generally move Phillipa around the visualised world more flexibly.

'I spy' can be thought of as a mental zoom tool, allowing finer details to be noticed. We pick up the visualisation just after Phillipa has crossed the busy Kenniston Pike:

Phillipa: Now I'm walking along the linear walkway. It's made from smooth black tarmac. It's raised above the ground on either side – it's the flat top of a grassy ridge about twelve to fifteen feet above the surrounding land.

Steve: OK. Notice other plants apart from grass.

Phillipa: OK. There are more trees bordering the golf course on the right – tall poplars and I think silver birch. Their leaves are all shimmery.

Steve: On the other side, to your left?

cont…

Phillipa: Oh, I'm coming to a line of bushes now – dogrose bushes. They are quite wild and untended. A few long runners are sticking out and waving gently in the wind. The cold weather has taken off most of the petals.

Steve: Describe the nearest rose.

Philippa: Um, there are two pale pink petals left about twice the size of my thumbnail. The centre of the flower is a little hard, green rosehip. It has a fringe of shrivelled strands or hairs which were the sticks where the pollen was attached – the stamens. They're brown and withered up now. They feel dry and gritty and they fall apart when I touch them.

Steve: Smell the flower.

Phillipa: Mm – no smell. I'm slicing the rosehip with my nail. It's white inside… Can't see any seeds. It smells bitter, and when I rub my fingers together they feel a bit sticky with the sap…

◆ The music man

Combine a prompted visualisation with a piece of music. Having chosen some prompt words (and perhaps a theme/genre, etc.) suggest that the music represents a person. As it plays, invite the children to scribble down their impressions of him or her. Read the list of prompt words during the music. Emphasise that the children can make whatever use of them they wish.

Extend the activity by replaying the music. This time, ask children to listen out for a particular instrument. Link the instrument with some detail of the scenario they have already created. So, for example, link violins to the wizard's thoughts/link drums to the weather outside the chamber/link a harp to the past/link a triangle to something important the wizard has to know, and so on.

See example using Purcell's *Music for the Funeral of Queen Mary*.

Legend has it (and this may be more than a legend!) that the scientist and inventor Nikola Tesla could visualise an engine and notice all of its component parts. He could start it up and leave it running for weeks in his subconscious, then bring it back to conscious awareness to see which components had worn.

The human ability to visualise has created the world we live in. Everything in the room where you sit was a thought before it became an actuality. Teaching children to visualise in the safe and enjoyable context of storymaking develops in them a powerful skill which can be transferred to all other areas of their lives.

The music man: Example

Musical extract: Henry Purcell's *Music for the Funeral of Queen Mary*

Theme – large consequences come from small beginnings

Genre – fantasy

Prompt words	Free writing
blue light	I see a tall man, though he is bent over by age or worry. He is dressed in long blue robes. They have a sheen to them, a blue-black sheen which changes as he moves. There is something special about these robes – there is an energy to them…There is magic in everything here, but the magic is like an energy and it has run low…
keen	Usually the whole place is bright and happy. But a darkness has come and this man – he is a wizard – has some responsibility for it. Maybe his responsibility is to keep the energy high, or somehow to keep the darkness out. This is a lot to do with the balance between darkness and light.
chance key wonder	He is wearing a blue skullcap. This is not his usual cap. I think this is some kind of punishment. He is punishing himself because he let the darkness in – not deliberately though. Something happened a long time ago. It was a chance meeting with a young girl who was travelling through his land. He fell in love and he thought she loved him. She enticed him, but really she was not innocent at all. As a token of his love for her, he gave her a secret some secret information, which was a key to some of the power he held. In a way he was showing off to her.
stone time	She promised to return to him, but she never did. As the years went by the wizard learned more of his craft and was given greater power by the lord of the land. The wizard was given control of the *vitality* that rises through all living things. Often he wondered about the girl he had loved so deeply. Why had she not come back to him? Where was her home, and why had he been unable to seek her out, despite his power?
seed grant	I see him now, an old man with long white hair and a beard like fleecy cobwebs. He is pacing about his gloomy stone chamber. Outside the darkness is sweeping over like a storm. Trees are dead and withered. Those animals still left alive are lying low. The wizard knows he has done a terrible thing, and only now when perhaps it is too late does he realise that the gentle girl from his long-ago past might be involved.
circle fall	Summoning his energy, he picks up his staff which leans against the wall. Atop the staff there is a perfect sphere of crystal. It is a living sphere, but not alive in the same way as him. It grants him a vision – of clouds and lightnings, of black dragons swirling in from far places, and the face of the wizard's lost love. She is as sweet and beautiful as ever, but her smile is evil. And now she is coming back with a vengeance.

Students are not here to worship what is known, but to question it.

Jacob Bronowski

Section Nine

Storytelling

Abra-cadabrah – I create as I speak

Ancient Aramaic saying

Section 9 — Storytelling

Page	Topic/activity	Story element covered	Accelerated learning link
291	The world of the story	*All elements*	Confidence and self-esteem/intra- and inter-personal intelligence

Section Nine

Storytelling

This short and concluding section of *ALPS StoryMaker* recommends the teaching of storytelling skills to teachers, parents and children, and offers some tips on the process and the benefits to be gained.

◆ The world of the story

The story is an analogue of life itself. Like any tale, our own existence moves along from its beginning towards its inevitable end: it has its themes, its subplots, its characters and settings. It has its particular phases – the chapters, scenes and paragraphs by which we mark our progress. It has its moments of fierce emotion, its conflicts and its resolutions. We are the story. We are the authors of our own being.

Educationally the world of the story incorporates the four key skills of reading, writing, speaking and listening. Furthermore, stories can and do cross subject boundaries: science, history, geography, maths come alive when we know something of the key figures within those fields and how they came to make their discoveries. The facts and figures of a subject's content are rooted in the lives of the people who contributed to that body of knowledge. Many of those people drew their inspiration from stories, making the themes and motifs they found there their life's work. The scientist and astronomer Carl Sagan had his imagination fired by the science fiction tales of Edgar Rice Burroughs. Two other SF writers, Arthur C. Clarke and Isaac Asimov, are also highly gifted communicators of scientific ideas. J. R. R. Tolkien, the fantasy writer, was also a professor of philology. The highly influential psychologist Carl Jung had many of his insights through studying myths and legends… And how many thousands more whose names have never touched the public imagination had their lives shaped by the power and wonder of stories?

Telling tales has probably been a fundamental human activity since language itself first appeared, spanning the great hierarchy of stories from garden-fence gossip to myths of creation and cosmos. We love to pass on what has happened to others, be they real or fictional characters. And in relating their stories, we find that we relate to one another. Storytelling, like learning, happens anyway. Storytelling as part of the great oral tradition, however, is an art which has long been neglected within the educational system. And yet it embodies a range of valuable skills which can easily be transferred to all other areas of a child's learning.

MOON

creation and origin myths
sacred stories
epic stories
wonder tales
legends
historical stories
fables
supernatural tales
folk tales
cumulative stories
animal stories
ancestor stories
family stories
personal anecdotes
shaggy dog stories
jokes

EARTH

'The Ladder to the Moon' – traditionally this hierarchy of stories links what is earthy and everyday to that which is universal, mysterious and wondrous (a similar structure, perhaps, to Dilts' neurological levels (see p.14) that connects environment to spirituality).

◆ Making a start

Storytelling is not story reading. Holding up a picture book and speaking the text more or less exactly is not storytelling. In order to tell a story truly, it needs to be personalised, rehearsed and performed. Personalising a story involves making it one's own, which, although that might mean it tells very differently from the way it reads, retains the essence of the original – that is to say, it preserves the author's intentions and purposes in creating the story in the first place.

Personalising a story

- Choose a story that you like. Reflect on why you like it.
- 'Unfold' the story (see p.66) to make its themes, motifs and structure more explicit.
- Chunk the story down into sections. Many tales break down quite naturally into a number of segments. Jot down the key ideas of each section on cards.

- Begin telling the story to yourself, a section at a time. Tell the story into a tape recorder. Tell the story to yourself as you look in a mirror.

- Satisfy the 'VAK factor'. Include visual, auditory and kinaesthetic details in your story.

- Begin to notice what works in the telling and what doesn't. Notice pace, notice the amount of detail and be aware of what you have chosen to include or leave out. Notice your own facial expressions and vocal qualities (Will you attempt the various characters' voices or not?) Remember that a told story need not sound anything like the same story being read out.

- Consider the use of props and visual aids. These may be elaborate and extensive – hats, items of costume, objects – or simple and minimal. Think about why you want to use any particular prop.

- Rehearse the story through a number of times until it feels familiar. Be aware of how the story begins to evolve. Follow your intuition. You may feel the need to introduce some further ingredients, while others tend to fade away quite naturally by themselves. Stories change over time with repeated tellings. Allow that process to work for you.

- Apply this same model to other stories so that you have a menu of tales to tell, some very short, others longer and more involved.

Performing a story

- Make sure the environment is suitable. Will people be comfortable? Are there likely to be distractions? Are your stories appropriate to the age-range and size (number) of the audience? Do what you can to ensure the conditions are right.

- Begin with a story you feel confident to tell, and choose a 'safe' audience (maybe just a few people you know well and who are aware of your endeavour).

- 'Go into' the story as you tell it. If you feel detached from the material you won't get the most out of it. If you are predominantly visual, notice the movie playing in your head. If you are auditory, listen to the characters and the sounds of the world they inhabit. If you are kinaesthetic, feel the shapes and textures of things. Weave these insights (lookings-in) into the tale, but continue to satisfy the VAK factor for the benefit of your listeners.

- Notice the audience responses and exploit those responses as far as you can. Use eye contact. React to people's facial expressions. If someone makes a comment (children especially often will) use it positively as part of the telling.

- Anticipate being flexible and feel easy and comfortable in that flexibility. If a new idea occurs to you as you tell a story, evaluate it in a moment and decide to try it out or discard it. If something happens in the immediate vicinity (a poster might fall off the wall, a bell might ring) is there a way you can use it to enhance the telling?

- Use 'hot buttons' (see p.122) in your storytelling. When someone's eyes light up with excitement, when your whole audience is hanging on to your every word, when they are 'in there with you', milk the moment without overdoing it. (This skill comes with practice.)

- Never become complacent. Tell the story afresh each time, and with sincerity and conviction. Your attitude should include enthusiasm, anticipation, excitement even. And you should exude an air of having authority and mastery over both your story and your audience: be in charge. Anticipate a pleasant and positive experience but be prepared to exercise your authority if needs be. Don't put up with rudeness. Stop the proceedings if people are talking while you're telling.

Finally —

The ability to tell a story boosts confidence and self-esteem. A storyteller has highly developed intra- and interpersonal skills: she can read herself and others with ease and elegance. A storyteller knows how to manipulate information. A storyteller is familiar and comfortable with the steady flow of insights and ideas that come as he develops his craft. A storyteller forges ahead with a sense of wonder and a sense of humour in equal measure. A storyteller is increasingly aware of the resonances between the elements within stories and those within his own life.

We learn what we do.

Marshall McLuhan

Bibliography

Aftel, M.	*The Story of Your Life: Becoming the Author of Your Experience*. Simon and Schuster 1996.
Alder, H.	*The Right Brain Manager* Piatkus 1993.
Alexander, M.	*The Earliest English Poems*. Penguin Classics 1970.
Angwin, R.	*Riding the Dragon: Myth and the Inner Journey*. Element 1994.
Bowkett, S.	*Meditations For Busy People* Thorsons 1996.
	For the Moon There's the Cloud: tales in the Zen tradition. Collins Pathways Reading Scheme, Collins Educational 1996.
	Imagine That: a handbook of creative learning activities for the classroom. Network Educational Press 1997.
	Self-Intelligence: a handbook for developing confidence, self-esteem and interpersonal skills. Network Educational Press 1999.
	What's the Story? Games and activities for creative storymaking. A. & C. Black tbp 2001.
Chetwynd, T.	*A Dictionary for Dreamers*. Thorsons 1993.
	A Dictionary of Symbols Thorsons 1993.
Claxton, G.	*Hare Brain Tortoise Mind*. Fourth Estate, 1998.
Crossley-Holland, K. and Walsh, J. P.	*Wordhoard*. Puffin 1972.
Day, J.	*Creative Visualisation with Children*. Element 1994.
Dennison, P. and Dennison, G.E.	*Brain Gym for Teachers*. Edu-Kinesthetics 1989.
Dilts, R. and Epstein, T.	*Dynamic Learning*. Meta Publications 1995.
von Franz, M-L.	*Shadow And Evil In Fairy Tales*. Shambala 1995.
Gawain, S.	*Creative Visualisation*. Bantam Books 1982.
Goldberg, P.	*The Intuitive Edge*. Turnstone Press 1985.
Goleman, D., Kaufman, P. and Ray, M.	*The Creative Spirit*. Dutton 1992.
Greenfield, S.	*The Human Brain: A Guided Tour*. Phoenix 1997.
Hall, C. and E., Leech, A.	*Scripted Fantasy in the Classroom*. Routledge 1990.
Hickman, D. E. and Jacobson, S.	*The Power Process: an NLP approach to writing*. The Anglo-American Book Company 1997.
James, T. and Woodsmall, W.	*Time Line Therapy and the Basis of Personality*. Meta Publications 1988.
Jung, C.	*Man and his Symbols* Picador 1978.
Knight, S.	*NLP at Work*. Nicholas Brealey Publishing 1997.
LeBoeuf, M.	*Creative Thinking*. Piatkus 1994.
Mellon, N.	*The Art of Storytelling*. Element 1999.

Meyer, R.	*The Wisdom of Fairy Tales*. Floris Books 1988.
National Advisory Committee on Creative and Cultural Education (NACCCE),	
	All Our Futures: Creativity, Culture and Education. DfEE 1999.
O'Connor, J.	*Extraordinary Solutions for Everyday Problems*. Thorsons 1999.
Pennac, D.	*Better Than Life*. Coach House Press 1994.
Porter, P. K.	*Psycho-Linguistics: The Language of the Mind*. ATG Publishing 1995.
Pullman, P.	*Northern Lights*. Book I of the *Dark Materials Trilogy*. Scholastic 1998.
Rose, C.	*Accelerated Learning*. Accelerated Learning Systems Limited 1991.
Rossi, E. L.	*The Psychobiology of Mind–Body Healing*. Norton, 1993
Rotsler, W. (compiler)	*Science Fictionisms*. Gibbs Smith 1995.
Rowshan, A.	*Telling Tales: how to use stories to help children deal with the challenges of life*) Oneworld Publications 1997.
Schnieder, M. and	
Killick, J.	*Writing for Self Discovery*. Element 1998.
Stock, G.	*The Book of Questions*. Equation (Thorsons) 1987.
Smith, A. and	*The ALPS Approach*. Network Educational Press 1999.
Call, N.	
Wallace, L.	*Stories for the Third Ear*. Norton 1985.
Williams, P.	*How Stories Heal*. European Therapy Studies Institute 1998 (ETSI, 1 Lovers Meadow, Chalvington, East Sussex, BN27 3TE).
Wilson, C.	*The Occult*. Granada 1978.
Zipes, J.	*Creative Storytelling*. Routledge 1995.

Index

Activities are shown in **bold** type.

Other Titles from Network Educational Press

THE SCHOOL EFFECTIVENESS SERIES

Book 1: *Accelerated Learning in the Classroom* by Alistair Smith

Book 2: *Effective Learning Activities* by Chris Dickinson

Book 3: *Effective Heads of Department* by Phil Jones & Nick Sparks

Book 4: *Lessons are for Learning* by Mike Hughes

Book 5: *Effective Learning in Science* by Paul Denley and Keith Bishop

Book 6: *Raising Boys' Achievement* by Jon Pickering

Book 7: *Effective Provision for Able & Talented Children* by Barry Teare

Book 8: *Effective Careers Education & Guidance*
by Andrew Edwards and Anthony Barnes

Book 9: *Best behaviour and Best behaviour FIRST AID* by
Peter Relf, Rod Hirst, Jan Richardson and Georgina Youdell

Best behaviour FIRST AID (pack of 5 booklets)

Book 10: *The Effective School Governor* by David Marriott
(including free audio tape)

Book 11: *Improving Personal Effectiveness for Managers in Schools*
by James Johnson

Book 12: *Making Pupil Data Powerful* by Maggie Pringle and Tony Cobb

Book 13: *Closing the Learning Gap* by Mike Hughes

Book 14: *Getting Started* by Henry Leibling

Book 15: *Leading the Learning School* by Colin Weatherley

Book 16: *Adventures in Learning* by Mike Tilling

Book 17: *Strategies for Closing the Learning Gap* by Mike Hughes with Andy Vass

Book 18: *Classroom Management* by Philip Waterhouse and Chris Dickinson

ACCELERATED LEARNING SERIES
General Editor: **Alistair Smith**

Accelerated Learning in Practice by Alistair Smith

The ALPS Approach: Accelerated Learning in Primary Schools
by Alistair Smith and Nicola Call

MapWise by Oliver Caviglioli and Ian Harris

The ALPS Resource Book by Alistair Smith and Nicola Call

Bright Sparks: Motivational posters for pupils by Alistair Smith
Over 100 photocopiable posters to help motivate pupils and help improve their learning.

Leading Learning: Staff development posters for schools by Alistair Smith
With over 200 posters which draw from the best in brain research from around the world.

Creating An Accelerated Learning School by Derek Wise and Mark Lovatt

EDUCATION PERSONNEL MANAGEMENT SERIES
These new Education Personnel Management handbooks will help headteachers, senior managers and governors to manage a broad range of personnel issues.

The Well Teacher – management strategies for beating stress, promoting staff health and reducing absence by Maureen Cooper

Managing Challenging People – dealing with staff conduct
by Bev Curtis and Maureen Cooper

Managing Poor Performance – handling staff capability issues
by Bev Curtis and Maureen Cooper

Managing Allegations Against Staff – personnel and child protection issues in schools by Maureen Cooper

Managing Recruitment and Selection – appointing the best staff
by Bev Curtis and Maureen Cooper

Managing Redundancies – dealing with reduction and reorganisation of staff
by Bev Curtis and Maureen Cooper

VISIONS OF EDUCATION SERIES

The Unfinished Revolution by John Abbott and Terry Ryan

The Child is Father of the Man by John Abbott

The Learning Revolution by Jeannette Vos and Gordon Dryden
The book includes a huge wealth of data and research from around the world.

Wise Up by Guy Claxton

THE LITERACY COLLECTION

Helping With Reading by Anne Butterworth and Angela White

Class Talk by Rosemary Sage

PRACTICAL RESOURCE BOOKS

Effective Resources for Able and Talented Children by Barry Teare

More Effective Resources for Able and Talented Children by Barry Teare

Imagine That... by Stephen Bowkett

Self-Intelligence by Stephen Bowkett